# COACHING BASEBALL

## SKILLS & DRILLS

The American Coaching Effectiveness Program
Level 2 Baseball Book

**Bragg A. Stockton, EdD**
University of Houston

**Human Kinetics Publishers, Inc.**
Champaign, Illinois

**Library of Congress Cataloging-in-Publication Data**

Stockton, Bragg A.
    Coaching baseball.

    (The American coaching effectiveness program.
Level 2)
        Rev. ed. of: Baseball skills and drills.
        1. Baseball—Coaching.        2. Baseball—Training.
I. Stockton, Bragg A.        Baseball skills and drills.
II. Title.        III. Series
GV875.5.S76        1984        796.357'07'7        84-6563
ISBN 0-931250-65-X

Developmental Editor: Fran Rivkin
Copy Editors: Kathryn G. Marshak and Peg Goyette
Production Staff: Fran Rivkin, Lezli Harris, and Sandra Meier
Typesetter: Yvonne Sergent
Cover Design: Jack W. Davis
Printed By: McNaughton and Gunn

ISBN: 0-931250-65-X

Printed in the United States of America        10   9   8   7

**Human Kinetics**
P.O. Box 5076, Champaign, IL 61825-5076
1-800-747-4457

*Canada:* Human Kinetics, Box 24040, Windsor, ON N8Y 4Y9
1-800-465-7301 (in Canada only)

*Europe:* Human Kinetics, P.O. Box IW14, Leeds LS16 6TR, England
0532-781708

*Australia:* Human Kinetics, P.O. Box 80, Kingswood 5062, South Australia
618-374-0433

*New Zealand:* Human Kinetics, P.O. Box 105-231, Auckland 1
(09) 309-2259

# Dedication

My help cometh from the Lord which made heaven and earth.
Psalm 121:2

Since everything that I am is because of God, and since every-thing which appears in this book is because of God, I dedicate *Coaching Baseball: Skills and Drills* to the glory of God. I pray that everyone who comes in contact with this book will be blessed, and in turn, will play the game of baseball as well as the game of life to the glory of God.

# CONTENTS

**PREFACE**

**PART I. OFFENSIVE PLAY**     **1**

CHAPTER 1. HITTING     3

Selection of a Bat     3
Grip     4
Stance and Stride     4
  *Distance From the Plate*     4
  *Stance and Stride Lengths*     4
  *Hands and Elbows*     5
  *Position of the Shoulders and Back Elbow*     6
Stride to Swing     6
  *Eyeballs on the Knees Concept*     7
  *Head and Hip Position and Movement*     7
  *Common Hitting Faults During Stride and Swing*     8
  *Throwing the Bat at the Ball*     9
  *Lead and Follow Hands*     10
Fundamental Hitting Analysis     12
  *Hitter's Checklist*     13
Hitting Fundamental Summary     14
Developing a Visual Tracking System     15
Strategies for Hitting     16
  *Aggressive Hitting*     16
  *Looking for a Pitch*     17
  *Hitting With Less Than 2 Strikes and With 2 Strikes*     18
  *Hitting Curve Balls and Hitting to the Opposite Field (Bat Control)*     18
  *Hit-and-Run*     18
In Sum . . .     19
How to Correct Hitting Problems     19
  *Diagnostic Chart*     19
  *Coaches' Evaluation of Hitters*     20
  *Getting Out of Slumps*     22
  *Characteristics Needed to Become an Effective Hitter*     22

Daily Practice Schedule                                    22
Hitter on Deck                                             23
  *Drills: Hip Turner • Wrist Roller • Throwing Bats • Lead and
  Follow Hand Swings • Bat Press • Three-Colored Home Plate
  and Contact Points • Hitting Off a Tee • Whiffle or Sock Ball
  • Whiffle or Sock Ball on a String • Contact Point (soft toss)
  • Simulating Swings (home drill) • Colored Ball • Number of
  Fingers • 30-Minute Daily Hitting Schedule*

## CHAPTER 2. BUNTING                                      25

Sacrifice Bunt                                             25
  *Mechanics of the Sacrifice Bunt*                        25
Mechanics of the Drag Bunt                                 26
  *Right-Handed*                                           26
  *Left-Handed*                                            27
  *Drills: Catch the Ball Bunt • Accurate Sacrifice Bunt • Rapid-
  Fire Bunting*

## CHAPTER 3. BASERUNNING                                  29

First Base Techniques                                      29
  *The Break From Home Plate and Overrunning First Base*   29
  *Rounding First Base — "Thinking Second"*                30
  *Leadoffs From First Base*                               32
  *Other Maneuvers From First Base*                        33
Second Base Techniques                                     34
  *Base Runner's Lead*                                     34
  *Advancing From Second to Third When the Ball is Hit*    34
  *Stealing Third*                                         34
Third Base Techniques                                      34
  *Base Runner's Lead*                                     34
  *Ground Balls*                                           35
  *Fly Balls*                                              35
Tagging Up on Foul Pop Flies                               35
Summary of Base Running Techniques                         35
Additional Steal Situations                                36
  *Runners Should Always Steal When . . .*                 36
  *Stealing Home Plate and the Squeeze*                    36
  *First and Third Steal Situations*                       36
Miscellaneous Base Running Policies                        37
  *Moving From First to Third on a Base Hit*               37
  *Ground Ball — Runners on First and Third — Less Than 2 Outs*  37
  *Getting Out of a Run-Down*                              37
Habits of Pitchers                                         38
  *Drills: Running Past First Base • Rounding First Base — Thinking
  Second • Running From Home Plate to First Base • Stop and
  Go • Lead and Pick-Off • Running the Bases • Assuming Leads
  and Baserunning Techniques • Complete Baserunning*

## CHAPTER 4. SLIDING                                      41

Stand-Up Slide                                             41
Decoy Slide                                                42
Hook Slide                                                 42
Head-First Slide                                           42
Sliding Summary                                            43
Practicing Sliding                                         43
Additional Drills                                          43
  *Drills: Sliding on Damp Grass • Around the Bases • Baserunning
  and Coaching*

**PART II. DEFENSIVE PLAY** **45**

The Glove 46
*Care and Selection* 46
*How to Use the Glove* 46
Basic Defensive Concepts 47
*Conditioning* 47
*Basic Rules of Defensive Play* 47

CHAPTER 5. INDIVIDUAL INFIELD SKILLS 49

Fundamental Fielding Analysis 49
Subcomponents 50
*Ready Position* 50
*Movement to the Ball* 51
*Fielding Position* 52
*Skip and Throw Position* 53
*Follow-Through Position* 54
Throwing Summary 54
Difficult Fielding Situations 56
*Short Hops* 56
*Ground Balls to the Backhand Side—Crossover Step* 57
*Fly Balls Overhead* 57
*Slow Rollers* 58
*Simulations* 59
Fielding and Throwing According to the Speed of the Runner
and the Speed of the Ground Ball 61
Tagging Runners 61
*Drills: Set-Sprint • Crossover Step • Crossover-Reaction • Flick
the Ball • Arm Action • Skip and Throw for Points • Rhythm
• Short Hop • Short Hop Goal • Backhand • Fly Balls Overhead
• Reaction-Position • Freeze • Simulation Drill for Specific Body
Positions • Shadow*

CHAPTER 6. POSITIONAL INFIELD SKILLS 63

First Baseman 63
*Qualifications* 63
*Fundamentals for Receiving Throws* 63
*Making Throws to Bases* 64
*Holding Runners on First* 64
*Fielding Ground Balls* 64
Third Baseman 65
*Qualifications* 65
*How to Play Third Base* 65
Second Basemen and Shortstops 65
*Turning Double Plays* 65
*Starting the Double Play—The Toss* 66
*Completing the Double Play* 66
Pitcher's Fielding Responsibilities 71
*Covering First Base* 71
*Backing Up Home and Third* 71
*Pitcher Starting the Double Play* 72
*Fielding Bunts* 72
*Defensing the Squeeze Play* 73
Catcher's Fielding Responsibilities 73
*Qualifications* 73
*Pop Flies* 73
*Steal and Pick-Off Situations* 74
*Tagging Runners Out at Home Plate* 75
*Backing Up First Base* 75

*Fielding Bunts*                                                          76
*Cutoffs and Relays*                                                      76
*Drills: Receiving Tosses • Ground Balls into Double Plays*
*• Double Play Practice • Double Play Practice With Runners*
*• Pop-Ups for Catchers • Catchers Throwing From the Stance*
*• Catcher Making Tag Plays at Home*

## CHAPTER 7. INFIELD PLAY                                               77

Run-Downs                                                                77
Bunt Coverage                                                            78
Pick-Offs                                                                79
Defensing First and Third Steal Situations                               79
   *Early First and Third Steal*                          79
   *Regular First and Third Steal*                        79
   *Delay First and Third Steal*                          79
   *In Sum . . .*                                         79
Play Action                                                              84
*Drills: Run-Down • First and Third Steal Situation • Scramble*
*• Stuffed or Wooden Glove*

## CHAPTER 8. OUTFIELD PLAY                                              85

Qualifications                                                           85
Ready Stance and Getting "The Jump" on the Ball                          85
Sun and Wind                                                             86
Fly Balls Overhead                                                       86
Circling Fly Balls                                                       87
Fielding Ground Balls                                                    87
Throwing                                                                 88
Playing Balls Off or At the Fence                                        89
Playing Line Drives                                                      90
Know the Hitter and the Pitch                                            90
Backing Up Plays                                                         90
Play Action                                                              90
Outfield Communication                                                   93
*Drills: Toe-Running • Outfield Ground Ball—Fly Ball • Balls*
*Lying At the Fence • Balls Hit Off the Fence • Outfield Teamwork*

## CHAPTER 9. TEAM DEFENSIVE PLAY                                        95

Pop Fly and Fly Ball Coverage                                            95
Cutoff and Relay System                                                  96
   *Situation: Runners at Second; First and Second; or First,*
   *Second, and Third; Less Than 2 Outs*                   96
   *Situation: Runners at First and Second; or First, Second, and*
   *Third*                                                 97
   *Situation: Sure Doubles to Left-Center Field, Center Field, or*
   *Right-Center Field*                                    97
   *Situation: Sure Doubles in the Left Field Corner or Right Field*
   *Corner*                                                97
Other Drills and Suggestions                                            100
*Drills: Five Player Cutoff and Relay • Cutoff and Relay System*
*• Team Throwing for Points • Three Player • Short Base*
*Situations • Individual Position • Game Situation (Simulation)*
*• Formal Infield and Outfield*

## CHAPTER 10. PITCHING                                       103

Physical Conditioning                                        103
Mental Aspects of Pitching                                   104
Two Basic Tenets of Pitching—Throw Strikes and Get the
Leadoff Hitter Out                                           104
Warming Up                                                   104
Pregame Warm-Up                                              104
The Pitcher's Motion                                         105
Common Denominators of All Effective Pitchers                107
Five Phases of the Pitcher's Motion                          107
  *Phase I*                                                  107
  *Phase II*                                                 107
  *Phase III*                                                108
  *Phase IV*                                                 108
  *Phase V*                                                  108
Angle of Delivery                                            109
Key Points for a Pitcher's Delivery                          110
Coaches' Analysis and Evaluation of Pitchers                 112
  *Phase I*                                                  112
  *Phase Ia*                                                 113
  *Phase II*                                                 113
  *Phase IIa*                                                113
  *Phase III*                                                113
  *Phases IIIa to IV*                                        113
  *Phase IV*                                                 113
  *Phases IVa to V*                                          114
  *Phase V*                                                  114
Different Pitches                                            114
  *Fast Ball*                                                114
  *Curve Ball*                                               114
  *Change-Up*                                                115
Pitching Strategies                                          116
  *Changing Angles*                                          116
  *Waste and Purpose Pitches*                                117
  *Hitters' Weaknesses*                                      117
  *Pitching Out of Trouble*                                  118
  *Pitching With Runners on Base*                            118
  *Pitching From the Stretch*                                118
  *Pick-Off Moves*                                           119
  *Balk*                                                     120
  *Signs and Shake-Offs*                                     120
Statistics                                                   121
  *Pitching Charts*                                          121
  *Drills: Pitcher's Bunny Hop • 50 Pitch Change-Up • Tarp
  Target • Hit the Spot Pitching • Pitcher's Control • Pick-Off*

## CHAPTER 11. CATCHING AS IT RELATES TO PITCHING            123

Catching Position                                            123
  *Giving Signs*                                             123
  *Giving the Pitcher a Target*                              123
  *Shifting on Low Pitches*                                  124
Communication Between Catchers and Pitchers                  125
  *Helping the Pitcher Establish Mental and Emotional Control* 125
  *Recognizing Weaknesses in Hitters*                        125

*Helpful Hints From a Catcher To a Pitcher*                    126
*The Catcher's Analysis of the Pitcher's Motion*              126
*Waste and Purpose Pitches*                                   126
*Helping the Pitcher out of Trouble*                          126
*Drills: Shift*


## PART III. PLANNING                                        **127**

### CHAPTER 12. DRILL SYSTEMS, MULTIPURPOSE
### DRILLS, AND STRATEGIES                                    129

Practices                                                     129
Creating a Learning Environment                              129
Drill Systems and Multipurpose Drills                        130
*Station Drill System*                                       130
*Fungo Stations*                                             132
*Pick-Offs — Bunt Coverage — Covering First Base*            132
*Batting Practice*                                           134
*Intra-Squad Games*                                          136
Offensive Game Strategy                                      138
*Hit-and-Run*                                                138
*Bunt-and-Run*                                               138
*Fake Bunt-and-Swing*                                        138
*Steals*                                                     138
*Sacrifice Bunt*                                             138
*Squeeze Bunt*                                               138
*Special First and Third Maneuvers*                          139
Defensive Game Strategy                                      139
Scouting                                                     140
Scouting Outline                                             140
Drill Summary                                                141
Seasonal Plan                                                142
*Drills: Must Swing Pitches • Pepper Game • Sacrifice Bunt
and Running Practice • Tagging-Up • Team Defensive
(Situations) • Mini Intra-Squad • One Pitch Intra-Squad •
Extended Bag Game*


## APPENDICES                                                 **143**

### APPENDIX A. BASEBALL CONDITIONING                         145

*Strength and Flexibility*                                   145
*Endurance*                                                  145
*How to Use Drills*                                          145
Strength and Flexibility Drills                              145
*Drills: Jumping Jacks • Three Point Stretch • Rise on Toes •
Bunny Hops • Scissor Claps • Sit Ups • Leg Rolls • Jack Knife
• Arm Rolls • Squat Thrusts • Squat Jump • Using the Rolley
• Using Hand Grippers • Isometric Swing Strengthener • Bat
Extension*
Endurance Drills                                             149


### APPENDIX B. CONSTRUCTING INSTRUCTIONAL AIDS              151

Half-and-Half Colored Baseballs                              151
Personal Strike Zone                                         151
Three-Colored Home Plate                                     152

Fold-Up Home Plate                                              152
Boxes and Triangles                                             152
   *Box*                                         152
   *Triangle*                                    152
Rolley                                                          152
Hitting Tees                                                    153
Jump Rope                                                       153
Stuffed or Wooden Glove                                         153
Tarp Target                                                     153
Colored Balls                                                   153

# PREFACE

Throughout the world sports play a significant role in the lives of participants and of those who follow the excitement, intrigue, and beauty which surround a competitive struggle. No other sport seems to influence its participants and fans as strongly as baseball. Baseball filters directly into the lives of millions, both in America and abroad. Baseball is unique. The skills of baseball have continued to challenge players of all ages throughout its history. Hitting, fielding, throwing, bunting, and pitching are not simple skills to master, even for professionals. And the challenge is even greater for the very young.

Young players must strive to strengthen their bodies, quicken their reactions, and increase their coordination if they hope to have a chance at mastering baseball skills. Their ability to successfully handle failure, adversity, and anxiety will be tested constantly. Opportunities to develop self-confidence, self-discipline, and sportsmanship are woven into all levels of baseball. Players of all ages and their coaches face a constant challenge to develop and maintain the skill levels necessary for consistent success on the baseball field. It is primarily this challenge that makes baseball fun for those involved. The challenge is also the basis for the joy and empathy that affect true fans as they identify with the dedicated preparation that precedes the beautiful performance of skills on the field.

It is for these reasons that *Coaching Baseball: Skills and Drills* was written and developed. The material in this book is designed to assist a coach working with any age level to help a player develop his natural abilities. Together, the coach and player should strive to perfect the necessary skills, and through this struggle, with the book's help, to achieve a high degree of self-realization and a rewarding baseball experience.

The book emphasizes methods of *teaching* skills with the intent of increasing the knowledge bases of both coach and player in order to equip them with the insights necessary to adequately implement a valid developmental program. Careful analysis of the text and illustrations may help a coach more effectively guide and direct his team's daily practice sessions. In a similar manner, a player should understand more vividly how to continue his skill development by pursuing an individualized home training program away from formal team practices.

Topics covered include baseball techniques and fundamentals, individual and team drills, motor skills development, physiology of exercise, and motivational and reinforcement techniques which relate to baseball skills. Other coaching competencies such as time management; organization of practices; analyses, evaluation, and diagnostic skills; and maintaining a learning environment are also highlighted.

## Special Note

An extensive research study was conducted in the Houston, Texas area with the intent of testing the validity of this book. Twenty-eight summer league coaches were selected at random and divided into two equal groups. One group of coaches served as the experimental group and used the book for 14 weeks while coaching their teams. The other group served as the control group and used their own methods for coaching their teams during the same 14-week period.

Following the 14-week period of coaching, a skills test composed of hitting, fielding the ball and throwing to a target, fielding short hops, and catching while running was administered to 84 12-year-old players, randomly selected with three from each coach's team. A Jugs pitching machine was used to control the speed and trajectory of balls thrown to the players during the test in order to control important variables.

The results of the study revealed that players whose coaches used *Coaching Baseball: Skills and Drills* as a coaching aid produced the highest scores on the skills test. The coaches who used the book were able to develop a significantly higher skill attainment in their players than those coaches who did not use the book. The fact that the experimental group only had 14 weeks to coach their players makes the book's value even more significant!

### How to Gain Maximum Benefits From the Book

The book uses numerous illustrative sequences and stick figure drawings in its analysis of baseball skills. Associating the stick figures and charts with the subject matter should provoke a vivid insight into the proper fundamentals. To achieve the clearest understanding of correct skill techniques and physical mechanics, the reader should examine and analyze the exact position shown for toes, heels, knees, hips,

hands, elbows, shoulders, and head. By becoming more conscious of each body part and its relationship to effective skill execution, the reader may imagine proper cause and effect relationships. Critical body positions will be emphasized throughout the book.

Coaches should be conscious that no single portion of this study is most important; each concept, drill, method, or procedure is equally significant and should warrant equal consideration and emphasis. In order for the training program to be effective, however, the coach should be enthusiastic with his coaching and leadership techniques. Similarly, players should be sensitive to their responsibility to maintain a vigorous self-training program. If such commitment by both coach and players continues throughout the season, they will realize success, achievement, and fun.

## Acknowledgment

I am extremely grateful to my wife, Judy, for her loving support and assistance in the development of both the first edition and this second edition. Special thanks to Judy for drawing the numerous stick figures that illustrate the text.

An expression of gratitude is also extended to Fran Rivkin and members of the Human Kinetics team for their skillful assistance in the organization and structuring of the content of this second edition.

*Bragg A. Stockton*

# PART I

## OFFENSIVE PLAY

The first four chapters cover the offensive aspects of baseball: hitting, bunting, baserunning, and sliding. Teams must be effective offensively in order to get any runs. Coaches should examine their team's strengths in order to determine the best way for the team to generate runs. Should the offense revolve around the team's speed or its power? A team with several power hitters can sometimes manage by relying on hitting, but most team members need to be good bunters and base runners. It is to every team's advantage to be adept at all phases of offensive play. With a full range of skills players will be able to take advantage of all opportunities.

# CHAPTER 1

# Hitting

Hitting, without a doubt, is the most difficult baseball skill to learn. It has even been stated that hitting a baseball is the single most difficult skill to master in all of sport. The combination of the round ball, round bat, and two human beings—the hitter and the pitcher—makes hitting a skill that demands great precision. Proper hand-eye coordination, reflexes, timing, weight distribution, kinesthetic awareness, and state of mind, all of which are needed to hit the ball effectively, require great dedication, concentration, and effort.

Since effective pitchers constantly try to change the ball's speed and position in the strike zone, the hitter faces a constant challenge to get contact between the best part of the bat and the best part of the ball while maximizing bat speed. Thus, a hitter needs to be able to concentrate, have visual discipline, and demonstrate self-control.

There is no shortcut or easy secret to successful hitting. Success comes from hours of meaningful practice and analysis. A player needs to have a positive state of mind, stimulated by a continuous desire to achieve in order to become a successful hitter. Failure can bring about discouragement and disappointment, and can diminish a player's drive. Coaches need to help players understand that failure is part of the learning process and help them to succeed.

## Selection of a Bat

The proper bat is important to insure effective hitting. The hitter must have complete control of the bat through the entire swing. It should be light enough to "throw" at the ball, but solid enough and possess enough hitting surface to be effective.

The speed of the bat's hitting surface determines how hard or how far the ball is hit. Players of all ages need to consider this when selecting bats. A hitter who doesn't have complete control over the bat, will not be able to swing it with the quickness required to hit the ball with authority.

Often on youth league teams the only bats available are too heavy. If this is the case hitters should experiment with each bat by choking it at different points to find the "balance point," the position where the bat feels comfortable in the hitter's hands. By varying the position of the hands on the bat handle, a hitter can find and mark the balance point with a piece of tape where the bottom part of the lower hand is positioned on the bat. The tape will remind the hitter where to hold the bat each time, thus increasing bat control. A bat is not always controlled best by holding it down on the knob.

*Key Point:* For hitters to maximize bat speed and maintain bat control, it is very important that they select the proper bat and know where to hold it.

Hitters also must consider their own styles of hitting. Because of differences in body structure, strength, coordination, and quickness, hitters vary considerably. Some players will specialize in hitting to all fields, while others may demonstrate a great deal of power at the plate. Hitters can increase their effectiveness considerably by choosing a bat which accentuates their strong points, helps them realize

3

their potential, but does not exceed their limitations.

Hitters should consider changing bats or altering the position of their hands on the bat if they continually pull the ball foul or if they frequently hit the ball late. Pulling the ball foul could indicate that the bat is too light or that it is being held too far away from the knob. Similarly, if hitters tend to hit the ball late, fouling the ball to the opposite field or striking out on fast balls, the bat could be too heavy or their hands could be too far down on the handle. In either case, hitters should consider their hands, the hands' relationship to the bat, and whether they are throwing their hands at the ball.

## Grip

Improper placement of the hands on the bat can reduce the whip action in the swing, thus limiting the hitter's power. Many hitters grip the bat too far back in their hands. A hitter should pick up a bat as though it were an ax, with the handle of the bat resting across the middle of the fingers (see Figs. 1-1, 1-2). This allows maximum wrist action.

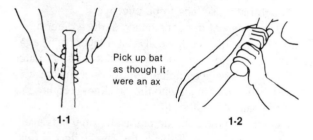

Pick up bat as though it were an ax

1-1     1-2

## Stance and Stride

### Distance From the Plate

The distance a hitter stands from the plate depends on his body structure and style of hitting. Basically, a hitter should stand far enough back from the plate so that his bat passes slightly across the outer edge of the plate when his arms are extended. This position encourages a hitter to "throw" the bat at the ball and to extend fully on all pitches. Standing too close to the plate makes it difficult for a hitter to execute a proper contact point position, and may lead him to swinging with his arms instead of throwing the bat at the ball (see Fig. 1-3).

The hitter's belt buckle should be in line with the center of the plate and the stance should be slightly closed (the front foot slightly closer to the plate than the back foot), with the stride going toward the pitcher's belt buckle. This position enables a hitter to hit all types of pitches more effectively. The hitter will

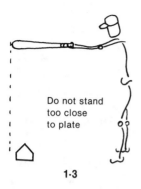

Do not stand too close to plate

1-3

be able to contact the curve ball before it reaches the maximum breaking angle, yet the position still permits the hitter to pull inside fast balls (see Figs. 1-4, 1-5).

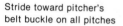
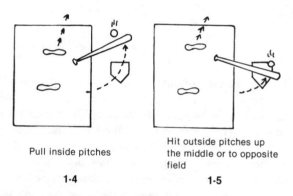

Stride toward pitcher's belt buckle on all pitches

Pull inside pitches

Hit outside pitches up the middle or to opposite field

1-4     1-5

### Stance and Stride Lengths

Stance and stride styles vary considerably among ball players. Hitters who are inconsistent should occasionally experiment with different stances. The stance and stride should feel completely comfortable to hitters so they can be relaxed at the plate. Generally, however, the stride should be executed slowly so that proper timing is maintained throughout the swing.

***Wide Stance—Short Stride.*** Effective timing techniques will be more likely if the hitter uses a *wide stance*, slightly wider than the width of the shoulders, with a *short stride*, approximately two thumb lengths (see Fig. 1-6). The hitter is less likely to be fooled by off-speed pitches when using the wide stance and short stride.

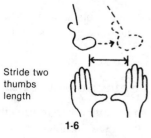

Stride two thumbs length

1-6

As the hitter takes the short stride, he should keep the front knee in. The stride should be directed toward the pitcher's belt buckle and the front shoulder should remain down and also pointed toward the pitcher's belt buckle (see Figs. 1-7, 1-8). The stride knee stays bent inward and only the "ball" portion of the stride foot lightly touches the ground. The rest of the stride foot firmly anchors itself in the ground as the hips turn and the hands are thrown at the ball (see Figs. 1-9, 1-10). By keeping the front knee inward and the front shoulder down, the hip weight and hands remain back in proper position so maximum bat speed and control can be obtained.

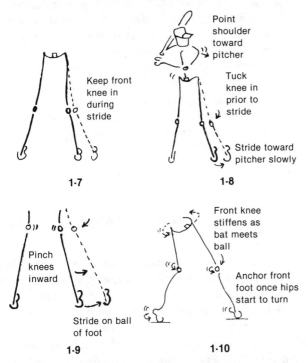

**1-7**

**1-8**

**1-9**

**1-10**

**Short Stance—Long Stride.** If the hitter uses a *short stance* with a *long stride*, he will need to pivot the back toe and hips quickly, simultaneously bringing the back toe forward slightly as he strides and turns at the moment of contact with the ball (see Figs. 1-11 to 1-14). This enables the head and shoulders

to remain on a plane level with the ball. If a hitter does not bring the back toe slightly forward, the head and shoulders drop, possibly causing the hitter to pop up. Pivoting the hips quickly as the bat meets the ball will automatically cause the proper rotation of the back toe and the knee and will keep the head and shoulders level. Therefore, hip speed should be emphasized frequently.

A short stance and long stride may lead to overstriding, which results in the hitter being off-balance and often fooled by change of speed pitches and curve balls. If a hitter's stride is initiated too early and is more than half the length of the stance, the hands and hips often start through the ball too soon, considerably restricting hip speed, bat speed, and bat control.

Proper timing consists of the hips snapping forward, the elbows and wrists extending, and the wrists snapping at the precise moment the bat contacts the ball. A hitter needs to practice these fundamentals in a seemingly unending pursuit of perfection so that the proper movement becomes a reflex.

**Hands and Elbows**

A hitter's hands and arms should be relaxed before each pitch. Stress and muscle tension can produce rigidity, which reduces flexibility and restricts bat speed and control. The force with which a hitter can "throw" the bat at the ball is directly related to the degree of relaxation maintained in the hands, wrists, and forearms.

The position of the hands and forearms before the bat moves through the ball can determine a hitter's effectiveness. Young hitters often have problems keeping their hands back and above the plane of the ball as the bat starts through the ball (see Figs. 1-15, 1-16). Hitters with weak hands and arms often drop their hands down low just before the stride, which leads to sweeping the bat upward toward the ball. A fitness program can develop strength in the hitter's hands and forearms and may alleviate the problem (see p. 22). Choking the bat also could help.

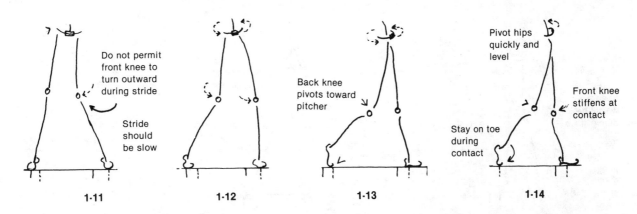

**1-11**

**1-12**

**1-13**

**1-14**

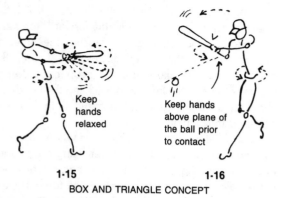

1-15                    1-16
BOX AND TRIANGLE CONCEPT

## Position of the Shoulders and Back Elbow

One of the most important rules of hitting is to keep the front shoulder down. When hitters keep the front shoulder down as they stride, they have a greater tendency to hit line drives because they are better able to keep the lead hand on top of the ball. The head is also in a better position to see the ball, and this helps keep the plane of the bat moving down through the ball. In baseball terms, this is called "getting on top of the ball."

Hitters usually are able to hit line drives when they get the barrel of the bat to hit through the top half of the ball with maximum wrist snap. In order to do this consistently, the front shoulder must remain down. Some hitters keep the back elbow slightly up and away from the body since that makes it relatively easy to keep the front shoulder down. As with other aspects of hitting, hitters may need to experiment to find the best solution for them. Hitters need to strive to *remain comfortable, yet maintain correct fundamental position*.

The hitter's stance may need to be adjusted to compensate for weak hands and arms. The hitter should start with the lead forearm basically parallel to the ground and the front shoulder slightly down while taking the stride. The "box" and "triangle" are effective coaching aids for keeping a hitter's body in the correct position during the stride. Using posterboard each player should cut a triangle which matches the position of his front shoulder, front knee, and back hip. A posterboard box should match the position of the lead forearm, lead upper arm, bat, and shoulders (see Figs. 1-17, 1-18 and Appendix B).

Hitters should practice in front of a mirror using the box and triangle in order to establish a mental picture of the proper body position during the stride phase of the swing. If the hitter's lead elbow straightens behind the plate during the turning phase of the swing, the bat will follow a slow and uncontrolled sweeping arc. If any of the three body parts in the hitter's triangle move away from their positions during the stride, the hitter will have slow hips and poor vision of the ball, resulting in loss of bat speed and bat control. The proper position illustrated by the box and triangle allow the hitter to maintain proper weight distribution, bat control, and quality bat speed, thus decreasing the number of ground outs, strikeouts, and pop-ups (see Figs. 1-17 to 1-19).

## Stride to Swing

The hitter's front shoulder remains down, the weight remains on the back hip, and the front knee turns inward as the stride foot moves forward (see Figs. 1-20 to 1-23). This keeps the hands back and cocked in a hitting position. As the hands start to extend to meet the ball, the hips turn quickly, the back toe and knee pivot with the back heel facing upward, and the head remains still as the ball meets the bat. These fundamentals can occur properly only if the hips and shoulders turn level quickly as the hitter swings through the ball. Hips and shoulder *never* turn upward during the swing (see Figs. 1-24 to 1-27).

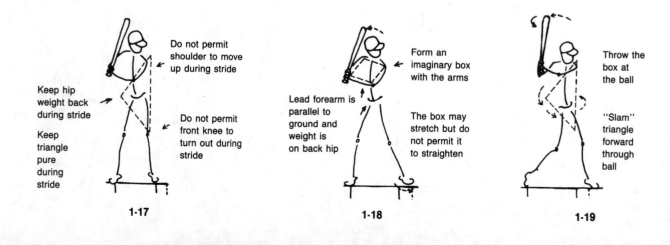

1-17                    1-18                    1-19

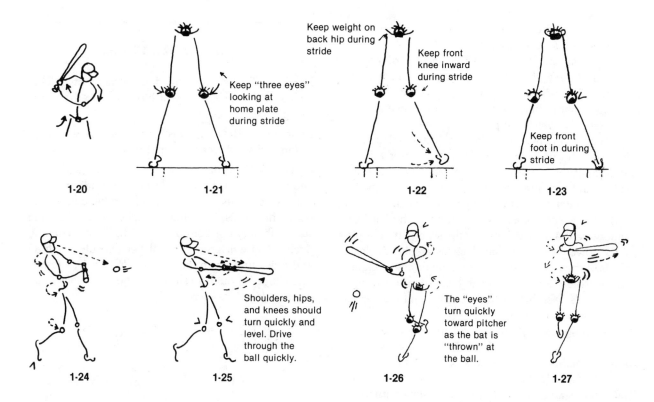

1-20    1-21    1-22    1-23

Keep "three eyes" looking at home plate during stride

Keep weight on back hip during stride

Keep front knee inward during stride

Keep front foot in during stride

1-24    1-25    1-26    1-27

Shoulders, hips, and knees should turn quickly and level. Drive through the ball quickly.

The "eyes" turn quickly toward pitcher as the bat is "thrown" at the ball.

## Eyeballs on the Knees Concept

Players learn better if coaches present a systematic training program which has descriptive elements that formulate pictures in the players' minds instead of only using verbal directions. The "eyeball concept" presents players with a clear visual image of the proper position and movement during the stride and swing. Players imagine that a hitter's knees and belt buckle area form three "eyeballs" (see Figs. 1-21 to 1-23). The coach should continually remind hitters to keep these three eyeballs looking at home plate during the stride and then turn them quickly as a *single unit* during the swing. The three eyeballs (the knees and belt buckle) should turn toward the pitcher with a quick snapping action *at the moment the elbows extend and the player contacts the ball* (see Figs. 1-26, 1-27).

Dividing hitting into the *stride* phase and the *swing* phase will help players achieve optimal bat speed and control. Hitters will pop up and strike out less often because they will be able to eliminate the slow back side, thus eliminating the tendency to drop under pitches, swing late, and pull the head out.

Coaches will find that players understand the cause and effect relationship of the mechanics of the swing when they use the visual image of the three eyeballs. It is poor psychology for the coach to harass the player verbally for popping up or striking out. The coach should always seek the most positive, educational approach to correcting mistakes. The

three-eyeball concept is an example of such a technique.

## Head and Hip Position and Movement

During the stance, stride, and throughout contact, the head should remain at a "one o'clock" position. That is, if the hitter visualizes a clock standing up, with the six on home plate and the twelve toward the sky, the head should point towards one o'clock (see Fig. 1-28). For a hitter to see the ball sharply it is important that the head stay still throughout the entire stride and swing. Once the hitter positions his head correctly, it helps to pretend there is a glass of water tied to his head and to try not to spill a drop through the entire stride and swing. When a hitter visualizes his swing he should see his body turning during the

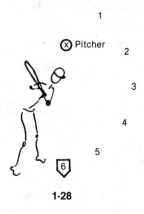

12

1

⊗ Pitcher

2

3

4

5

6

1-28

turn phase of the swing and see his head positioned in a vise—absolutely still.

*The hitter must see the ball sharply in order to hit the ball sharply.* If the head is constantly moving forward, to the side, or up and away from the pitch, it is difficult for the hitter to maintain the concentration necessary to watch the pitch effectively.

Keeping the head still is not a difficult skill to learn by itself, but when proper hip movement is added, stability of the head may be affected. The hips must rotate and face the pitcher as the hitter contacts the ball. In order for this to happen, the back toe and back knee should also rotate toward the pitcher; otherwise the hips lock during the swing and the hitter's power will be reduced considerably. At least 60% of the hitter's weight should be on the back hip as the stride begins. This will help keep the weight and hands back before the hips turn and the hands are thrown at the ball.

Rotating the bottom part of the body tends to cause the head and neck to move away from the ball, so the head and hips must work in opposition to one another. As the hips rotate forward and horizontally, the head and eyes must remain stationary to insure proper contact (see Figs. 1-29, 1-30.)

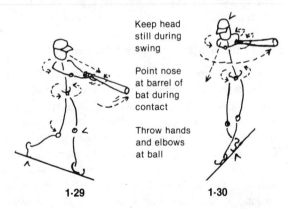

1-29          1-30

The faster the hips turn, the more power the hitter can generate in the swing. Also, the hitter is less likely to drop under the pitch, so there is a greater possibility of hitting line drives (see Figs. 1-31 to 1-34). Hitters should use the Hip Turner Drill to help develop quicker hips.

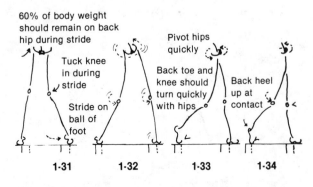

1-31          1-32          1-33          1-34

## HIP TURNER DRILL

*Purpose:* To facilitate the development of quicker hips and the relationship of hip speed to the entire swing.

*Equipment:* Bats or substitute bats (for example, broomsticks), gloves for home plates.

*Procedure:* The hitter places a bat or substitute bat behind the waist, horizontal to the ground, and uses a glove as home plate. While holding the ends of the bat in the hands, the hitter assumes a normal batting stance (hitting position) and "watches" an imaginary pitch being delivered. The player executes a stride and quick turn *using the bat to help turn hips faster.* The player should finish in a proper contact point position (see Figs. 1-35 to 1-38).

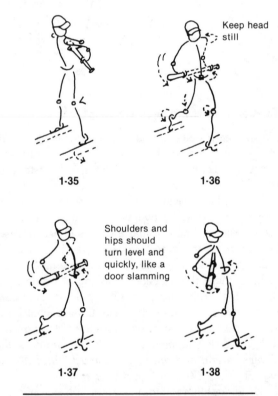

1-35          1-36

1-37          1-38

### Common Hitting Faults During Stride and Swing

Hitters are apt to make the following mistakes in the areas already discussed. Coaches should watch for them and know how to correct them.

1. The stride foot moves too far. (Hitter must wait for the ball.)

2. The stride knee moves out and turns too soon. (Stride knee should stay in during stride.)

3. The front shoulder moves up during the stride and swing. (Front shoulder must stay down, pointed at pitcher's belt buckle.)

4. Back elbow and hands drop down during the stride and swing. (Keep back elbow and hands up for proper hitting position.)

5. Back shoulder, back hip, or back knee move slowly during the swing. (Body should "snap" around and forward as the bat meets the ball.)

These mistakes result in loss of vision of the ball, lack of bat control, and restricted bat speed, which often lead to strikeouts, pop-ups, and ground outs.

### Throwing the Bat at the Ball

*As the bat makes contact with the ball, the elbows and wrists should extend* to supply the whip necessary to hit the ball with authority and power. Proper extension will be easier if the hitter pretends to "throw" the bat at the ball. The Wrist Roller Drill can help players generate maximum efficiency in throwing the bat at the ball and the Throwing Bats Drill establishes the feel of throwing the bat at the ball.

---

### WRIST ROLLER DRILL

*Purpose:* To enhance bat speed and control by facilitating maximum efficiency in "throwing" the bat at the ball.

*Equipment:* Bat (one per player).

*Procedure:* Players place themselves in the contact position, and then roll the bat forward and backward causing the bat to touch each shoulder as it completes a full arc. Players should use only their wrists and forearms to rotate the bat. Approximately 60-80 of these wrist rollers should be done in 60 seconds (see Figs. 1-39 to 1-44).

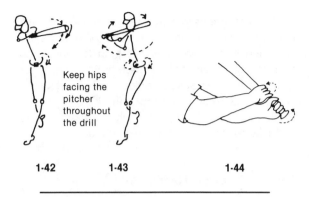

Keep hips facing the pitcher throughout the drill

1-42          1-43                    1-44

---

### THROWING BATS DRILL

*Age Group:* 8 and up.

*Purpose:* To establish the feeling of throwing the bat at the ball to get more power into the swing.

*Equipment:* Bat.

*Procedure:* Two players take a bat and move to a vacant area where there will be no danger of hitting anyone or anything. The two players stand facing one another at a distance of about 150 feet. The player with the bat assumes a batting stance and visualizes an imaginary pitcher. As the imaginary pitcher delivers an imaginary pitch, the hitter actually *throws* the bat toward the pitch.

If the player's timing is correct, the bat should sail directly towards the imaginary pitcher. The hitter should *keep hands and wrists loose and relaxed and extend the elbows quickly* to promote the flexibility necessary for effective bat control and bat speed. Also, the bat thrower should try to develop a strong, *downward-level turn with both front and back shoulders* to ensure balance, timing, and power (see Figs. 1-45 to 1-47).

The other player must remain totally alert to stay out of the way of the thrown bat, retrieve the bat after it drops, take a stance, and throw it back at an imaginary pitch towards the original thrower.

The more bats a hitter throws in this manner, the greater the probability will be of attacking the ball properly in a game. Using an old bat with the knob cut off will help avoid hurting fingers as players release the bat.

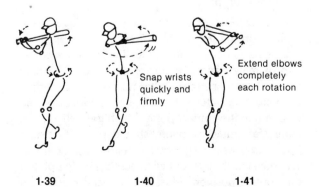

Snap wrists quickly and firmly

Extend elbows completely each rotation

1-39          1-40                    1-41

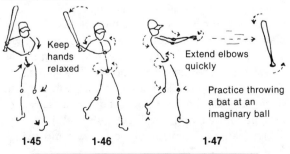

Keep hands relaxed

Extend elbows quickly

Practice throwing a bat at an imaginary ball

1-45          1-46                    1-47

Two arcs are used in the swing—an *arm arc* and a *wrist arc*. The majority of the swing should be concentrated in the wrist arc, but both the wrists and arms should extend fully at the moment the bat contacts the ball. As stated earlier, the easiest way to capture this action is simply to "throw" the bat straight at the ball using primarily the hands, wrists, and elbows, to propel the bat at the ball.

## Lead and Follow Hands

While the arms are extending during the swing, the hitter turns with the lead side. The muscles of the lead side of the back, shoulder, and whole arm pull the bat firmly and quickly "through" the ball. The action of the lead side largely determines how the bat will contact the ball. If the hitter is having trouble making proper contact with the ball, it will be helpful for him to take some swings using the *lead hand only*. As the hands start through the ball the hitter should visualize his lead hand as an airplane landing. If the lead hand turns upward prior to contact, the bat barrel will drop and a fly ball, pop-up, or foul ball may result.

---

## LEAD AND FOLLOW HAND SWINGS DRILL

*Purpose: Lead hand swings* enable a hitter to establish proper timing and power with the lead side of the body, thus giving the hitter proper contact with the ball. *Follow hand swings* establish the feeling of throwing the bat at the ball.

*Equipment:* Bat, other equipment varies on how drill is used.

*Procedure:* Depending on their level of ability and availability of other players and equipment, hitters can hit an imaginary ball, hit off of a batting tee (see Appendix B for instructions), or hit a ball thrown at half speed by another player.

When executing swings with the lead hand, the hitter should concentrate on keeping the hand above the plane of the ball. If the lead hand drops under the plane of the ball, a pop-up, strikeout, or fly out will generally occur. The hitter must also turn the hips quickly for proper timing and power. The lead elbow should *not* extend fully before contact with the ball, since that will promote a slow bat due to an excess of arm arc in the swing (see Figs. 1-48, 1-49).

The same concepts apply to follow hand swings (see Figs. 1-50, 1-51).

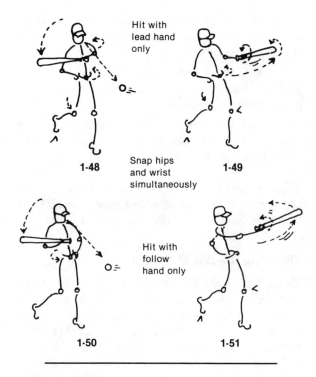

By concentrating on keeping the *lead hand on top of the ball and turning the hips quickly,* a hitter can establish proper timing and power with the *lead side of the body.* The lead hand/follow hand action creates timing and power. Both hands should snap straight into the ball at precisely the same instant. This will help a hitter to establish proper bat speed and control.

The Bat Press is another good drill for working on hitting fundamentals.

---

## BAT PRESS DRILL

*Purpose:* To help develop hitting strength and promote better awareness of proper hitting fundamentals.

*Equipment:* Bat (one for each pair of players), glove (one for each pair).

*Procedure:* Players work in pairs. One player places a glove on the ground to represent home plate and stands 12 inches in front of the glove to represent the approximate contact point for the hitter. The hitter uses the partner's rear end to represent the plane of the ball. The hitter simulates a *slow motion* swing, stopping at the contact point. The hitter, while maintaining a contact position, should press the bat as firmly as possible against the partner's rear for 10 seconds and think about all the critical body points at the contact position. More experienced players can act as "coaches" for each other, checking to see if the hitting fundamentals are correct.

After the count of 10, the player serving as the ball should walk slowly around the partner's body, being rolled around only by the force of the bat supplied by the strength of the hitter's wrists and forearms (see Figs. 1-52 to 1-54).

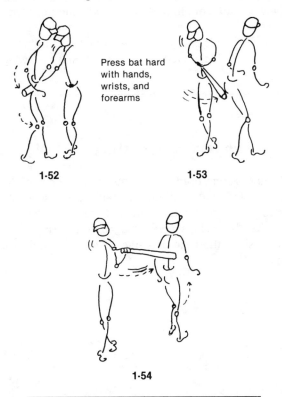

Press bat hard with hands, wrists, and forearms

**1-52**

**1-53**

**1-54**

Players can use a three-colored home plate to develop their understanding of contact points.

### THREE-COLORED HOME PLATE AND CONTACT POINTS DRILLS

*Purpose:* To develop a hitter's ability to hit the ball according to proper contact points.

*Equipment:* Three-colored home plate (see Appendix B for instructions), other equipment varies.

*Procedure:* Players use this home plate while practicing hitting off a tee, hitting whiffle balls, or simply simulating swings in front of a mirror or personalized strike zone. Before hitting, a player should check to make sure the belt buckle area is lined up with the center of the plate and that the feet are placed behind the knob of an imaginary bat laying in the center of the plate (see Fig. 1-58). Study the drawings for clarification of the three contact points and where the

bat should meet the ball (see Figs. 1-55 to 1-58). It is equally important to observe the position of the feet in relation to home plate.

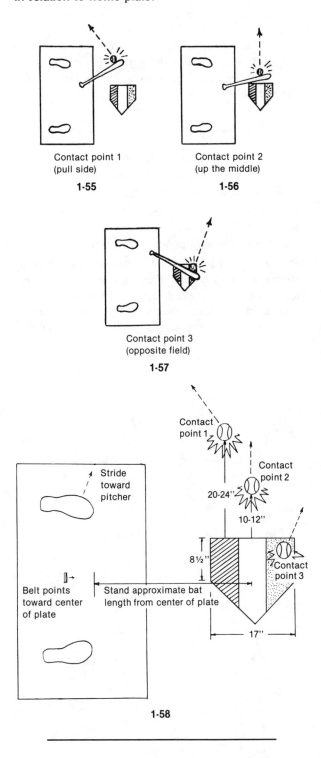

Contact point 1 (pull side)

**1-55**

Contact point 2 (up the middle)

**1-56**

Contact point 3 (opposite field)

**1-57**

Stride toward pitcher

Belt points toward center of plate

Stand approximate bat length from center of plate

Contact point 1

Contact point 2

20-24"

10-12"

8½"

Contact point 3

17"

**1-58**

By perfecting their ability to hit according to proper contact points, players will stop "pulling" outside pitches or getting "jammed" on inside pitches, and thereby decrease their number of pop-ups, strikeouts, and ground outs. A hitter's success is largely determined by the ability to hit according to proper contact points and the development of a sensitive visual tracking system, a concept developed later in this chapter (see p. 15).

The Hitting Off a Tee Drill is an excellent way for players to work on their hitting mechanics and contact points without having to be concerned about a moving ball.

---

### HITTING OFF A TEE

*Purpose:* To develop the mechanics of players' swings using a stationary ball.

*Equipment:* Batting tee (see Appendix B for instructions), baseballs or soft training balls, three-colored home plates (see Appendix B for instructions).

*Procedure:* Players can construct a "hitting laboratory" in a garage. Balls can be hit into a net, tarp, sheet, or blanket draped from the ceiling. Players place a three-colored home plate in front of the "backstop" and carefully place a tee at the

desired contact point. By moving the *tee* to different contact points in front of the plate, the hitter cycles through many swings, developing bat control and the ability to hit the ball to all fields.

The hitter should alternate between one-handed (using both lead and follow hand) and two-handed swings to establish the proper timing and relationship between the bottom part of the body and the hands. This drill can help a player develop a feel for striding with the hands and hips cocked, and then turning the hands and hips together as a unit during the swing.

---

## Fundamental Hitting Analysis

Hitting is comprised of two phases, the *stride* and the *turn*. During the stride, the body stays slow and closed. During the turn, the body turns quickly with the hands and hips working together. Figures 1-59 to 1-70 show the front and side view of the stride and turn.

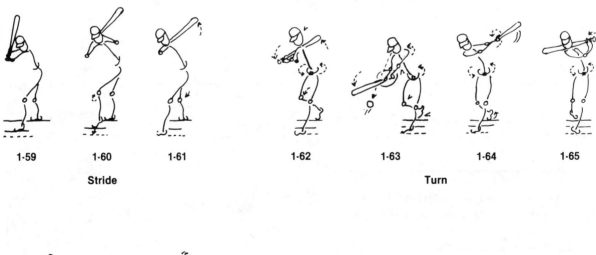

| 1-59 | 1-60 | 1-61 | 1-62 | 1-63 | 1-64 | 1-65 |
|------|------|------|------|------|------|------|
| **Stride** | | | **Turn** | | | |

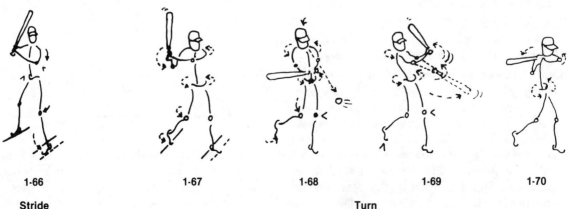

| 1-66 | 1-67 | 1-68 | 1-69 | 1-70 |
|------|------|------|------|------|
| **Stride** | | **Turn** | | |

## Hitter's Checklist

1. *Establish a comfortable stance.* Try using a stance that is several inches wider than the shoulders. The wider the stance, the smaller the stride. Thus, the hitter will not be off-balance on off-speed pitches and can wait longer on the pitch before swinging (see Fig. 1-71).

2. *Keep hands in proper hitting position.* They should be in a comfortable position near the shoulders, ready to swing down through the ball. The hitter must have maximum wrist action. If the hip weight remains back and the front knee in during the stride, the hands will stay back (see Figs. 1-72, 1-73).

3. *Keep front shoulder down during the stride and swing* to hit down through the ball and hit sharp line drives. This also prevents the hitter from pulling the head away from the ball too frequently and keeps the lead hand on top of the ball (see Fig. 1-74).

4. *Weight should lean slightly toward the plate, the head should be in a "one o'clock" position, and the hitter should stride toward the pitcher's belt buckle* (see Fig. 1-75).

5. *As stride toe moves toward the ball, back hip weight should stay back, the front shoulder down, and the bat back* to prevent lunging or being off-balance on off-speed pitches, and is the basis of timing on all pitches (see Fig. 1-76).

6. *Establish proper timing; the hands and hips should move through the swing together as the bat meets the ball.* The hitter must turn the hips and shoulders levelly through the swing to establish proper weight distribution, maximum bat speed, and control in the swing (see Fig. 1-77).

7. *Pivot the back toe and back knee as the bat contacts the ball* to allow the hips to open into the hitting position and prevent the head from dropping (see Fig. 1-78).

8. *Focus sharply on the ball all the way to the bat.* The head and eyes should stay in an effective hitting position and should remain as still as possible throughout the swing to help the hitter track the ball from the pitcher's fingers to the bat (see Fig. 1-79).

9. *"Throw" the bat at the ball.* The arms, elbows, and wrists should snap into an extended position at the moment the ball meets the bat. The hitter should "throw" the bat at the ball to achieve proper timing in the swing (see Fig. 1-80).

10. *Follow through.* Both wrists should elongate and extend through the ball quickly. Following contact the wrist should roll over, causing the bat to complete a full arc around the body during the follow-through to complete the entire wrist arc of the swing (see Fig. 1-81).

1-71     1-72     1-73

1-74     1-75     1-76

1-77     1-78     1-79

1-80     1-81

The fundamentals summarized above must be simulated frequently throughout the season so they become habits for hitters. If a hitter develops and maintains good mechanical habits, concentration on body parts will be minimized while hitting and the hitter's eyes and mind can concentrate on each pitch more intensely, and hitting will be more effective.

Players can have fun and practice hitting fundamentals in their backyard, a gym, or any other confined area with a hitting game using whiffle balls or old socks.

## WHIFFLE OR SOCK BALL DRILLS

*Purpose:* For batting practice, to make the hitters keep their eyes on the ball. Especially useful where space is limited.

*Equipment:* Bats, whiffle balls or sock balls (old socks tied into knots the size of a ball).

*Procedure:* Whiffle balls or sock balls should be thrown at a distance of about 40 feet. A point system can be used to add some competition among participants. A line drive is worth three points, a fly ball or ground ball is worth two points, a pop fly or easy ground ball is worth one point, and a foul tip or a missed swing does not receive any points. The player or team with the most points wins.

## WHIFFLE OR SOCK BALL ON A STRING

*Purpose:* To help players learn to keep their heads still and their eyes on the ball while swinging.

*Equipment:* Bat, whiffle ball or sock ball (old socks tied into knots the size of a ball).

*Procedure:* A sock ball is suspended by a string from the ceiling of a room or garage. Several of these at different heights will give players practice hitting balls of various heights.

The Contact Point Drill helps players polish all of their hitting fundamentals.

## CONTACT POINT DRILL (soft toss)

*Age Group:* 10 and up.

*Purpose:* To develop bat control and refine fundamentals of the swing.

*Equipment:* Bats, balls, three-colored home plates (see Appendix B for instructions), fence (or screen, backstop, or net), helmet.

*Procedure:* Players work in pairs. One player is the tosser and the other the hitter. The tosser stands slightly to the side of the hitter, and tosses a ball in the direction of a specific contact point. Every 3 to 5 seconds the tosser tosses another ball to a different contact area. The hitter hits each pitch at the specific contact point into the fence and strives for proper bat control at each contact point (see p. 11). The hitter should execute this drill both using the lead and follow hand only and using both hands.

The player tossing the balls should *wear a batting helmet and stand safely to the side*, being careful to toss each ball softly to a specific contact point. The tosser can help the hitter smooth and perfect hitting mechanics by cuing the hitter on such important fundamentals as: (a) slow stride, (b) maintaining the hitter's "triangle," "box," and "eyeballs" during the stride, (c) turning hips and knees together, (d) "throwing" the bat at the ball, (e) keeping eyes still, and (f) finishing with the back heel up. The tosser can also help the hitter analyze the movement. Once the hitter hits 25 balls, players switch roles.

## Hitting Fundamental Summary

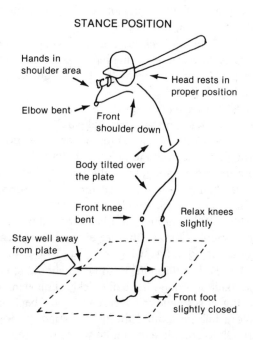

STANCE POSITION

Hands in shoulder area

Head rests in proper position

Elbow bent

Front shoulder down

Body tilted over the plate

Front knee bent

Relax knees slightly

Stay well away from plate

Front foot slightly closed

1-82

## STRIDE POSITION

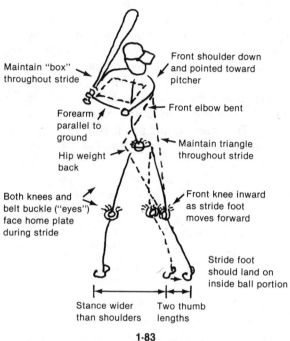

Maintain "box" throughout stride

Front shoulder down and pointed toward pitcher

Forearm parallel to ground

Front elbow bent

Hip weight back

Maintain triangle throughout stride

Both knees and belt buckle ("eyes") face home plate during stride

Front knee inward as stride foot moves forward

Stride foot should land on inside ball portion

Stance wider than shoulders

Two thumb lengths

**1-83**

## CONTACT POINT POSITION

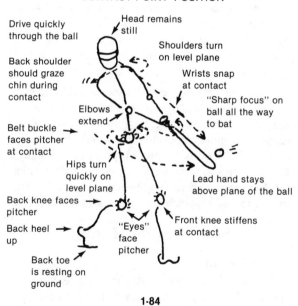

Drive quickly through the ball

Head remains still

Shoulders turn on level plane

Back shoulder should graze chin during contact

Wrists snap at contact

"Sharp focus" on ball all the way to bat

Elbows extend

Belt buckle faces pitcher at contact

Hips turn quickly on level plane

Lead hand stays above plane of the ball

Back knee faces pitcher

Back heel up

"Eyes" face pitcher

Front knee stiffens at contact

Back toe is resting on ground

**1-84**

Hitting is a two-phase act: (a) the stride, and (b) the swing. The stride phase should be completed before the hands start forward in the swing. The stride is performed slowly and the swing (contact) phase is performed quickly. Remember:

Slow Stride—Quick Bat

The stride phase of hitting must be performed correctly in order for the back shoulder, hips, knees, and hands to drive through the ball correctly.

# Developing a Visual Tracking System

The position of the head is important because it allows the player to track the ball effectively with the eyes (refer to p. 7). If the head is in the correct position and remains still, and if the stride and swing are correct, the hitter should feel the back shoulder touch the chin during the turn portion of the swing. Only if the head position is correct will a hitter be able to develop an effective tracking system.

*Developing a quality tracking system is probably the most important phase of hitting.* A hitter must focus sharply on the ball from the time it leaves the pitcher's fingertips until it hits the bat. Any lapse during the ball's flight can lead to failure.

The hitter must first learn to determine the *speed of the pitch* and then identify the *rotation of the ball.* To figure out the speed and rotation of each pitch as early as possible, the hitter should pretend the pitcher is delivering the pitch through a window near the pitcher's release point, and train himself to focus on the ball at that point. If the hitter determines the velocity first and spin second, he is more likely to be in a proper hitting position on all pitches, whether they are fast balls, curve balls, sliders, or change-ups. If the hitter is not mindful of the speed of the pitch, he will be off-balance and will swing too soon at curve balls and change-ups. The hitter should determine the spin as the pitch comes to the plate and should adjust the plane of his bat for curve balls and high or low fast balls.

By studying the angle of the pitcher's release point, the hitter can often determine whether the pitch will sink, sail, or jump, as well as the arc of a breaking curve ball. For example, if a pitcher's release point is overhead, the fast ball will usually jump if thrown hard, and the curve ball will break down. If, however, the pitcher's release point is more to the side, often the fast ball will sink and the curve ball will break flat across the strike zone. This type of information is vital for a complete tracking system.

The following three drills can help hitters develop their tracking systems. The Colored Ball Drill is especially good for young players.

## SIMULATING SWINGS DRILL (home drill)

*Purpose:* To develop and refine a player's tracking system—the ability to determine the speed, rotation, and correct contact point of each pitch.

*Equipment:* All players on the team should construct a personal strike zone and three-colored home plate (see Appendix B for instructions). Bat or half bat is optional.

*Procedure:* At home the player hangs the personalized strike zone on a wall next to a full-length mirror and places the three-colored home plate on the floor in front of the strike zone. The hitter assumes a hitting stance and focuses on one of the "pitches" on the strike zone. The player pretends a pitcher is throwing that pitch. The hitter imagines a game setting and visualizes the path of the ball while performing the proper swing for that pitch. A bat is not necessary, but can be used if there is sufficient room.

After several swings in front of the strike zone, the hitter should move the three-colored home plate over in front of the mirror and study the elements of the swing, being especially careful to keep the head still. The combination of practicing the swing in front of the strike zone and the mirror provides an optimal learning environment for developing hitting skills.

## COLORED BALL DRILL

*Purpose:* To develop visual tracking skills in hitters by teaching them to watch the ball from the time it leaves the pitcher's hand until it reaches the contact point.

*Equipment:* Four or five differently colored baseballs per group (see Appendix B for instructions), *no* bats, home plate, helmets. Colored tennis balls may be used for all ages, and should be used by all players younger than 10.

*Procedure:* Players work in groups of four; one player serves as a pitcher, one a catcher, and two players *without* bats are hitters. If both hitters hit from the same side, one stands behind the other. If one is a left-handed hitter and the other a right-handed hitter, they stand on their respective sides of home plate.

The pitcher selects one of the colored balls from a container, carefully hiding the ball from the hitters. The hitters compete on each pitch to determine who can call the color of the ball first and whether the pitch has a fast ball or curve ball spin. If the pitch is a strike, the hitters simulate a correct swing. However, if the pitch is not a strike they should "take" the pitch. The catcher calls balls and strikes. A point is awarded to the first hitter (a) calling the correct color, (b) calling the correct spin, and (c) if the hitter takes the pitch if it is a ball, or simulates a swing if it is a strike. After five pitches players change roles. The player with the most points wins the contest.

## NUMBER OF FINGERS DRILL

*Purpose:* To develop a hitter's visual tracking system.
*Equipment:* Glove as home plate.

*Procedure:* One player kneels 2 feet in front of home plate and passes his hand through the strike zone, showing various numbers of fingers. The other player practices simulating the proper physical mechanics of the swing *without* a bat, while calling out loud the number of fingers the partner passes through the strike zone. The players passing their hands through the strike zone also serve as "coach," correcting improper body position in their partners' swing. The coach should pay particular attention to the position of the "hitter's" head (see Fig. 1-85).

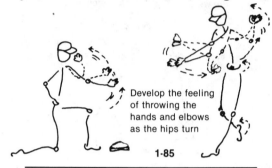

Develop the feeling of throwing the hands and elbows as the hips turn

1-85

Hitters can refine their tracking systems by looking for cues before the pitcher's release. For example, pitchers may "expose" their pitch before the delivery by changing the position of the throwing hand either during the delivery, at the top of the delivery, or by holding the ball differently for different pitches. This advance information can aid a hitter tremendously in tracking the pitch to the bat.

*Key Point:* In summary, the successful hitter concentrates on *physical mechanics* and the *visual tracking system* simultaneously. Of these two areas, visual discipline is more important and should be stressed accordingly. However, proper physical mechanics allow the eyes to remain still during the swing which permits proper tracking, and promotes bat speed and bat control, all of which contribute to quality hitting.

## Strategies for Hitting

### Aggressive Hitting

*A hitter should always go to the plate with an aggressive, optimistic attitude, ready to attack the ball.* Taking too many strikes leads to a defensive attitude and often leads to hitting slumps. A passive, defensive hitting philosophy often results in called third strikes. Hitters must be mentally ready to hit when they step into the batter's box. They must know that they are better hitters than the pitcher is a pitcher. This positive outlook will lead to an aggressive swing.

Hitters need to be aggressive, but also need to force the pitcher to throw strikes by *swinging only at pitches which are in the strike zone*. Swinging at "balls" only helps the pitcher and likewise can lead to hitting slumps. Since one of a pitcher's main objectives is to keep pitches on the edges of the plate with "something on them," hitters need to be selective to the point of swinging not only at strikes, but also only at pitches they can hit effectively

*Key Point:* All hitters should step to the plate with enthusiasm and eagerness to attack the ball with fundamental precision.

## Looking for a Pitch

*Hitters should go to the plate looking for a particular pitch.* They should have a definite idea about the types of pitches the pitcher is throwing and the effectiveness of those pitches. Keeping a record of each pitch, as on the Pitching Chart, is an effective means for learning this information.

### Pitching Chart

| Name of Pitcher: | | | Game: | | | Date: | | |
|---|---|---|---|---|---|---|---|---|
| Inning | Fast ball | Curve ball | Change-up | Slider-Sinker | Hitter & Pitch | Cum. % | Leadoff Hitter |
| 1 | 57 % | 63 % | 50 % | % | 1. ⓕ Cu C ⓒ 6-3<br>2. ⓒF Cⓤ F-9<br>3. ⓕ C F C ⓕ 1B<br>4. ⓒ F C ⓒ K | 59% | YES |
| 2 | 63 % | 50 % | 100 % | 100 % | 1. ⓕ ⓒ C F ⓒ F-7<br>2. ⓒ F ⓒ C ⓕ 6-3<br>3. F ⓕ ⓒ C ⓢ Sl F-4 | 63% | Yes |
| 3 | % | % | % | % | | | |

#### PITCHING CHART KEY

Strike Zone — Place a mark in the exact location the pitch entered the area. This information is used to calculate the percentage of strikes for each type of pitch, and to give batters an idea of where the pitcher locates pitches.

% — To determine the percentage of strikes for each type of pitch for each inning, divide the number of strikes by the number of total pitches for that particular type of pitch.

Hitter & Pitch — Record each pitch as it is thrown to each hitter. Circle the strikes. Use abbreviations such as F for fast ball, C for curve, CH for change, SL for slider and SN for sinker. Also note what happened to the hitter. This information can be very beneficial in determining a trend or what type of pitch the pitcher may throw in various situations. By studying the chart each inning, a hitter can soon discover what type of pitch is thrown when the count is 0-0, 2-0, 3-1, or 3-2 or maybe what the pitch will be after the pitcher misses with a curve ball.

Cumulative % — Divide the total number of pitches in all of the columns into the total number of strikes for each inning. This figure helps hitters learn the nature of the pitcher's control and it can help them analyze how to approach their next turn at bat in terms of aggressiveness, patience, and visual selection.

Leadoff Hitter — Record whether the pitcher got the leadoff hitter out each inning. Winning pitchers usually get the leadoff hitter out.

After a few innings, the chart will reveal the pitcher's patterns. The example used in the sample Pitching Chart shows that during the first 2 innings the pitcher threw 15 fast balls, 14 curves, 3 change-ups, and 1 slider. It also shows that the pitcher threw about the same number of fast balls and curve balls for strikes. The hitter now knows that he needs to be prepared for both curve balls and fast balls but that the first pitch will probably be a fast ball.

Since the chart shows that the pitcher mixes the pitches well and gets both the fast ball and curve over the plate consistently, the hitter has to go to the plate concentrating on the speed and spin of the ball and bear down on all pitches. Charts may indicate that a pitcher tends to throw mainly fast balls or mainly curves, or only throws fast balls for strikes. In this case, the hitter can go to the plate looking for a particular pitch. Of course, as is discussed further below, if the hitter has 2 strikes he should not rely as much on the chart as when he has less than 2 strikes.

### Hitting With Less Than 2 Strikes and With 2 Strikes

*With less than 2 strikes hitters should look for "their pitch."* They should be patient enough to wait for a pitch which would increase the probability of a good hit, such as a belt-high fast ball across the middle of the plate. They should not allow themselves to be tempted to swing at pitches which are difficult to hit well, such as low curve balls or high fast balls.

Once hitters have 2 strikes, they must concentrate on *making contact, staying on top of the ball*, and *thinking about driving the ball up the middle*. The mental adjustment will allow them to protect the plate and remain a "tough out."

### Hitting Curve Balls and Hitting to the Opposite Field (Bat Control)

By tracking the ball carefully a hitter can determine first the speed and then the spin of the ball. Once the pitch is determined to be "off-speed," and then the spin to be that of a curve ball, the hitter must think about reacting instantly to the angle of the break. *The bat arc must match the angle of the curve ball to increase the hitting area on the bat.*

The important point to remember, when hitting an overhand curve which breaks down, is to match up the arc of the bat with the angle of the break in order to permit the ball to break into the quality part of the bat. The same bat arc used to hit most curve balls cannot be used to hit most fast balls. *The bat arc*

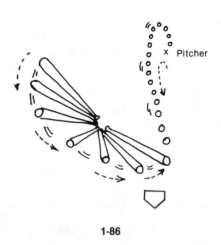

**1-86**

*used on an overhand curve is somewhat similar to a golfer's swing* (see Fig. 1-86). When hitting flat-breaking curves, sliders, and outside fast balls, hitters should try to *drive the ball up the middle or to the opposite field*. If hitters try to pull these pitches, they will contact the ball improperly, have poor weight distribution, and timing will be off (see Contact Points, p. 11).

### Hit-and-Run

If executed properly, the hit-and-run can advance runners and help produce more runs. A hitter must follow certain guidelines when attempting the hit-and-run play.

*A hitter's primary concern in the hit-and-run should be getting on top of the ball and not popping up.* The hitter should attempt to hit a line drive behind the moving base runner so that the base runner can advance more than one base on a base hit. A right-handed hitter should wait slightly longer before starting to swing to enhance his chances of "slicing" the ball to right field. A left-handed hitter should try to pull the ball sharply to right field or punch the ball through the shortstop's area if the shortstop moves toward second to cover the bag as the runner breaks from first base. A hitter should increase his strike zone slightly and swing at any pitch he thinks he can meet capably with the bat.

Learning the bat control necessary to execute a hit-and-run is not easy and needs to be practiced frequently during batting practice. As the hitter learns more effective bat control, he will be able to advance a runner on second base to third base, when there are no outs, by hitting the ball to the right side. Also, the hitter will find that the increased bat control helps him get hits he would not previously have gotten.

## In Sum . . .

Whether hitters are trying to hit curve balls, fast balls, sinkers, or sliders, and whether the pitches are high, low, inside, or outside, the hitter needs good *bat control* and *bat speed*, and a well-developed *visual tracking system*. Bat control and bat speed require proper execution of several precise body movements. A player cannot become a proficient hitter by performing one or two simple fundamentals; rather, there are numerous significant mental and physical elements which must be perfected. As players practice, many of the separate elements will blend together into a smooth precise unit. Such precision requires almost unlimited simulation of the swing and hitting practice accompanied by meaningful internal feedback.

*Hitting should eventually become a reflex so that the mind can concentrate solely on tracking the pitch.* Only then can a hitter successfully handle all types of pitches. A hitter should think only about tracking the ball when at the plate in a game. A hitter may review fundamentals while in the dugout, or on deck during the game, or during practice, in the back yard, in front of a mirror, or anywhere practice occurs—*not while at bat during a game*.

## How to Correct Hitting Problems

### Diagnostic Chart

Occasionally a hitter encounters problems that are baffling to both player and coach. The following diagnostic chart should prove useful for solving many of those problems. It should be emphasized that symptoms, causes, and corrections are often multiple in nature; therefore, coaches and players must realize that a *combination of several factors may need to be taken into consideration in order to correct the problem.*

### Diagnostic Chart

**Problem: Inconsistent Contact**

| Symptoms | Possible Causes | Suggested Solutions |
|---|---|---|
| Striking out<br>Popping the ball up<br>Grounding out<br>Getting jammed<br>Hitting late | Not tracking the ball properly<br>Not concentrating on the ball; mind wanders<br>Poor fundamentals<br>Not being aggressive at the plate<br>Swinging at pitches out of the strike zone<br>Not looking for a specific pitch to hit<br>Lack of confidence<br>Allowing anxiety and tension to dominate state of mind | Simulate swings against an imaginary pitcher<br>Practice simulating swings in front of a personal strike zone on a wall, using 3-colored home plate<br>Analyze the type of pitch hit and where it entered the strike zone<br>Develop better visual and mental control<br>Review fundamental body position during the swing<br>Encourage hitter to relax and think "lazy body—quick bat"<br>Encourage hitter to turn back and front shoulders level through the ball<br>Player should "throw" the bat at the ball, not simply swing<br>Encourage hitter to drive the ball right back through the pitcher<br>Build confidence through success experiences and positive reinforcement |

## Diagnostic Chart (Continued)

### Problem: Slow Bat

| Symptoms | Possible Causes | Suggested Solutions |
|---|---|---|
| Striking out<br>Fouling the ball back<br>Hitting late<br>Not hitting the ball hard | Not turning back and keeping front shoulder down and level during the swing<br>Gripping bat too tightly<br>Holding bat too far down on knob<br>Bat too heavy<br>Hitter too weak<br>Allowing the arms, instead of wrists and forearms, to dominate swing<br>Sweeping the bat rather than "throwing"<br>Overstriding with a fast body movement towards the ball<br>Lead elbow straightens out too soon before contact<br>Not simulating enough swings<br>Not tracking the ball properly<br>Not concentrating on pitch | Simulate proper stance, stride, and contact point positions<br>Keep hands and body relaxed before the swing<br>Choke up on the bat<br>Develop strong hands and forearms<br>Practice Wrist Roller drill<br>Practice throwing the bat<br>Simulate proper swings<br>Practice Hip Turner Drill<br>Practice hitting with lead and follow hands separately<br>Focus more and concentrate on ball |

### Problem: Dropping Under

| Symptoms | Possible Causes | Suggested Solutions |
|---|---|---|
| Popping the ball up<br>Flying out<br>Fouling the ball back | Overstriding causing head to drop and leading to dropping under pitch<br>Dropping hands or back elbow before swing<br>Picking front shoulder up and dropping back shoulder during stride and swing<br>Permitting lead hand to move up prior to contact<br>Not permitting back toe to turn freely as bat contacts ball<br>Not "throwing" bat at ball<br>Not turning hips quickly enough or horizontally<br>Not keeping knees pointed toward home plate during stride<br>Not striding on ball of front foot | Practice stance and stride drills with tape<br>If hitter drops hands before swing, encourage him to start hands lower before swing (only direction for hands to travel will be through the ball)<br>Practice striding with front shoulder down and knee in<br>Practice hitting off a batting tee with lead hand and follow hand swings; lead hand should land at contact area like an airplane<br>Simulate swings in front of mirror, check back toe<br>Practice throwing bat with lead and follow hands<br>Practice Hip Turner Drill<br>Simulate swings against an imaginary pitcher |

## Coaches' Evaluation of Hitters

Coaches should continually evaluate and carefully analyze their players while they perform their skills. All players should be encouraged to evaluate and analyze their own performance as well. Frequently an observant coach or player will be able to spot problems in a hitter's style or selection of pitches to hit. Early identification of problems makes them easier to correct, and presumably will help the hitter's performance.

Following are some questions that coaches and players should ask themselves as they evaluate and analyze a player's performance. These questions involve some of the most common mistakes young players make. They are followed by the condition the mistake can create, and a method for correcting the mistake.

*Question #1:* Is the hitter's grip too tight?
*Condition:* If the grip is too tight, the lack of flex-

ibility in the hands and wrists will restrict bat speed and control.

*Solution:* Encourage hitter to keep *hands loose.*

*Question #2:* Is the hitter holding the bat too far down on the knob?

*Condition:* Bat speed and control could be hampered since many young hitters' hands and forearms are too weak to hold most bats down on the knob.

*Solution:* Encourage hitter to *choke the bat.*

*Question #3:* Does the hitter lift the front shoulder or drop the back shoulder during the stride?

*Condition:* If the front shoulder moves up during the stride, the hands will drop under the ball and the head will pull away from the ball.

*Solution:* Encourage the hitter to keep the *front shoulder down* during the stride and emphasize the importance of a *quick, level turn of the hips and both shoulders.*

*Question #4:* Is the hitter aggressive at the plate?

*Condition:* If hitters aren't aggressive at the plate, they will tend to take too many pitches. Hitters will not only fail to swing at prime pitches, but will begin to take called third strikes.

*Solution:* Encourage the hitter to *attack the ball.*

*Question #5:* Does the hitter hit the ball with elbows bent and close to the body?

*Condition:* If the hitter makes contact with the ball when his elbows are bent and close to his body, he will be restricting his bat arc and wrist arc. Such a condition is related to lack of flexibility of the arms and hands.

*Solution:* Encourage the hitter to *"throw" the bat at the ball* to increase the power in the swing.

*Question #6:* Does the hitter drop the back elbow or hands before the swing?

*Condition:* If the hitter drops the back elbow or hands before the stride, the front shoulder tends to go up and the head pulls away from the ball. The hands will be under the ball at contact causing pop-ups and fly outs.

*Solution:* Encourage the hitter to start with the *lead forearm parallel to the ground* and to keep the *front shoulder down during the stride.*

*Question #7:* Does the hitter overstride?

*Condition:* Overstriding can lead to slow hips, sweeping the bat, moving the eyes, and dropping under the ball.

*Solution:* Encourage the hitter to keep the *front shoulder down, front knee in,* and *weight on the back hip while striding,* and use a *wider stance with a shorter stride.*

*Question #8:* Does the hitter's back toe turn as the bat meets the ball?

*Condition:* If the back toe does not turn as the bat meets the ball, the turning action of the hips is limited, which restricts bat speed and leads to dropping under the pitch.

*Solution:* Encourage the hitter to allow the *back toe to turn quickly* while *"throwing" the bat at the ball.*

*Question #9:* Does the hitter straighten out the lead elbow too soon?

*Condition:* Straightening the elbow early in the swing can lead to sweeping the bat with the arms, restricting bat speed and bat control.

*Solution:* Encourage the hitter to *relax the arms* and *"throw" the bat at the ball.*

*Question #10:* Does the hitter keep the front knee in and the weight on the back hip while striding?

*Condition:* If the front knee turns out and the hip weight starts forward early in the stride, the hands will start forward too soon. This reduces bat speed and control and makes hitting a curve ball or going to the opposite field difficult.

*Solution:* Encourage the hitter to have a *slow, relaxed body during the stride,* and to keep the *body weight back until the hips start to turn.*

*Question #11:* Do the hitter's hands and hips work together throughout the swing?

*Condition:* Frequently, young hitters fail to coordinate the hands and hips together during the swing. As the contact of the bat with the ball occurs, the hips should turn at the precise moment the elbows and wrists extend.

*Solution:* Encourage the hitter to *simulate hundreds of swings each week* while being conscious of correct timing and the refinement of correct mechanical principles.

*Question #12:* Does the hitter swing at pitches he can hit effectively?

*Condition:* If a hitter swings at almost any pitch, the average pitcher becomes far more effective because of the "enlarged" strike zone.

*Solution:* Encourage hitters to look for a *certain type of pitch* in a *certain area of the strike zone* when there are less than 2 strikes and *to attack all pitches within the strike zone* when there are 2 strikes.

*Question #13:* Does the hitter hit the ball to the opposite field when the pitches are on the outside corner of the plate?

*Condition:* Attempting to pull all pitches leads to improper contact with the ball and often results in ground outs and strikeouts because the hitter turns through the ball too quickly.

*Solution:* Encourage the hitter to practice hitting outside pitches to the opposite field by *squaring the hips to that field* as the bat contacts the ball and *not completing the full turn of the hips.* Make sure the hitter keeps the hands above the plane of the ball since dropping under the ball is much easier on outside pitches.

### Getting Out of Slumps

There is no definitive solution for getting out of a hitting slump, but the points listed below can help to correct most hitting problems.

1. *Analyze the tracking system.* Before making any mechanical adjustments, the hitter should analyze the quality of his tracking system. Total concentration on the ball is necessary along with a strong positive attitude. If the hitter dwells on mechanical problems or the possibility of failure during a plate appearance, the ability to concentrate on the ball will decrease and lead to inconsistent contact. *The most important hitting fundamental is to keep the mind and eyes concentrating on the ball.*

2. *Swing at pitches that can be hit effectively.* Some hitters fall into slumps because they start swinging at pitches that are not in the strike zone. The hitter must be disciplined enough to swing only at pitches that can be hit effectively.

3. *Change bats.* Occasionally a change of weight, length, or balance of a bat helps to improve a hitter's timing.

4. *Adjust the stance.* A wider stance may eliminate head movement and lunging, and result in better timing.

5. *Hit the ball up the middle.* By trying to hit the ball back through the pitcher's mound, the hitter is less likely to pull the eyes away from the ball, and will wait longer on the pitch.

6. *Meet the ball.* Try to get the best part of the bat on the ball. "Throw" the bat down at the ball quickly with the hands. Watch the ball hit the bat and try to stay on top of the ball.

7. *Confidence.* In the midst of failure, a hitter must believe that he is an effective hitter, capable of hitting any pitch.

8. *Analyze fundamentals.* A hitter should be able to diagnose fundamental mistakes by taking an inventory of the body positions and their relationship to the swing. Mistakes such as dropping the hands or back elbow, lifting the front shoulder, overstriding, or turning the stride knee too soon can all lead to pulling the head out, dropping under the ball, and failure to track the ball properly. By simulating on a daily

basis hundreds of properly executed swings in front of a mirror and a personal strike zone, hitters will maintain and reinforce effective hitting habits. Such a training procedure will help prevent or eliminate many hitting slumps. Coaches should insist that their players pursue this type of program away from formal team practice in order to increase good habits and enhance muscle memory.

### Characteristics Needed to Become an Effective Hitter

1. *Confidence*—awareness of one's cultivated talents

2. *Poise*—being able to perform under pressure

3. *Aggressiveness*—wanting to attack the ball

4. *Self-control and discipline*—being able to wait for an appropriate pitch

5. *Desire to excel*—keeping one's individual goals high

6. *Alertness*—being able to identify the speed and spin of pitches

7. *Enthusiasm*—always being ready to perform with maximum effort

8. *Observant*—able to notice movements in the pitcher's motion which tip off different pitches

9. *Positive outlook*—able to keep discouragement to a minimum

10. *Competitiveness*—able to accept a challenge on every pitch

11. *Consistency*—able to fulfill the responsibility of a steady performer

## Daily Practice Schedule

Hitting is a motor skill requiring precision, reflexes, strength, flexibility, and concentration. Proper habits must be formed for a hitter to be consistently effective. Since organized workouts do not provide a sufficient amount of time for proper development, coaches should encourage their players to perform a daily, supplementary home training program. The following schedule is a suggested daily workout for players 10 years old and older. Younger players may want to practice hitting off a batting tee and hitting whiffle balls.

---

### 30-MINUTE DAILY HITTING SCHEDULE

*Always practice with the intent to improve.*

• 50 simulated swings in front of a mirror. The hitter should be conscious of the primary body parts such as toes, heels, knees, hips, hands, elbows, shoulder, and head, and relationship of the body parts to the swing.

• 50 simulated swings in front of a personal strike zone (see p. 15). The hitter should practice tracking an imaginary pitch into the strike zone and hitting the pitch with the lead hand, follow hand, and both hands.

• 60 seconds of Wrist Rollers (see p. 9).

• 10 repetitions of Throwing Bats (see p. 9).

• 25 Hip Turners (see p. 8).

• Daily review of stance, stride, and contact point positions using Contact Point Drill (see p. 11).

• 5 minutes of Rolley (see Appendix B for instructions), bat extension drills, hand grippers, and other bat fitness drills (see p. 148).

• 15 repetitions of each of the fitness calisthenics (see Appendix A).

---

Hitters should condition themselves by swinging a leaded bat which weighs 15-20 ounces more than their regular bat. This makes all of the hitting muscles stronger and also makes hitting actions quicker. Simulating swings with a regular bat is also an effective conditioner. If a ball player simulates at least 100 swings a day, making sure to execute the proper mechanics on each swing, performance will increase tremendously. Wrist Rollers and Hip Turners are also excellent conditioners when done in large numbers.

From a mental standpoint, the best conditioner for a ball player is to constantly think and talk hitting. Players who mentally place themselves into various hitting situations and imagine performing successfully will be more apt to perform successfully in actual situations than players who simply think hitting when at the ball park.

As emphasized previously, hitting is an extremely intricate skill. The tougher the pitching, the more complex hitting becomes. Thus ball players who desire futures in baseball should condition themselves totally—physically, mentally and emotionally. Through dedication and preparation, a player will develop greater confidence and understand proper hitting techniques.

## Hitter on Deck

The hitter on deck serves as the base coach at home plate on all plays at home. If a close play is developing at home plate after a base hit, the on-deck hitter should hustle out to pick up the bat and get behind home plate to tell the runner whether to slide or stand up.

The on-deck hitter should know what the pitcher has been throwing and should be concentrating on every move the pitcher makes. The on-deck hitter needs to get "psyched" into a positive state of mind ready to step aggressively to the plate and attack the ball. Even though a few practice swings with a weighted bat or something comparable is useful, the primary concern should be mental and emotional readiness to hit.

# CHAPTER 2

# Bunting

*The weaker a player's hitting is, the stronger his bunting must be.* This concept is just as true about weak hitting teams. Each member of the team should work as diligently on bunting technique as on hitting. One of the best ways to become an efficient bunter is to practice bunting various types of pitches frequently. Just as with other phases of baseball, repetitious work on fundamentals is often the key to success.

## Sacrifice Bunt

A properly executed sacrifice bunt enables one or more runners to advance successfully to the next base, placing them in a more advantageous scoring position. This fundamental point is often forgotten by hitters attempting to lay down the sacrifice bunt. Runs can be lost because hitters fail to lay down a bunt successfully when needed. Each player needs to learn the following rules governing bunts.

1. *The hitter should bunt strikes only.* The hitter should not attempt to bunt pitches out of the strike zone. Trying to bunt pitches out of the strike zone only helps the pitcher and leads to inconsistent bunting.

2. *The hitter should lay down a successful bunt on the first attempt,* but must make sure the ball is in the strike zone.

3. *The ball should not be bunted back to the pitcher.* The most effective place for the bunted ball is

3 to 4 feet inside the foul lines and about 15 to 20 feet from home plate (see Fig. 2-23).

4. *The hitter should not pop up the bunt.*

5. *The hitter should not try to run until after the bunt is laid down.*

### Mechanics of the Sacrifice Bunt

The proper mechanics of the sacrifice bunt are shown in Figures 2-1 through 2-6. The bunter in the figures is executing the following key points of the sacrifice bunt:

1. The hitter turns his feet and starts the bat forward as the pitcher is ready to release the ball.

2. The hitter keeps the lower hand near the knob and slides the upper hand up approximately 12 inches from the lower hand.

3. Both hands, especially the upper hand, are firmly in control of the bat. The lower hand is slightly relaxed to help soften the bunt.

4. The hitter gets the bat well out in front at eye level.

5. The knees are relaxed and the bunter is bent in a semi-crouched position.

6. The hitter allows the ball to hit the bat and is careful not to push the bat at the ball.

7. The hitter assures a more effective sacrifice bunt by not running to first base until after the bunt is laid down.

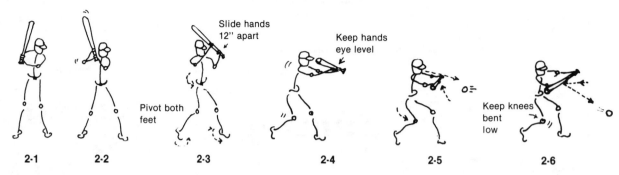

Figures 2-1 through 2-6  Hitter pivots feet, slides upper hand 12" up bat, gets bat at eye level, keeps knees bent, points elbows down, and catches ball with bat.

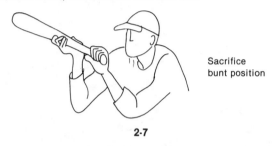

2-7

The Catch the Ball Bunt Drill is an excellent way for players to learn proper bunting fundamentals.

## CATCH THE BALL BUNT DRILL

*Age Group:* 10 and up.

*Purpose:* To teach the bunter to bend the knees and not push the bat at the ball.

*Equipment:* Bat, ball, home plate (see Appendix B for fold-up), glove.

*Procedure:* Place a glove at the end of the bat. Coach pitches. Bunter pivots into a sacrifice bunt position and kneels down on the ground. (Right leg on ground for right-handed batter.) Have the batter try to catch the ball with the glove while in the kneeling bunting position. Emphasize keeping hands 12 inches apart on the bat, with the lower hand loose and the upper hand firm, holding the bat at eye level, and keeping the hand next to the knob base (see Figs. 2-8, 2-9).

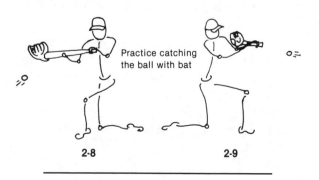

## Mechanics of the Drag Bunt

### Right-Handed

The drag bunt is designed to give the hitter a quicker start toward first base and is meant to produce base hits. The hitter has an additional advantage since the defense doesn't know a hit will be a bunt until after the pitcher releases the ball. The hitter steps back with the right foot while bending both knees. The right hand slides up the barrel of the bat to the label while the hitter simply extends the bat across the plate. The hitter bunts the ball down the third base line, and immediately shoves off hard with the right foot toward first base. The front knee must bend thoroughly for a successful drag bunt. Bending the knee permits the bunter to place the bat in a proper plane with the ball (see Figs. 2-10 to 2-14). The bunter should not think of running until after the bat meets the ball.

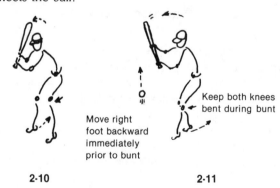

Another method a right-hander may use to drag bunt is similar to the sacrifice bunt. The primary difference between the two methods is that the bunter crosses the back foot over in the direction of the pitcher, and "pushes" the bunt past the mound. This bunt might be thought of as a running sacrifice.

Drag bunt position (right-handed)

2-15

### Left-Handed

The left-hander's drag bunt is similar to the running sacrifice. The left-handed bunter crosses the left foot over, pointing it towards the pitcher after extending the bat across the plate (see Figs. 2-16 to 2-21). The bunter should be careful not to cross over with the back leg too soon, or lean towards first base too severely as the pitch comes to the plate; this tends to reduce bat control and timing, thus restricting bunting effectiveness.

The drag bunt should go to the same area as the sacrifice bunt (see Fig. 2-23). Hitters can raise their batting averages several points by becoming proficient drag bunters, so it would be to their advantage to put in as many practice hours on bunting as they do on hitting.

The following two drills are effective ways for players to work on their bunting skills.

## ACCURATE SACRIFICE BUNTING

*Age Group:* 10 and up.

*Purpose:* To develop players' bunting skills.

*Equipment:* 140 feet of rope, stakes to hold rope, infield area, bats, balls, helmets.

*Procedure:* Each bunter bunts ten pitches, attempting to have the ball "die" in the designated area. A rope is placed in the infield to denote the appropriate areas for bunting. If a rope is not available, use bats, balls, or helmets to outline the designated area. Players can get points for each good bunt.

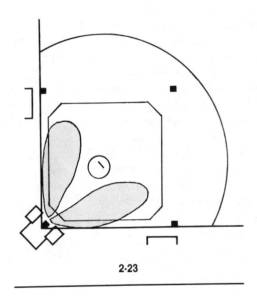

2-23

2-16

Do not start bunt until after ball is released by pitcher

2-17

Cross left leg over toward pitcher after contact with ball

2-18

Do not bunt ball back to pitcher

2-19

2-20

2-21

Drag bunt position (left-handed)

2-22

## RAPID-FIRE BUNTING DRILL

*Age Group:* 10 and up.

*Purpose:* To provide players many opportunities to bunt in a short period of time. Helps develop sacrifice bunting and drag bunting skills. Defensive players also have an opportunity to develop and quicken defensive reactions.

*Equipment:* Bats, balls, gloves, helmets.

*Procedure:* Players work in groups of four. One member of each group serves as the bunter, while the others serve as defensive players and "pitchers." The bunter places a glove on the ground to use as a home plate. The defensive players form a line approximately 40-50 feet in front of the bunter.

Each defensive player pitches a ball to the bunter, fields the bunt, and returns to the end of the line. The defensive player must field or retrieve the ball no matter where it goes, even if the bunter fouls the ball back or misses the ball. The next defensive player should deliver the pitch to the bunter as soon as the previous defensive player fields the ball and is out of the way. The bunter lays down 5 sacrifice bunts and 5 drag bunts before switching with one of the defensive players. The drill moves at a brisk pace, giving everyone a challenging workout.

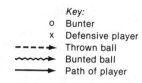

Key:
o   Bunter
x   Defensive player
- - - →   Thrown ball
∿∿∿→   Bunted ball
——→   Path of player

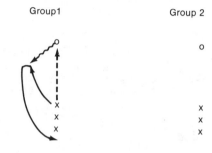

Group1                          Group 2

*Each defensive player:*
1 - Has his own ball
2 - Throws a pitch to
    the bunter
3 - Fields the bunt
4 - Returns to end
    of line

**2-24**

# CHAPTER 3

# Baserunning

Baserunning is one of the most important aspects of baseball, but one which many coaches neglect. For various reasons, individual ball players and teams as a whole do not include baserunning as much as they should in their workouts. Baserunning is especially important for teams which lack sound hitting. If a team has *adequate pitching, excellent defensive play, effective bunting,* and *if they are knowledgeable base runners,* they will not need many hits to win games.

## First Base Techniques

### The Break From Home Plate and Overrunning First Base

Getting a quick start from home plate after making contact with the ball is essential for all hitters. Slow rollers and high chops can often be turned into base hits by players with speed and determination. If a base runner puts forth maximum effort down the line, there is added pressure on the infielders to rush the play. Also, a hard-running runner seldom grounds into a double play. Therefore it is important for every ball player to get as fast a start from home as possible after making contact with the ball.

As players run to first base, they should perform the following fundamentals:

1. keep *weight leaning forward*
2. *feet and hands move in a straight line* instead of diagonally

3. *toes should point straight ahead*, not outward, to insure proper shove
4. run with *enthusiasm*

Movements by the arms and legs across the straight line of the body can limit speed.

When base runners run to first after hitting a ground ball, they should always turn the head to the right as they touch first base to see if there is an overthrow on the play. Runners who fail to check often are not able to advance to second base on an overthrow because they are not aware of the ball's location until it is too late to advance.

Players should realize that failure to run out a fly ball, pop-up, or ground ball at top speed is an indication of a poor attitude and can hurt their image. Also, it is possible that the ball may be misplayed, and the base runner should be ready to take advantage of every opportunity. Players should understand that quality base runners are *aggressive, alert, observant, and confident.*

The Running Past First Base Drill accustoms players to not slowing down as they reach first base.

---

### RUNNING PAST FIRST BASE

*Purpose:* To teach players to overrun first base.

*Equipment:* Three first bases, three home plates (see Appendix B for instructions on fold-up home plates).

*Procedure:* Three home plates and three first bases are set up at regulation distance. A line of players stands at each home plate. Players begin by standing in the batter's box, simulating a swing, and then jogging past first base.

Each time players touch first base they should turn the head to the right in order to develop the habit of checking for overthrows by infielders during a real game situation. This will help the runner to advance to second base quicker. Once past first base, players jog back, avoiding the next player in their group and other groups. Running gets progressively faster. Finish with some relay races where the next player in line starts as soon as the preceding player steps on first base.

## Rounding First Base—"Thinking Second"

When any ball is hit into the outfield, whether it is a base hit, fly ball, or an error through the infield, the runner should "think second." Thinking second means that the runner rounds first base at top speed while looking for a defensive bobble or slow play by an outfielder. The runner should sprint approximately one-third of the distance to second base at full speed and then make a decision whether to continue to second base or return to first. If the runner returns to first, it should be done cautiously, *always keeping eyes on the ball.* The throw to the infield could go astray, enabling the runner to advance, and quite often a single base can make the difference in a close game.

A base runner should "circle out" of the base path about 15 feet before first base to get a maximum shove off the base and also to head straight toward second base. The runner tags the center of the base while shifting the weight toward the pitcher's mound to help build momentum towards second. To help shift the weight, the left arm is pulled down hard as the runner tags the bag. Runners must be moving at top speed, otherwise they will not be able to "think second" properly (see Figs. 3-2 to 3-11).

*Note:* The same procedure is used when runners advance from first base to second base "thinking third," or when they go from second base to third base "thinking home."

Players can perform the Rounding First Base—Thinking Second Drill to practice rounding bases.

3-1

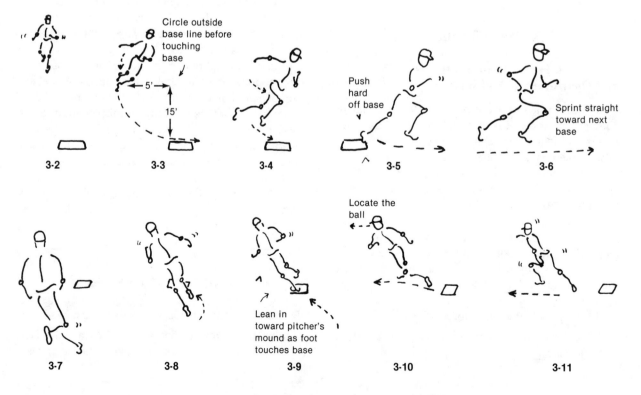

3-2    3-3    3-4    3-5    3-6

3-7    3-8    3-9    3-10    3-11

## ROUNDING FIRST BASE—THINKING SECOND

*Purpose:* To teach players how to round first base.

*Equipment:* Three cones or other markers, three first bases, three home plates (see Appendix B for instructions).

*Procedure:* Three home plates and three first bases are set up at regulation distance. A line of players stands at each home plate. Players begin by standing in the batter's box, taking a swing, and jogging to first base and rounding the base. Place a marker 15 feet before first base so players know where to begin the turn. Running gets progressively faster.

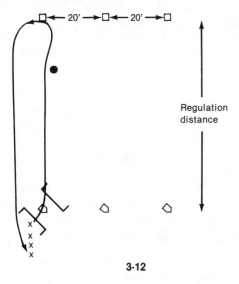

**3-12**

In the following two drills runners need to listen to the coach to find out whether they should stop at first base or continue to second. These two drills are designed for 5- to 9-year olds who are just learning to run bases effectively. Older players should execute baserunning drills against a defense, fielding a ball in a simulated real game setting. Older players need to learn to make baserunning decisions depending on how the ball is hit and how the defense fields the ball.

## RUNNING FROM HOME PLATE TO FIRST BASE

*Age Group:* 5-9.

*Purpose:* To teach players to react to the first base coach.

*Equipment:* Three first bases, three home plates (see Appendix B for instructions).

*Procedure:* Three home plates and three first bases are set up at regulation distance. A line of players stands at each home plate. Players begin by standing in the batter's box, taking a swing, and running to first base. Coach calls out either "sprint" or "take the turn" when the player is 25 feet from the base. Players react appropriately.

Each time players sprint through first base they should turn the head to the right in order to develop the habit of checking for overthrows by infielders during a real game situation. This will help the runner to advance to second base more quickly.

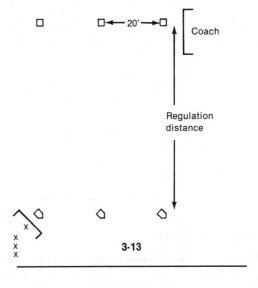

**3-13**

## STOP AND GO

*Age Group:* 5-9.

*Purpose:* To have players practice running through first base, rounding first base and stopping, and rounding first base and proceeding to second base.

*Equipment:* Four bases, three home plates (see Appendix B for instructions).

*Procedure:* Bases are set up as indicated in the figure, with a line of players at each home plate. Players begin by standing in the batter's box with a bat, swinging and running toward first base. Coach calls out one of the following.

1. "Sprint"—to have player run through first base. (Player should check for "overthrow" as he touches first base by looking to the right.)

2. "Take the turn"—player takes the turn and returns to first. (Player should "watch" the imaginary ball, never losing sight of it while returning to first base.)

3. "Go to second"—player correctly rounds first base and goes to second base (the base directly to the left of their group), all at top speed.

4. "Take the turn," pause, "go"—player takes the turn, slows, goes to second base at top speed.

Players should go into second base standing, *without* running past second. After their turn they return to their group, avoiding other runners. Once players learn to slide they can slide into second base.

```
□                □←— Regulation —→□ [ *
                   distance            ┌─┐
                                       │ │ Regulation
                                       │ │ distance
                                       │ │
                                       ▼
```

★  Coach
x  Players

3-14

## Leadoffs From First Base

***Defensive Lead From First Base.*** The defensive lead is designed to learn about the pitcher's move to first base. The first base runner in the game takes an extra long lead in order to draw a throw from the pitcher. The runner is not attempting to steal, so the weight is leaning back towards first base to assure that he will not get picked off. The whole team should watch as the runner attempts to gather information about the pitcher's move so they will know how much of a lead they can get off that pitcher. How high the pitcher picks up the foot during the delivery, how quickly the pitcher releases the ball, how quickly the pitcher throws to first on an attempted pick-off, and how often the pitcher attempts a pick-off are all valuable pieces of information for opposing base runners.

***Offensive Lead From First Base Including the Regular Steal.*** Any time runners will be moving with the pitch, they should assume an offensive lead. It should be used on steals, hit-and-runs, bunt-and-runs, and fake bunt-swings. An offensive lead is the *maximum distance* runners can safely lead off from first base. Body position should be comfortable with weight distributed equally on both feet. A runner's eyes should be fixed on a right-handed pitcher's left heel or a left-handed pitcher's right shoulder. As soon as that part of the pitcher's body moves in a direction that dictates a pitch to home plate, the runner takes a quick crossover step to initiate the attempted steal. This split-second "jump" on the pitcher is often the difference between being safe or out at second (see Figs. 3-15 to 3-19). If the hitter is performing a hit-and-run, bunt-and-run, or fake bunt-swing, the runner should glance toward home plate while running to see where the ball was hit or bunted. If the ball was popped up, there still might be time to stop and return to first base.

***Walking Lead From First Base.*** The walking lead is effective primarily against pitchers who *seldom* throw to first base or who maintain a set time pattern in the stretch and delivery. It can be used for the same situations as the offensive lead. Observant base runners know exactly how long it takes the pitcher to go from the pause in the stretch to the move toward the plate. The runner should slowly start walking off the bag as the pitcher starts the stretch to get the maximum "jump" off the pitcher.

***Sacrifice Bunt Lead From First Base.*** When the hitter is going to perform a sacrifice bunt, the runner should stay on the base until the pitcher starts the stretch. The runner then takes a lead of about two strides, constantly watching the pitcher. As the pitch is delivered, the runner takes a sideways "crow hop" or a side jump and comes to rest with the weight on the balls of the feet. Before breaking for second, the runner waits to see where the ball is bunted, or if it is bunted at all. This should eliminate double plays on pop bunts as well as pick-offs from the catcher following a missed bunt (see Figs. 3-20 to 3-25).

Focus on pitcher

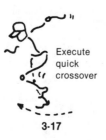

Execute quick crossover

Strive to obtain maximum speed in two strides

3-15            3-16            3-17            3-18            3-19

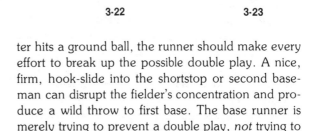

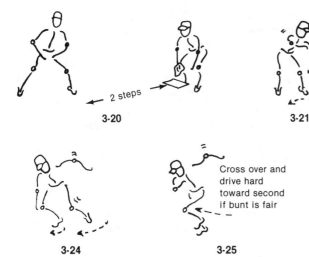

The sacrifice bunt lead is also effective when the bases are loaded with no outs. If a hitter hits a line drive, the runners should be able to get back to their bases safely, thus preventing the double play. The runner must *see the line drive go through* the infield before attempting to advance.

### Assuming a Lead and Moving Back to First Base.

Runners should take their lead from first base by executing quick side steps to the desired distance. The quick side steps allow a runner to maintain proper balance and return successfully to first base if the pitcher attempts a pick-off while a runner is getting a lead. The base runner should concentrate on the right-handed pitcher's left heel and the left-handed pitcher's right shoulder while assuming a lead.

Once the runner has the proper lead and sees the pitcher start a pick-off move to first, the runner should either go back into first base standing up or diving. If the runner decides to go back to first base standing up, he should take a quick crossover step with the right foot and step on the outside corner of the base with the left foot. If, however, the runner had an extra long lead, he may have to dive back to first base by taking a quick crossover step with the right foot and diving toward first base. The runner cushions the fall with the left hand turned inward, and touches the outside corner of the base with the right hand.

Assuming appropriate leads from first base and returning safely on attempted pick-offs requires considerable practice and repetition. Players must develop proper habits in this important phase of the total offensive plan so that they will make fewer mistakes during the game.

## Other Maneuvers From First Base

### Breaking Up the Double Play.

Any time a runner is on first with less than two outs and the bat-ter hits a ground ball, the runner should make every effort to break up the possible double play. A nice, firm, hook-slide into the shortstop or second base-man can disrupt the fielder's concentration and pro-duce a wild throw to first base. The base runner is merely trying to prevent a double play, *not* trying to injure the shortstop or second baseman.

### Fly Balls.

When the batter hits a fly ball with less than two outs, the base runner at first should move half to three-quarters of the way to second base and watch the outfielder play the ball. From this point the runner should be able to return easily to first base if the ball is caught, or advance one or more bases if the ball is misplayed.

If there is a runner on third base and the score is close, the runner on first base has an excellent op-portunity to advance on a fly after tagging up. Since the fielder will generally throw either to home or the cut-off person, the defense's attention will not be primarily on the runner at first. Whether a runner should tag up and attempt to advance from first to second in other situations depends on the speed of the runner, the position of the fly ball, the velocity of the wind, and how well the outfielder throws.

### Fake Steal.

Another effective move at first base is the fake steal. It is a simple maneuver, yet if used appropriately, it distracts the pitcher, catcher, short-stop, second baseman, and first baseman. To per-form the fake steal, the base runner takes a short lead from first, and as the pitcher pitches, the runner takes a quick crossover step followed by two extra strides toward second base. Then the runner quickly pivots, faces home plate, and gets ready to get back to first base in case the catcher attempts a pick-off.

The fake steal keeps the defense off balance. It may pull them out of position slightly which will help the hitter. It may also draw an occasional throw from the catcher or pitcher, which provides a possibility for a wild throw. Also, the fake steal helps set up the delayed steal.

### Delayed Steal.

The essential component of the delayed steal is deception. The runner actually steals second base because of a defensive lapse by the shortstop or second baseman and not by the catcher or pitcher. The runner first must execute a fake steal on one pitch, and then a full extended lead after each of the next two pitches. On the fourth pitch the runner extends the lead as usual, but this time continues to extend the lead using a sideways crow hop, being careful to keep head, shoulders, and hips parallel to the third base foul line until halfway to second base.

If the delayed steal is performed properly, the shortstop and second baseman will not realize the runner is stealing and will reach the bag too late to take the throw. This type of steal is generally effective only once or twice a game. The delayed steal is most effective if *every* base runner executes the fake steal or the proper extension of the lead after each pitch so the defense never really knows which runner will try the delayed steal. It also helps the hitter because the shortstop and second baseman may concentrate too much on the runner and will not get a quick jump on ground balls.

## Second Base Techniques

### Base Runner's Lead

The base runner's lead at second base depends on the position of the shortstop and second baseman. It is often a constant adjustment between the base runner and the defense. The further the shortstop and second baseman move from the bag, the longer the lead the runner should get, but the runner must always keep in mind that the pitcher or catcher could throw to second for an attempted pick-off. While taking the lead, the third base coach should tell the base runner what the shortstop is doing, and the runner should concentrate on the second baseman and pitcher.

As the pitcher pitches, the runner should increase the lead by 10-12 feet (less for very young players). Increasing the lead after the pitch is an important aspect of baserunning. A base runner needs the longest lead possible in order to score from second on a base hit. Runners should extend their leads after pitches at *all bases* to get the best jump after the ball is hit.

### Advancing From Second to Third When the Ball is Hit

*Ground Balls.* If there is a runner only on second, less than 2 outs, and the ball is hit on the ground and to the runner's right, the runner should go back towards second base *only* as far as the second baseman or shortstop make him. Occasionally, with a runner on second base, no one will cover second when a ground ball is hit to the third baseman,

so if the runner does not retreat too much, it might be possible to advance to third base after the third baseman throws to first. The runner must make sure that all ground balls go past the pitcher's mound before attempting to advance. An alert pitcher could spring off the mound, field the ball, and throw the runner out. The basic rule for baserunners is: *advance to third base if the ground ball is hit either directly at them or to their left and past the mound.* If runners follow this rule they should never get thrown out at third by a shortstop, second baseman, or pitcher after they field a ground ball.

*Fly Balls.* If a batter hits a fly to right, right center, center, or deep left center with less than two outs, the runner should tag up and try to advance to third base—of course, depending on the throwing ability of the outfielder, the wind conditions, the distance and direction the ball is hit, and the speed of the base runner. If the ball is hit to the shallow part of the outfield, the wind is blowing in, the outfielder has a strong, accurate arm, and the base runner is rather slow, it would be unwise to try to advance. If the ball is hit to medium left field, the runner should move about one-third of the distance toward third base and react to the outfielder's play. The runner should be able to advance if the ball is misplayed, but if it is caught the runner will be able to get back to second.

### Stealing Third

If the pitcher has a habit of checking the runner only once or twice in the stretch position, or the shortstop and second baseman allow the runner a lengthy lead, and a right-handed hitter is at bat, the runner should try to steal third base. Third can be easier to steal than second when runners are aware of these three conditions and have developed a sense of timing for when to break for third. The runner should practice stretching the lead at second. If the shortstop and second baseman allow a lead of six steps, the runner should try to lengthen the lead one more step as the pitcher turns his head towards home, and then instantly break toward third as the pitcher starts the motion toward home. The important key to a successful steal of third base is the base runner's awareness of the pitcher's habits.

## Third Base Techniques

### Base Runner's Lead

The base runner on third base should take the lead in foul territory, so that if hit by a batted ball, he will not be out. Also the traction is usually better on the grass than on the dirt in the base path.

If the pitcher goes into the full motion, the base runner should take a *walking lead* and advance six to seven steps down the line. With less than two outs, an alert base runner with a good walking lead might be able to score on bunts, slow rollers, high chops, ground balls up the middle and past the mound, or passed balls. In the walking lead, the base runner's weight and momentum should be *forward*, toward the plate, as the pitcher delivers the ball. The runner watches the ball cross the plate and returns to third quickly if the hitter takes the pitch or swings and misses. Although the lead is in foul territory, the runner should return to third base in *fair* territory to disrupt any pick-off attempts by the catcher.

If the pitcher takes the stretch and the third baseman holds the runner close to the base, the runner should take a *safe offensive lead* and quickly increase it two or three steps after the pitcher pitches. This should put the runner in approximately the same position as the walking lead does by the time the pitch crosses the plate.

### Ground Balls

If the ball is hit on the ground, the runner must decide instantly whether to try to score or hold at third base. Usually a runner will not be able to score on a moderately hit ball to the pitcher, first, or third baseman. There might be an opportunity to score on a ground ball hit to either side of the shortstop or second baseman. The runner's decision is based on three factors: (a) the *depth of the infielders*, (b) the *type of ball hit*, (c) the *score and which hitters are coming up*. If the infielders are near the infield grass, the runner probably will not be able to score on moderately hit or hard hit ground balls, but might be able to score on any ball hit with very little speed (bunts, high chops, or slow rollers) with an appropriate walking lead.

The score and which hitters are coming to bat also affects the runner's decision. For example, if the defensive team is ahead several runs, they may play at regular infield depth to insure getting the out at first on a ground ball and let the runner score. However, if the defensive team is only one run ahead, the score is tied, or they are behind, they probably will pull the infield in close and try to throw the runner out at home plate.

If there are no outs and the third, fourth, and fifth hitters are coming to the plate, the runner should be cautious about trying to score. The stronger hitters in the line-up are apt to get a base hit or hit a sacrifice fly and then the runner on third will be able to score without risk. If the seventh, eighth, or ninth hitters are coming to the plate, the base runner should try

harder to score on a ground ball, because other opportunities may not emerge. Regardless of the hitter, scoring from third on a ground ball in a close game is a pressure situation for both the fielders and the base runner and should be practiced often.

### Fly Balls

The runner on third base *must* go back and tag up on all line drives and fly balls. Too often, inexperienced base runners assume that line drives or long drives will fall in for hits and thus they impatiently streak for home. This is poor baserunning since an alert outfielder might make an outstanding catch. If the runner starts for home as the bat meets the ball, and an outfielder catches the ball, the runner may not have time to return to third base, tag up, and still score, or worse still, the runner might be doubled off of third. The best policy for a base runner on third with less than two outs is simply to tag up on all balls hit in the air and then either *draw a throw* or *try to score*.

## Tagging Up on Foul Pop Flies

Anytime a pop fly is hit foul, all base runners should return to their bases, tag up, and draw a throw from the defensive player who caught the ball. The defensive player could throw the ball away, and this is the *only* constructive move the runner can make in this situation. Therefore, regardless of where the ball is popped foul, the runner should tag up instantly and bluff an advance.

## Summary of Base Running Techniques

1. Hitters should get a quick start from home plate. "Think Second" on all balls hit into the outfield.

2. Runners on first base should try to break up double plays by sliding into the pivot person.

3. Runners on first should move about halfway to second on fly balls hit to the outfield.

4. Runners on second should make sure the ground ball is either hit at them, or to their left, and past the mound before advancing to third with less than two outs.

5. Runners' leads at second should vary according to the distance the shortstop and second baseman are positioned from the bag. Runners should listen to the third base coach.

6. Runners should use a walking lead at third base with less than two outs.

7. All runners should tag up on foul pop-ups and flies, and bluff toward the next bag to draw a throw from the fielder.

8. Runners on third base should tag up on all fly balls and line drives with less than 2 outs, regardless of how deep the ball is hit.

9. Runners should always make sure that line drives move through the infield before advancing in order to prevent double plays.

10. Runners on second base should tag and advance or draw a throw on all balls that are hit to the right, right center, center, or deep left center with less than 2 outs.

11. Runners should know when to use the defensive, offensive, walking, and sacrifice bunt leads.

12. Runners on third base with less than two outs should not try to score on ground balls to third or first base. The ball must be hit up the middle, past the pitcher's mound before the runner tries to score.

13. Runners should never get hit by a batted ball and should never interfere with an infielder fielding a ball.

14. Runners should extend their leads two to three steps after each pitch.

15. Runners should use fake steals frequently.

The Lead and Pick-Off Drill can be used to work on proper fundamentals of base running at all bases.

---

## LEAD AND PICK-OFF DRILL

*Age Group:* 10 and up.

*Purpose:* To promote proper development of base running fundamentals.

*Equipment:* Base (glove can be used), ball (optional).

*Procedure:* A pitcher and runner position themselves anywhere in the outfield or off the field. The runner practices all types of leads demanded by various game situations at all the bases, while the pitcher works on simulating the pick-off motion or the motion to the plate. The runner should think about quickness, timing, alertness, aggressiveness, and precision. The base runner and pitcher should pretend they are in a real game so they will be highly sensitive to every fundamental movement necessary for successful performance.

---

## Additional Steal Situations

### Runners Should Always Steal When . . .

When there are runners on first, first and second, or first, second, and third and there are two outs, runners should always be stealing on a 3-2 pitch. Whatever happens to the hitter, the runners will be ready to take advantage of the situation.

A runner on first or second base should always steal when an inexperienced pitcher forgets to deliver from the stretch and instead pitches with a full wind-up. An alert base runner should spot this error quickly and respond immediately with an attempted steal.

### Stealing Home Plate and the Squeeze

An observant base runner can steal home plate if the pitcher uses a big, easy motion with a high leg kick. The runner usually can get a quick break for the plate, especially if the pitcher is left-handed. The runner should get a long, walking lead and at the precise moment the pitcher makes the first move, the runner should make an instant break for the plate. It helps if a right-handed hitter is up when the runner attempts the steal so it will be more difficult for the catcher to tag the base runner sliding into home.

The squeeze is executed slightly differently from the steal. The runner on third should get the longest lead possible and as the pitcher starts the motion to the plate, either the full motion or the stretch, the runner should extend the lead and then stop. Just as the pitcher releases the ball the base runner should break quickly for the plate. The hitter must bunt the pitch on the ground. This type of squeeze is very difficult to defend against.

### First and Third Steal Situations

The first and third steal can produce valuable runs if executed properly. There are three variations: the early, regular, and delayed versions, each designed to baffle and harass the defense.

*Early Steal.* The early first and third steal starts with the runner at first base breaking for second just as the pitcher pauses in the stretch. The runner is attempting to get into a run-down between first and second. Occasionally, an inexperienced pitcher may balk at this point. If the pitcher doesn't balk, he will probably step off the rubber and throw to the shortstop. The runner on third should have a safe lead and should make a break for home as soon as the pitcher throws the ball to the shortstop. Another opportune time for the runner on third to break is when the shortstop and first baseman are preoccupied with the run-down created by the runner from first base. A run might be scored without a ball even being hit.

*Regular Steal.* In the regular first and third steal, the runner at first base breaks for second as the pitcher starts the delivery to the plate. The runner's primary objective is to steal second base. Meanwhile, the runner on third assumes an offensive lead and *instantly* decides whether to break for the plate or remain at third as the catcher makes the throw to second. The third base runner must make this decision as the ball passes the pitcher's mound, since the pitcher could cut off the throw and pick off the runner at third.

The third base runner also should watch the second baseman and the shortstop, as they might break into the infield grass area, cut off the ball, and try to pick him off at third, or throw him out at the plate. The runner also needs to be aware of the possibility of a fake throw to second by the catcher as he extends his lead from third. The entire maneuver requires split-second timing and quick decisions by both the defense and the base runners and will need to be practiced by both frequently.

*Delayed Steal.* The late or delayed steal is executed in a manner similar to the early steal. The runner on first base waits until the catcher receives the pitch and then breaks for second, attempting to get in a run-down in order to give the runner from third an opportunity to score. The runner on third follows the same procedure as explained for the early and regular steal. He assumes a safe offensive lead, making sure that the throw from the catcher goes past the pitcher's mound, and attempts to score only if the shortstop, second baseman, and first baseman are occupied with the run-down between first and second. Like the early and regular first and third steal, timing and quick thinking are necessary for a successful performance, so hard work and practice are required to perfect it.

## Miscellaneous Base Running Policies

### Moving From First to Third on a Base Hit

When a runner is on first base and a base hit is driven into right field, the runner should quickly check the position of the outfielders and the ball. The runner needs to determine the type of throw the outfielder will make. If the outfielder is coming towards the ball, the throw will be much quicker and stronger than if the fielder has to retreat back and to the side. This information will help a runner decide whether to advance to third or only go to second.

Immediately after touching second base, the runner should look at the third base coach to find out whether to advance to third or hold at second base. To make sure that the outfielder will not throw behind the runner, the runner should not round second more than a few feet unless intending to advance.

### Ground Ball—Runners on First and Third— Less Than 2 Outs

*Runner on First.* The runner on first should try to create a possibility for the runner on third to score. If the ball is hit to the second baseman, the runner should make sure that the second baseman can't tag him out and throw to first base for a quick double play. If necessary, the runner should stop and run back to first, forcing the second baseman to throw the ball either to first or second base. The second baseman may waste time trying to tag the evasive runner, and forget about the runner on third. The fielder eventually may not have time to get the double play and will only get one out. The runner at first should force the defense into the most difficult double play possible, in order for the runner to try to score from third.

*Runner on Third.* The runner on third should break for home on all ground balls regardless of where the ball is hit, and attempt either to score or to get in a run-down. When the runner breaks for the plate, the defense's attention might be diverted from the other runners, and a fielder may throw to the plate. If the runner on third successfully remains in a run-down between third and home long enough, (a) the possible double play will be eliminated, (b) the runner from first will be able to go to third and the hitter will be able to advance all the way to second, and (c) the runner on third might be able to score on a wild throw. If this maneuver is executed properly, runners will advance to second and third base and may be able to score on a single.

### Getting Out of a Run-Down

A runner should never get tagged out in a run-down without maximum effort to get out of the situation. First of all, the runner should try to stay in the run-down as long as possible to create the greatest possibility for a wild throw from a defensive player. Secondly, the runner should try to run into a defensive player who is standing in the base path without the ball, since this would be defensive interference on the fielder and the runner would be awarded the next base.

# Habits of Pitchers

Successful baserunning depends on the base runner's knowledge of the pitcher's habits. Most pitchers, especially inexperienced ones, occasionally display in their delivery flaws which will help observant base runners. Base runners should check for the following items when studying a pitcher.

1. How high does the pitcher lift the stride foot?

2. How long does the pitcher pause in the stretch before each pitch?

3. How many times does the pitcher check the runner on second base?

4. Does the pitcher use a full motion or stretch with a runner on third base and less than two outs?

5. What type of pick-off moves does the pitcher have to all bases?

6. How often does the pitcher attempt pick-offs?

Every player on the team should study the pitcher carefully while sitting in the dugout.

Coaches can use the following two drills to get the whole team to practice baserunning techniques. Running the Bases is an especially good drill for younger players. Assuming Leads and Baserunning Techniques allows runners to work on their technique with a pitcher on the mound.

---

## RUNNING THE BASES

*Age Group:* 5-9.

*Purpose:* To give players practice running bases.

*Equipment:* Infield bases.

*Procedure:* Player starts in the batter's box, simulates swing, and runs for first base. The coach at first says "sprint through first base," "take the turn," "take the turn and go," or "go to second." The player responds appropriately, then stays at that base. The next player "comes to bat" and goes through the same procedure. The base runner takes off with the simulated swing and advances two bases, rounding or overrunning as appropriate.

---

## ASSUMING LEADS AND BASERUNNING TECHNIQUES

*Age Group:* 10 and up.

*Purpose:* To develop the proper techniques of assuming leads and executing offensive maneuvers from each base.

*Equipment:* Infield setup, gloves (for pitchers).

*Procedure:* Pitchers form a small circle around the pitcher's mound and face home plate. A group of runners stands at each base. The pitchers simulate pitching from the stretch position and either deliver an imaginary pitch to the plate or execute a pick-off move to the base closest to them. After five moves, the pitchers rotate around the "circle" one space so that each pitcher gets to execute pick-off moves to each base.

While the pitchers are simulating their moves, the runners execute offensive maneuvers at the base where they are stationed. After all offensive maneuvers, the runners rotate to the next base (see Fig. 3-26). The drill should last approximately 10-12 minutes.

Base runners should rotate to the next base after all offensive maneuvers have been performed.

---

The Complete Baserunning Drill provides players with an opportunity to practice all the fundamentals of baserunning at each base with a hitter at the plate. Runners should be encouraged to work with hitters on various signs and game situations.

---

## COMPLETE BASERUNNING DRILL

*Purpose:* To practice all baserunning skills.

*Equipment:* Complete infield.

*Procedure:* After the last swing in batting practice a player runs to first, rounds it, and "thinks second." The runner then returns to first base and either gives the hitter a sign or the hitter gives the base runner a sign. The sign could be for a steal, hit-and-run, sacrifice bunt, delay steal, fake steal, or any other maneuver from first base the runner should be able to perform.

Following proper execution of several baserunning skills at first base, the runner advances to second and responds to all game situations which occur during batting practice. For example, the base runner

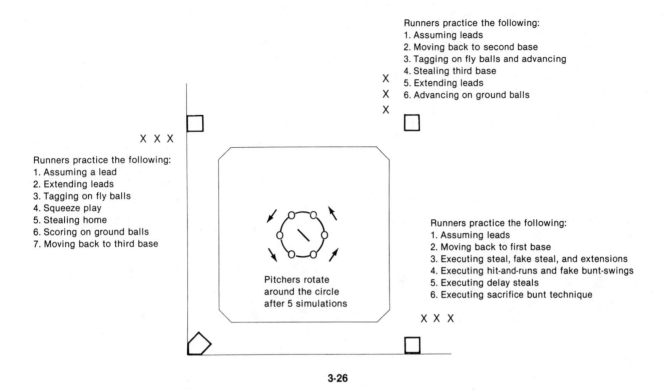

Runners practice the following:
1. Assuming leads
2. Moving back to second base
3. Tagging on fly balls and advancing
4. Stealing third base
5. Extending leads
6. Advancing on ground balls

Runners practice the following:
1. Assuming a lead
2. Extending leads
3. Tagging on fly balls
4. Squeeze play
5. Stealing home
6. Scoring on ground balls
7. Moving back to third base

Pitchers rotate
around the circle
after 5 simulations

Runners practice the following:
1. Assuming leads
2. Moving back to first base
3. Executing steal, fake steal, and extensions
4. Executing hit-and-runs and fake bunt-swings
5. Executing delay steals
6. Executing sacrifice bunt technique

**3-26**

may want to tag up on fly balls, or get a lead and advance on various types of batted balls.

After both physically and mentally reviewing baserunning techniques at second base, the runner moves to third and practices the fundamentals required of a runner on third. Once again the runner may want to give the hitter a sign for such game situations as a safe or "all out" squeeze, or a steal. Runners should practice each primary technique and fundamental at each base before completing the drill.

# CHAPTER 4

# Sliding

Sliding is often a neglected aspect of the player's development. A player must practice slides to perform them safely and effectively during a game. There are several types of slides, each with its own specific advantages. Four types of slides are discussed here: the stand-up slide, the decoy slide, the hook slide, and the head-first slide.

## Stand-Up Slide

The stand-up slide is the most versatile of the four slides. Runners can avoid tags effectively and still get to the next base quickly. It is also basically a safe slide and relatively easy to learn. The stand-up slide is illustrated in Figures 4-1 to 4-5. While studying the figures, the following points should be noted:

1. The right knee is bent slightly and the left leg positioned under the right knee;

2. The base runner slides on the hip pockets;

3. Hands are held high;

4. The slide starts about four steps from the base.

By keeping the *right leg on top*, runners can plant the right foot into the base or the ground and allow momentum to carry them into a standing position, ready to advance to the next base. The stand-up and advance is the primary feature of the slide. Runners should not leap at the base to initiate the slide, but rather perform a *quick sitting movement*. Gravity pulls the runner down, so leaping or jumping at the base only limits the quality of the slide.

As runners approach a base, they should notice on which side of the base the infielder's glove is posi-

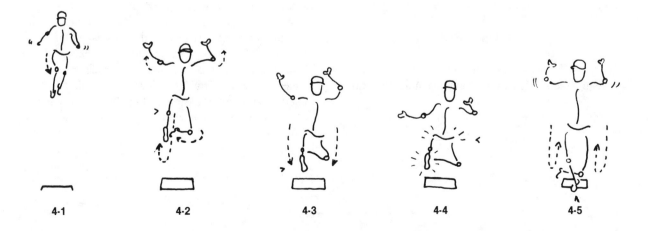

| 4-1 | 4-2 | 4-3 | 4-4 | 4-5 |

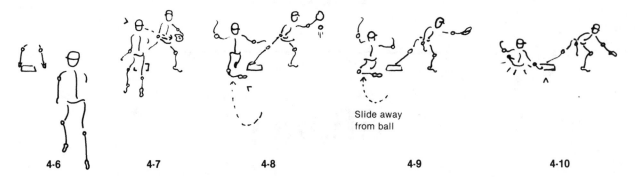

Slide away
from ball

4-6            4-7            4-8            4-9            4-10

tioned to determine which way to slide (see Figs. 4-6 to 4-10). In the figures, the runner slides away from the base and tags it with the hand, which is one of the versatile features of the stand-up slide.

Players should learn the stand-up slide by "walking" through it. During the preliminary learning session runners should concentrate on *keeping both knees bent, landing only on the hip pockets, keeping the right heel off the ground*, and *keeping both hands off the ground*.

*Important:* Runners should cup their hands when executing any slide in order to help prevent injuring their fingers.

## Decoy Slide

If the infielder already has the ball in the glove and is waiting for the insliding base runner, the only remaining move for the runner is the decoy slide. The runner slides away from the base, using the stand-up slide position, and then just as the infielder is about to put on the tag, the runner quickly draws back the outstretched hand, rolls over, and reaches for the back side of the base with the other hand as he slides past the base.

The decoy slide should start a fraction sooner and go further to the side than the regular stand-up slide, so that the infielder's tag is drawn out away from the base. Evading the tag like this requires hours of practice, but often pays dividends in close ball games.

## Hook Slide

The hook slide is a natural slide which is relatively easy to execute. Runners simply leave the ground as

they approach the base, lean back, and extend both legs to one side in a hooked or bent position. Runners can slide to either side, but should always finish by tagging the base with the back foot (see Figs. 4-11, 4-12). Unlike the stand-up slide, which requires upright balance, a runner executing a hook slide should tilt his weight to the side on which he is sliding. The hook slide is an excellent slide to use when trying to break up a double play or slide away from a tag.

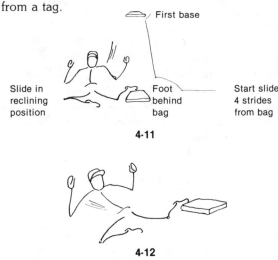

First base

Slide in          Foot          Start slide
reclining         behind        4 strides
position          bag           from bag

4-11

4-12

## Head-First Slide

The head-first slide is both exciting and effective when done properly. It requires only a diving, lunging movement in a completely prone position begun four strides away from the base (see Figs. 4-13 to 4-15). Most base runners think they reach the bag fastest with this type of slide, especially in straight steal situations. The head-first slide should not be used when going into home plate since the possibility of injury is too great with the catcher blocking the plate.

Cup hands
to prevent finger injury

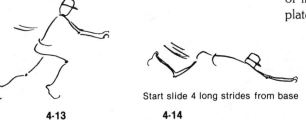

Start slide 4 long strides from base

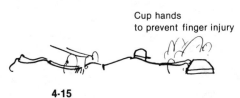

4-13            4-14            4-15

## Sliding Summary

- Start to slide approximately four long steps from the base.
- Slide away from tags.
- Be ready to advance on overthrows.
- Keep both hands cupped during slides to avoid injuries to fingers.
- Do not jump or leap at the base.
- Break up double plays with clean hook slides.
- Execute the decoy slide if the infielder or catcher has the ball ready for the tag.
- Wear some type of sliding pads under the uniform to eliminate abrasions.

## Practicing Sliding

Base runners should perfect all four slides so that, when various sliding situations arise, the runner will instantly be able to use the proper slide. When a player is practicing sliding either at home in the backyard or at organized team practice, he may want to slip jeans on over his uniform pants to help prevent abrasions while practicing. During a game a player may want to wear sliding padding under his uniform pants, such as three-quarter-length jockey underwear or longjohn thermal underwear. Also, most sporting goods stores stock various types and sizes of sliding pads which players may wear under their uniforms. The following drill will facilitate the development of all slides.

### SLIDING ON DAMP GRASS

*Purpose:* To teach sliding with minimal possibility for injury.

*Equipment:* Water grass briefly, extra bases, gloves.

*Procedure:* Players should be wearing long pants or some kind of sliding pads, and can begin in stocking feet. They should practice "walking through" a slide several times before trying it at full speed.

Players should walk through the fundamentals of the stand-up slide while holding a bat over their head to learn to keep their hands off the ground during the slide. The right knee should be bent upward and right heel be off the ground as players land softly on their rears. Once players obtain the "feel" of these specific fundamentals, they should execute stand-up slides into a base or into a glove serving as a base.

As players begin to develop the proper rhythm and timing of executing slides at full speed, they

should attempt to master the skill of sliding to either side of the base and touching the base with the hand. They should also master the method of sliding into the base, popping up and advancing to the next base, or decoy sliding around a base to avoid a tag. The versatility of the stand-up slide permits players to slide away from tags by using the decoy, or to quickly advance to the next base on overthrows.

## Additional Drills

Coaches can use the following two drills to incorporate sliding and, gradually, other baserunning skills, into baserunning drills. Baserunning and Coaching accustoms players to listening to base coaches and to acting as base coaches while encouraging them to work on their running.

### AROUND THE BASES

*Purpose:* To practice quickly leaving bases and the batter's box, and practice stopping, rounding, or running through appropriate bases.

*Equipment:* Three bases, home plate.

*Procedure:* Diamond is set up as usual. Can be set up in any field where running and sliding will not be dangerous (possibly on a soft grassy area). Players split into four groups, one 5 feet away from each base. The first player in each of the groups at first base, second base and third base start in a running postion at their base, using various leadoffs when permitted. The first player in the home plate group starts in the batter's box. On the coach's command "go," all players sprint to the next base. Players must round second and third base and stop, but run through first base and home plate.

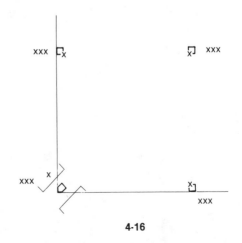

**4-16**

Additional stipulations can be made on later rounds, for example, players perform a hook slide into second, a stand-up slide into third, and a decoy slide going into home. Or, players round appropriate bases as long as they retreat back to that base. Players join the group at the base to which they ran.

---

## BASERUNNING AND COACHING

*Age Group:* 8 and up.

*Purpose:* To have base coaches practice handling runners and have base runners practice looking for and listening to base coaches' signals.

*Equipment:* Infield bases.

*Procedure:* Two players act as base coaches and other players line up at home plate. At the slap of a coach's hands, the first runner breaks for first base. The first base coach imagines where the ball has been hit and based on that knowledge tells the runner what to do: sprint through first base, make the turn, go for second, or make the turn and go for second with a slide.

Prior to hitting second base, runners must look for the third base coach's signal to hold up or go on to third. When runners come into third, the coach tells them to slide, hold up, make the turn, or go to home.

---

# PART II

# DEFENSIVE PLAY

A consistently effective defense is absolutely essential for a team to be successful. All players must strive to master their own position and establish an effective working relationship with other members of the team. Players need to master proper fielding and throwing mechanics for their position, and also need to know where to be in different defensive situations, such as cutoffs, relays, bunt coverage, double plays, attempted steals, and pick-offs.

Effective fielders need to be strong, flexible, coordinated, and rhythmical. They need quick hands and feet to refine the fundamental skills of fielding and throwing. Competitive spirit and general effort will go a long way in helping a player embark on a personal program of skill development.

During games, players' minds should be constantly active. They need to be ready to respond to the many varieties of balls that are hit and to make plays which require quick decisions and intense concentration. Players need to learn to judge the speed and spin of hit balls quickly in order to field them most successfully. Their entire mental and physical energy should be primed, ready to respond to the next play.

Players need to spend many meaningful hours of practice on the basic fundamentals and mechanics of their position. Unless a player's fundamentals are sound, the player will not be able to make the many plays necessary to help the team perform well. The challenge confronting all coaches is *to make their players want to prepare properly* and be completely ready for each game.

The defensive section integrates the analysis of motor skills of basic defensive play with an effective drill system which will facilitate the development of skills in players of all ages. Reading through the drills as well as the other material will provide the clearest understanding of the skills.

Part II, Defensive Play, is divided into a discussion of general defensive concepts, three chapters covering infield play (including the pitcher's and catcher's fielding responsibilities), one on outfield play, one on team play, and one each on the pitcher's and catcher's responsibilities in pitching.

## The Glove

### Care and Selection

Proper care and use of the glove is often misunderstood or neglected by young players. Because of young players' small structure and limited finger, hand, and forearm strength, they are not able to use most gloves effectively. Most young players select gloves which are too large and cumbersome for them to handle, and consequently, the glove is a liability rather than an asset. Most fielding errors at this age level stem from the players' inability to keep the glove open wide enough to allow the ball to enter the glove.

Young players should be encouraged to choose a glove which is medium-sized and manageable. Players should make sure their glove is clean after each practice and game. They should dampen the glove occasionally in order to loosen the fiber in the leather. Players should also treat the glove with saddle soap or some other leather conditioner often during the season to keep the glove clean, soft, and pliable.

### How to Use the Glove

Players should *place each finger in the designated spot in the glove and cup the hand slightly*. This will make the glove maneuverable and will soften the hands while they field the ball. Players need to keep the glove open like a "pancake" while fielding (see Figs. II-1, II-2). Players should help train the glove to stay open by laying the glove face down in a flat open position when not in use, or by placing a soft-

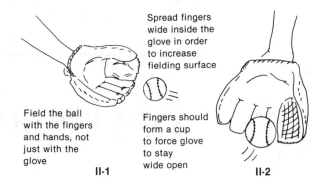

Field the ball with the fingers and hands, not just with the glove

Spread fingers wide inside the glove in order to increase fielding surface

Fingers should form a cup to force glove to stay wide open

II-1                          II-2

ball or volleyball in the pocket, instead of allowing the glove to fold shut.

## Basic Defensive Concepts

### Conditioning

Players, especially those who have gone through puberty, need to pursue a fitness program which emphasizes strengthening fingers, hands, and forearms. Hand grippers, squeezing soft rubber balls, and the rolley (see p. 148) should all be part of a daily program. Supporting body weight in a push-up position on the finger tips and working with light dumbbells (2-5 pounds), also adds muscle tone in appropriate areas. Any exercise done with dumbbells should be done *only in the off season when the players are not throwing*. Dumbbell exercises should be done slowly and in several directions for five minutes every other day. Other conditioning exercise ideas can be found in the conditioning section (see p. 145). Players will be able to use the glove properly only if they have the necessary strength, so this part of a player's development must not be ignored.

### Basic Rules of Defensive Play

Every player should clearly understand the basic rules of defensive play. Each member of the team should train mentally as well as mechanically to promote consistency in performance. As part of their preparation, every player should understand the following:

1. At all times, each player should know the *number of outs, location of the runners, the score,* and the *inning*.

2. Each player should be *eager* to be involved in the next play.

3. Players should *charge all ground balls*.

4. Players should use *both hands* on plays whenever possible, and the hands should be *carried low before fielding ground balls*.

5. Players should *throw to a specific target*, not a general area.

6. Players should *make sure of the first out on a double play*, even though it may take a split second longer.

7. With runners on base, players should try to *knock down all potential base hits* and try to keep them in the infield.

8. With runners on base, infielders should be ready to *take the proper cutoff or relay position* on base hits.

9. Players should keep the glove *wide open* when fielding *all ground balls*.

10. The player's hips should be *low* and hand stretched *well in front of the body* to field the ball.

11. Players should call pop flys *after* the ball has reached its peak.

12. Players should field all ground balls with the *quickness necessary to succeed* against runners of various speeds.

13. Players should *concentrate on the proper mechanics of fielding* on every ball.

# CHAPTER 5

# Individual Infield Skills

Chapters 5, 6, and 7 all involve infield skills. Chapter 5 includes the general skills every infielder must understand; Chapter 6, the specific skills required at different positions (other than those involved in pitching); and Chapter 7, plays that all infield players execute together. All pitching skills, including the skills catchers need to catch pitches, are presented in Chapters 10 and 11.

## Fundamental Fielding Analysis

*Note:* Although this section pertains to infield play, outfielders perform many of the same skills and therefore should become familiar with the fundamentals of fielding. All differences are included in Chapter 8, Outfield Play.

To perform effectively, players must concentrate on all the details of fielding. The whole fielding and throwing movement is presented first, and then each aspect is analyzed separately. Figures 5-1 to 5-14 illustrate the basic mechanics for fielding a ground ball

from the ready position all the way to the follow-through of the throw. The following fundamentals should be noted:

### Fielding

1. The *stance* is straight forward with knees pointed slightly inward and weight leaning forward in a ready position. The primary concerns at this point are to get the *maximum jump* on the ball and to *concentrate* on the speed and bounce of the ball (Figs. 5-1, 5-2).

2. Charge the ball, staying *as low as possible*, keeping the belt buckle lined up with the ball (Fig. 5-3).

3. Feet are *comfortably apart* while fielding, spread slightly wider than the shoulders (Fig. 5-4).

4. The *glove foot is several inches in front of the throwing foot* as the ball enters the glove (Fig. 5-4).

5. Rear is *low*, close to the ground (Fig. 5-4).

6. Hands are well *out in front* as ball enters the glove (Fig. 5-5).

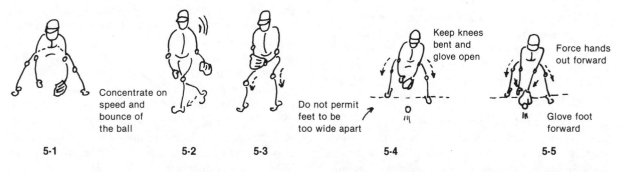

5-1    Concentrate on speed and bounce of the ball

5-2    5-3    Do not permit feet to be too wide apart

5-4    Keep knees bent and glove open

5-5    Force hands out forward    Glove foot forward

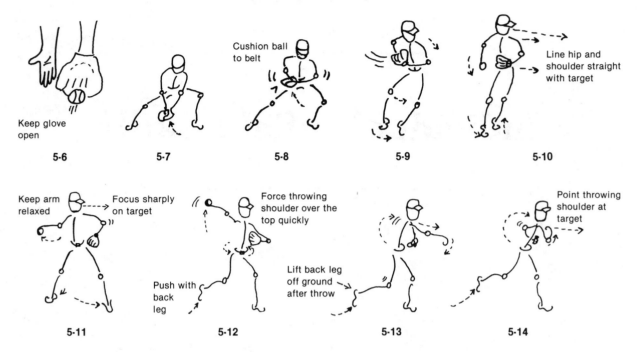

Keep glove open

5-6

5-7

Cushion ball to belt

5-8

5-9

Line hip and shoulder straight with target

5-10

Keep arm relaxed    Focus sharply on target

5-11

Force throwing shoulder over the top quickly

Push with back leg

5-12

Lift back leg off ground after throw

5-13

Point throwing shoulder at target

5-14

7. Glove remains *wide open* (Fig. 5-6).

8. Eyes *concentrate squarely* on the ball as it enters the glove (Fig. 5-7).

9. As soon as the ball enters the glove, it should be brought *straight back* to the belt in order to *cushion the ball*, and assume a skip and throw position (Figs. 5-8, 5-9).

### Skip and Throw

10. Point the glove side shoulder *straight at the target* before throwing (Fig. 5-10).

11. Keep the *glove and throwing hand together* in the center of the chest while starting the skip and throw (Fig. 5-11).

12. Use the *entire throwing side* during the skip and throw for a good throw, bringing the throwing shoulder quickly *over the top* of the throw to insure both power and accuracy (Fig. 5-12).

13. Complete a successful fielding effort by making a perfect throw, *keeping eyes on the target*, and *following through* with the throwing shoulder towards the target (Fig. 5-13).

14. *Back leg moves up from the ground about one foot* after the ball is released, to allow the body to roll properly during the follow-through. Many young players tend to drag the back foot as they throw, which contributes to a lazy throwing shoulder and often results in a high throw (Figs. 5-13, 5-14).

The entire fielding effort can be divided into two basic components—*fielding* and *skip and throw*. Players need to concentrate on one component at a time during the fielding effort. Young players may

rush through the play and think about throwing before the ball is successfully fielded, or they may execute the fielding component successfully and then fail to concentrate on the throwing component. They need to *concentrate on each component as they perform it* for a successful total effort.

## Subcomponents

Five subcomponents of fielding and the skip and throw are discussed in detail here. They are the *ready position, movement to the ball, fielding position, skip and throw position*, and the *follow-through position*. To communicate effectively during analyses and evaluation, both coaches and players should have a vivid picture of the body position for each subcomponent in their minds. Following the analysis of various subcomponents are drills which will facilitate the development of the fundamentals in young players.

### Ready Position

Infielders must be in a ready position before every pitch, since they must be ready to move in any direction the moment the ball is hit. Different players may be comfortable with different ready positions. Essentially, the proper ready position for a player is the position the player would take if preparing to race someone in a 60-yard dash in any direction. Generally, the feet are slightly wider apart than the shoulders, the knees are bent and slanted slightly in, and the weight is leaning forward in a relaxed position. From this position a player will be able to move quickly in any direction.

Various styles of the ready position are illustrated in Figures 5-15 to 5-19. *Players must develop a ready position which allows them maximum quickness and starting power.* An effective method for teaching the ready position is the Set-Sprint Drill.

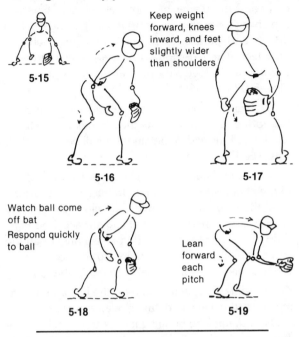

5-15

Keep weight forward, knees inward, and feet slightly wider than shoulders

5-16          5-17

Watch ball come off bat

Respond quickly to ball

Lean forward each pitch

5-18          5-19

## SET-SPRINT

*Purpose:* To teach the proper ready position.

*Equipment:* None needed, can be done with gloves.

*Procedure:* The coach instructs the players to get into a position to sprint in any direction. Once the players assume their ready positions, the coach, positioned in front of the players, quickly points in any direction.

The players instantly sprint 5 yards in that direction. Competition can be held between players to create greater enthusiasm and improve reaction time.

---

Both infielders and outfielders should move around a bit between pitches to prevent the body from tightening. Keeping the body loose can help a player successfully complete a difficult play.

## Movement to the Ball

As the pitcher pitches, all infielders and outfielders should be in a ready stance, leaning slightly forward as the pitch reaches the plate. If the hitter makes contact, each fielder must be able to get an instant break towards the ball. When the ball is hit to either side or overhead, players should instantly execute a crossover step in the direction of the ball (see Figs. 5-20 to 5-23 and 5-26 to 5-28).

Infielders and outfielders often have difficulty with ground balls because they don't concentrate on the ball. If a ground ball is hit in the direction of a fielder, the fielder should *focus sharply on the speed and spin of the ball* in order to know how fast to move to the ball and exactly when to assume a fielding position. If a player doesn't charge the ball properly or fails to get into a proper fielding position soon enough, the player could make an error or field the ball too late to make the play.

Players will learn optimal movements and fielding habits necessary for consistent success only by fielding great numbers of all types of ground and fly balls. Coaches should be constantly alert for opportunities to help players learn how to move to the ball (see Figs. 5-20 to 5-31).

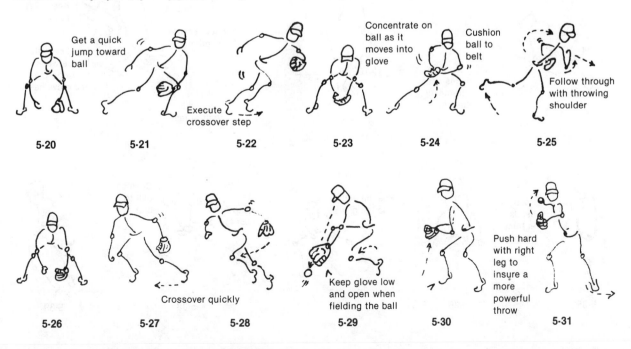

Get a quick jump toward ball

Execute crossover step

Concentrate on ball as it moves into glove

Cushion ball to belt

Follow through with throwing shoulder

5-20     5-21     5-22     5-23     5-24     5-25

Crossover quickly

Keep glove low and open when fielding the ball

Push hard with right leg to insure a more powerful throw

5-26     5-27     5-28     5-29     5-30     5-31

Coaches can use the Crossover Step Drill to work on movement to either side.

## CROSSOVER STEP DRILL

*Purpose:* To help develop a coordinated relationship between the ready position and the crossover step.

*Equipment:* None needed, or use gloves.

*Procedure:* Players spread out in front of the coach and assume a ready position. The coach points either to the left or right and players perform a crossover step, face their belt buckles in that direction, and take three strides.

### Fielding Position

The fielding position is one of the most important positions to master in the entire training program. The fielder's whole body must be in the proper position before fielding a ground ball to decrease the probability of an error. Coaches should stress the following points when teaching the proper fielding position (see Figs. 5-32 to 5-34 and 5-35 to 5-39).

1. Players should be in the fielding position *before* the ball reaches the glove. The speed of the ball, the direction it is moving, and the speed with which the play must be made all influence when players should stop charging the ball and when they should get in the fielding position. Game situation drills can help a player develop the correct timing (see Fig. 5-35).

2. In the fielding position, a player's feet should be *approximately shoulder width apart*. The *glove side foot should be further out in front than the throwing side foot*. With the feet in this position, the glove hand can stretch out further in front of the body and the player has optimal balance. Coaches can check for proper foot position by placing a bat on the ground parallel to players' shoulders, between their feet. The bat should touch a player's throwing side toe and glove side heel at the same time (see Figs. 5-32 to 5-34).

3. Players' knees should be *bent* and the rears low to the ground to allow their hands to reach out for the ball instead of fielding the ball between their legs (see Figs. 5-36, 5-37).

4. Players' hands should be *at least 1 foot in front* of their bodies to enable them to track the ball visually all the way into the glove. The glove should stay wide open to increase its fielding surface (see Figs. 5-36, 5-37). Too often young players only open the glove partially as the ball enters, so they commit errors because the ball is unable to get in the glove.

5. While sharply focusing on the ball and *watching it all the way* into the glove, a player should *cushion the ball* by bringing it back to the belt buckle (see Figs. 5-37 to 5-39). In other words, the glove and the ball should continue in the same path until the hands are stopped by the belt buckle. This is an important phase of fielding and should be practiced often by using activities like the Short Hop Fielding Drill. Soft hands and flexible elbows and knees are essential for infielders and outfielders.

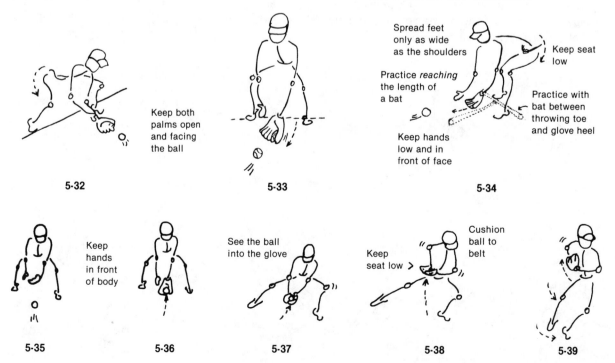

Keep both palms open and facing the ball

5-32

5-33

Spread feet only as wide as the shoulders

Practice *reaching* the length of a bat

Keep hands low and in front of face

Keep seat low

Practice with bat between throwing toe and glove heel

5-34

Keep hands in front of body

5-35

5-36

See the ball into the glove

5-37

Keep seat low >

Cushion ball to belt

5-38

5-39

6. The player should play through the ball by continuing to move the body toward the glove as the hands start to cushion the ball back in the glove.

Coaches can use the Crossover Reaction Drill to get players to use crossover steps and in a fielding position quickly.

## CROSSOVER-REACTION DRILL

*Purpose:* To work on fielding agility, specifically the crossover step.

*Equipment:* Balls (one for every two players), gloves.

*Procedure:* Players work in pairs starting at the right field foul line about 25 feet apart, facing one another. Players with their backs to the infield start by rolling the ball to their partner's right. Partners field the balls and return them to the left of the original roller. Players continue in this fashion until they move 150 feet, they then return towards the right field foul line. Do at medium speed.

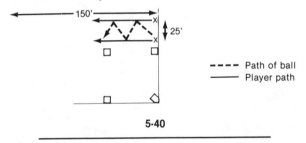

**5-40**

Once the player cushions the ball to the belt, the *fielding* component is complete and the *throwing* component begins.

### Skip and Throw Position

The two most important factors in the skip and throw are *to get an instant, sharp focus on the chest* of the player the fielder is throwing to, and after releasing the ball, *to point the throwing shoulder directly at that same spot.* Players must learn the following mechanics as well:

1. While cushioning the ball to the belt and playing the ball through at the end of the fielding component, the player immediately starts to *line up the glove side shoulder and hip in the direction of the throw* (see Fig. 5-41). While the eyes focus sharply on a specific spot, and the glove stays in the center of the chest, the player can perform one of two movements with the feet—either the player takes a step with the throwing side foot and then skips, or simply skips forward without a step and prepares to throw. The step-skip and throw is slightly slower than the skip and throw, so it should not be used if the play must be made quickly (see Fig. 5-42).

2. During the skip, the player should have the *fingers placed comfortably on the ball and the throwing arm relaxed.*

3. Once the throwing hand leaves the glove, the arm should extend down and back quickly in a comfortable, relaxed manner to prepare for the throw (see Fig. 5-43). The arm extends quickly and starts forward instantly, like the action of a yo-yo. The *arm and wrist must stay flexible and loose* to keep throws accurate and to prevent players from experiencing arm strain (see Figs. 5-44, 5-45).

4. As the arm starts forward the throwing shoulder and back should be forced quickly *over the top* of the motion (see Fig. 5-46). Many young players lazily drag the throwing shoulder rather than moving it quickly.

5. As the player releases the ball, the arm should be extended well overhead with the flat portion of the throwing wrist facing the throwing target. There should be a *strong wrist snap* at the point of release to facilitate accuracy and velocity.

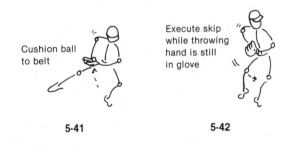

**5-41**        **5-42**

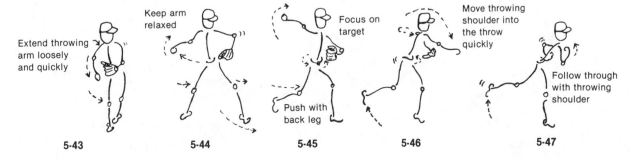

**5-43**      **5-44**      **5-45**      **5-46**      **5-47**

### Follow-Through Position

After the player releases the ball, the throwing shoulder should follow through toward the target and the back leg should lift off the ground about one foot (see Fig. 5-47). Young players often forget these two fundamentals and as a result lose accuracy and velocity in their throws. Simulating the follow-through position frequently will help players execute properly.

## Throwing Summary

Figures 5-48 through 5-54 diagram the throw from both the glove hand and throwing hand sides.

The Flick the Ball Drill, Arm Action Drill, and Skip and Throw for Points Drill all help develop the skip and throw segment of the fielding effort.

## FLICK THE BALL DRILL

*Purpose:* To develop throwing skills by emphasizing strong wrist action and proper spin on the ball.

*Equipment:* Gloves, half-and-half colored baseballs (see Appendix B for instructions).

*Procedure:* Players work in pairs with one colored baseball. Partners stand only 10-12 feet apart and face one another. They flick the ball back and forth, aiming at each other's chest. Each time players flick the ball they place the throwing elbow in the glove hand and hold it stationary out in front of the body (see Fig. 5-55). This restricts players to using only the wrist and forearm to "flick" the ball. Each time they flick the ball, players should try to get maximum spin on the ball and keep the ball's colors side-by-side as it travels to the partner.

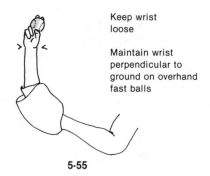

Keep wrist loose

Maintain wrist perpendicular to ground on overhand fast balls

**5-55**

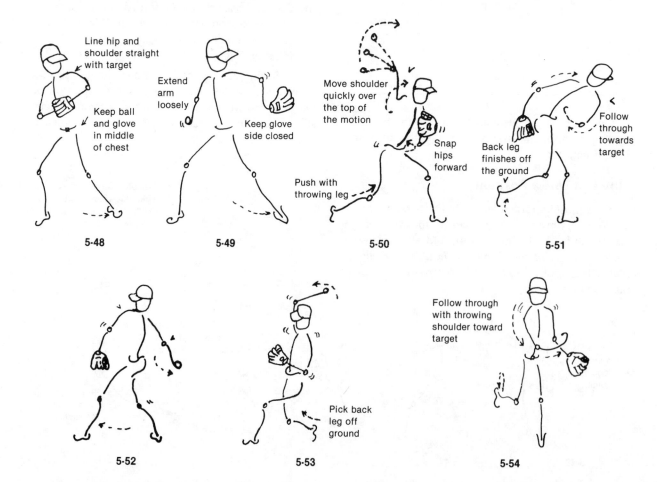

**5-48** Line hip and shoulder straight with target / Keep ball and glove in middle of chest

**5-49** Extend arm loosely / Keep glove side closed

**5-50** Move shoulder quickly over the top of the motion / Snap hips forward / Push with throwing leg

**5-51** Follow through towards target / Back leg finishes off the ground

**5-52**

**5-53** Pick back leg off ground

**5-54** Follow through with throwing shoulder toward target

The players hold the ball by placing the first two fingers on either side of the colors and the thumb exactly on the midline underneath the ball (see Fig. 5-56). Young players with very small fingers may have to use three fingers on top of the ball instead of two. The drill should continue until each player has executed at least 20 "flicks."

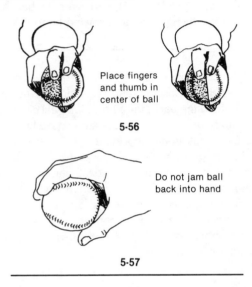

Place fingers and thumb in center of ball

5-56

Do not jam ball back into hand

5-57

## ARM ACTION DRILL

*Purpose:* To develop loose, fluid arm action while throwing.

*Equipment:* Gloves, half-and-half colored baseballs (see Appendix B for instructions).

*Procedure:* Players work in pairs with one colored baseball. They kneel down to one knee and face each other 40-60 feet apart. Partners throw to one another aiming at each other's chest, holding the ball as in Figures 5-56 and 5-57.

As the players complete each throw they analyze the spin of the colored ball. The colors should spin side-by-side as the ball travels to the target. If the midline of the colors doesn't remain perpendicular to the ground, and the colors don't stay side-by-side during the throw, the player should examine the fingers on the ball and the position of the wrist. The wrist, elbow, and shoulder of the throwing arm should be loose and flexible, never tight and rigid. As the arm starts downward behind the body, the extension should be full and loose, and as the arm comes around and the ball is about to be released the flat portion of the throwing wrist should be facing the target. At this point the flick of the wrist and follow-through of the throwing shoulder completes the throw. Each player should execute at least 20 throws.

## SKIP AND THROW FOR POINTS

*Purpose:* To teach players to focus visually on a specific spot before throwing and to throw to that spot effectively.

*Equipment:* Gloves, half-and-half colored baseballs (see Appendix B for instructions).

*Procedure:* Players work in pairs with one colored ball. They stand 60-90 feet apart and face one another. Players earn points by throwing to specific spots on the partner's body. Throwing directly to the partner's chest earns the thrower 5 points, to the partner's head earns 3 points, to the partner's arms or legs earns 1 point, and any spot away from the partner's body takes a point away from the thrower's score. Each time players catch a throw, they hold the glove exactly where they caught the ball so that they and their partners can evaluate the score of that throw. A player wins by reaching 50 points.

As they proceed through the drill players should analyze the spin of the colored ball. If the ball is held as in Figure 5-56 and thrown properly, the colors remain on opposite sides and the center division line remains perpendicular to the ground. The colors should neither twirl in various directions nor should one of the colors ever face the thrower. Each player gets visible feedback of throwing effectiveness by watching the ball. If the colors do not remain side-by-side during each throw, the player should analyze the position of the fingers on the ball, as well as the action of the arm and wrist behind and in front of the body during the throw.

Review pages 53-54 for a thorough understanding of the skip and throw mechanics. Note the glove and throwing hand are always held in the middle of the chest area prior to the throw. The glove side shoulder and hip are in a straight line with the target. Following the skip, the hand breaks downward from the glove and moves smoothly and quickly through the entire throwing motion. The throwing shoulder should always follow through directly toward the target.

The first two fingers and thumb of the throwing hand should be on the center line of the ball. The arm and wrist action should be *quick, loose,* and *relaxed.* The arm should follow a path similar to the pitcher's delivery (see p. 105).

The Rhythm Drill incorporates all elements of the fielding effort, all the fielding and skip and throw components. It is one of the drills most basic to baseball and should be repeated at all practices.

### RHYTHM DRILL

*Purpose:* To create a smooth deliberate fielding effort.

*Equipment:* Balls (one for every two players), gloves.

*Procedure:* Players pair up, stand 70-90 feet apart, and roll various types of ground balls to their partners. Partners field the ground ball and throw back using the skip and throw. After fielding 5 balls, the players switch roles. Each player should field about 15 balls in 5 minutes.

Players should concentrate on the ready position, proper movement to the ball, and maintaining effective fielding and throwing positions. Coaches should remain alert for opportunities to positively reinforce those players who execute the drill smoothly and to help players who are having problems.

## Difficult Fielding Situations

Four specific types of hit balls that can be especially difficult for fielders are discussed here: short hops, fly balls overhead, ground balls to the backhand side, and slow rollers. The drills included in these areas should be practiced frequently so players will feel comfortable making these difficult plays.

### Short Hops

A short hop is a ball which is hit or thrown and first lands on the ground slightly in front of the infielder. An infielder must have quick hands and flexible actions in order to field short hops effectively.

The essence of the Short Hop Drill is improving glove action. The glove needs to stay wide open, low, and well out in front of the body. The player's knees should be bent with the rear low to the ground. The player should focus sharply on the ball from the time it is thrown all the way into the glove, and then cushion the ball back into the belt with a smooth, flexible movement. *The ball and glove should flow in the same direction.*

### SHORT HOP DRILL

*Purpose:* To develop quick glove action and soft hands, and to practice fielding "short hops."

*Equipment:* Balls (one for every two players), gloves.

*Procedure:* Players get into pairs and throw each other difficult short hops. Throws should include various speeds and directions in order to challenge the player receiving the throw.

Players should keep their feet stationary and should rely only on the flexibility of their knees, hips, back, elbows, and hands to catch the difficult short hop throws. All players should learn to backhand short hops which go to the throwing hand side.

By encouraging players to keep their feet stationary in a fielding position, and by placing the throwing hand behind the back, the Short Hop Drill challenges the players' *glove action* and *dexterity* (see Figs. 5-58 to 5-61). This is an important drill in the player's training program and should be performed often. In order to simulate interest the coach can occasionally administer a brief short hop tournament in a workout. The more competitive the drill becomes, the more effective it will be for participating players.

The Short Hop Goal Drill is a fun way for players to work on short hops.

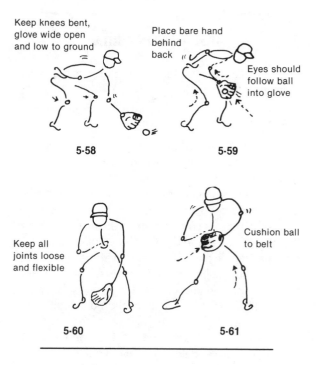

Keep knees bent, glove wide open and low to ground

Place bare hand behind back

Eyes should follow ball into glove

**5-58**          **5-59**

Keep all joints loose and flexible

Cushion ball to belt

**5-60**          **5-61**

### SHORT HOP GOAL DRILL

*Purpose:* Players work on short hops in a competitive situation.

*Equipment:* Cones or other markers, balls, gloves.

*Procedure:* Partners stand within a goal about 10 feet across, facing another pair about 50 feet away. The object is to throw the ball through the other pair's

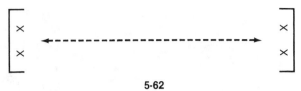

**5-62**

goal. The throwing team gets a point for each ball that gets through the opponents' goal.

---

## Ground Balls to the Backhand Side — Crossover Step

Fielding a ground ball to the backhand side is one of the most difficult plays infielders make, and they must practice it often in order to execute it smoothly. The player needs to take a quick crossover step to get in position quickly to field the ball. The crossover step is executed by quickly pivoting the feet to get the hips and shoulders facing the direction the ball is traveling. It is essential to make this move quickly (see Figs. 5-63 to 5-68). Players can practice fielding to the backhand side by using the Backhand Drill.

---

### BACKHAND DRILL

*Purpose:* To practice fielding balls on the throwing hand side.

*Equipment:* Balls (one for every two players), gloves.

*Procedure:* Players pair up and stand about 75 feet apart. One player rolls a ground ball to the throwing hand side of his partner. The player should roll the ball so that the fielder is forced to backhand the ball every time. Fielders should assume a quality ready position before each ground ball.

As the ball is rolled, the fielder should execute a quick crossover step to the throwing hand side. Upon reaching the ball, the fielder should *plant the throwing foot hard; bend the back and legs low, open the glove* wide and low to the ground; *see the ball enter the glove, cushion* the ball backward and upward; and finally, *raise up* and make a hard, overhand throw. The fielders should *shove off* with the throwing side leg in order to generate power in the throw. The player does not have time to skip and throw on this play because the runner will beat the throw (see Figs. 5-63 to 5-68).

Players should field five throws and then switch roles with their partners.

---

## Fly Balls Overhead

Infielders and outfielders need to retreat quickly on fly balls and line drives hit overhead. Players should use the crossover step to get the quickest possible jump on the ball.

---

### FLY BALLS OVERHEAD

*Purpose:* Facilitates development of proper habits for retreating quickly on fly balls and line drives.

*Equipment:* Balls (one for every two players), gloves.

*Procedure:* Players pair up and stand about 75 feet apart. One player throws fly balls and line drives over his partner's head so that the fielder must retreat quickly for the ball. The fielder should assume a quality ready position before each throw.

As the ball is released, the fielder should execute a quick, deliberate crossover step in the direction the ball is traveling. The quickness of the initial step is very important. The player should be at top speed after two steps and should watch the flight of the ball at all times, if possible. By watching the ball, the fielder will be able to adjust more effectively if the wind affects the ball's flight.

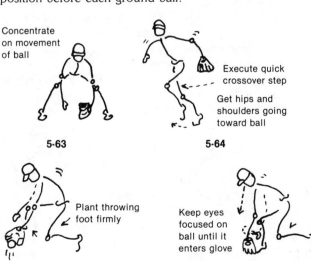

Concentrate on movement of ball

Execute quick crossover step

Get hips and shoulders going toward ball

**5-63**          **5-64**

Plant throwing foot firmly

Keep eyes focused on ball until it enters glove

**5-65**          **5-66**

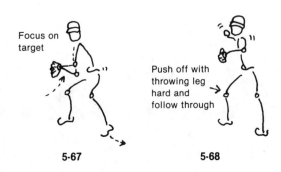

Focus on target

Push off with throwing leg hard and follow through

**5-67**          **5-68**

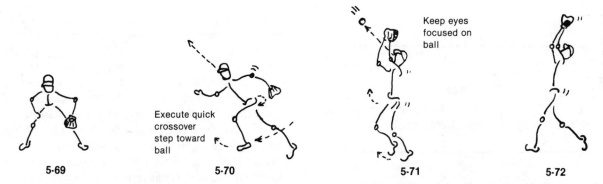

5-69          5-70          5-71          5-72

The fielder should catch the ball with two hands whenever possible, to increase the probability of a catch and to get off a faster, more coordinated throw after the catch (see Figs. 5-69 to 5-72).

Players should field five throws and then switch roles.

———————————

Players have to make sure they practice the initial crossover step and don't simply raise up and back step to the ball, a common mistake among young players. Players should reach for the ball with the glove only at the *last instant*. Often, young players try to run after the ball with their glove arm out-stretched, which reduces their speed considerably and restricts coordination and balance. Players should sprint to the ball and then reach to make the catch.

### Slow Rollers

Fielding a slow roller is another challenging play for an infielder. Coaches should stress the following aspects when teaching this skill: (a) players need to charge the ball quickly; (b) they should get into a low fielding position with the glove out in front and wide open; (c) they should field the ball just to the inside of the glove side foot; (d) they should bring the ball back quickly into a throwing position; and (e) while in the crouch, they should complete the throw as the throwing side foot comes forward.

If possible the player should try to field the ball with both hands and execute a three-quarter sidearm

throw to first base. However, if the ball has come to a complete stop, the player may field it with only the throwing hand. The player fields the ball with the glove foot forward and throws as the throwing foot comes forward. He fields and throws the ball in one step (see Figs. 5-73 to 5-78). If a player has difficulty mastering this method, it might be better to have the player execute a short, quick skip and throw from the crouched position.

Infielders must be alert to get the maximum jump on the ball and then charge the ball quickly. Infielders should move straight for the ball and reduce their speed just before reaching it in order to have better control of the play.

The following two drills help players learn how to move quickly from a ready position to a fielding position. They can be modified easily to incorporate whatever fielding skills have been taught.

———————————

### REACTION-POSITION DRILL

*Purpose:* To teach proper movement from a ready position to a fielding or backhand position.

*Equipment:* Gloves.

*Procedure:* Players spread out in a ready position in front of the coach. The coach tosses a ball up ap-proximately 12 inches and lets the ball fall to the ground. Before the ball hits the ground, players get in a fielding or backhand position.

To increase the complexity of this drill the coach can toss the ball up with either hand and catch the

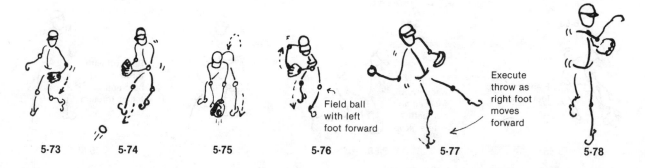

5-73          5-74          5-75          5-76          5-77          5-78

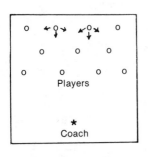

5-79

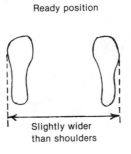

Ready position

Slightly wider
than shoulders

5-80

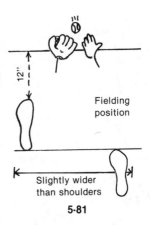

12"

Fielding
position

Slightly wider
than shoulders

5-81

ball. The players must assume a ready position and jump off the ground each time the coach tosses the ball. After a few tosses the coach lets the ball drop to the ground. If the coach's right hand touched the ball last, the players quickly assume a fielding position, but if the coach's left hand touched the ball last, the players assume a backhand position. Each time the players assume a backhand or fielding position, the coach should pause and help players make any necessary adjustments to their positions (see Figs. 5-79 to 5-81).

By performing this drill often, players will become familiar with their most effective ready position and with the importance of reacting quickly to get into a proper fielding position.

The Freeze Drill helps players develop a coordinated relationship between their ready position, reaction time, movement to the ball, and fielding position.

## FREEZE DRILL

*Purpose:* To help develop a more coordinated relationship between a player's ready position, reaction times, movement to the ball, and fielding position.

*Equipment:* Gloves.

*Procedure:* The coach has players spread out and assume a ready position. The coach points either to the right, left or to the ground. Players execute a crossover and three quick steps in the designated direction, and assume a proper fielding position. The players freeze in the fielding position until the coach yells "cushion." Players then bring both hands straight back to their belt buckles and simulate a skip and throw. Players remain in the frozen fielding position for about 15 seconds, analyzing and evaluating the position of their own feet and hands.

The coach can point over the players' heads to have them execute a quick crossover step and pur-

sue an imaginary fly ball over their heads. The coach should make positive comments to players executing correctly and offer constructive criticism to players who need help.

The Freeze Drill helps players learn to assume a proper ready position, move quickly in the direction the coach points, and develop a proper fielding position. If repeated often, this learning will transfer to games where players need to get a quick jump on ground balls and fly balls, in order to field them effectively.

### Simulations

Simulating correct fundamentals is very beneficial for players. Simulation provides them unlimited opportunities to practice many aspects of the game quickly without any equipment or other players. It can help a player develop a kinesthetic image—a mental picture and feel for fundamental skills—which will help the player to perform successfully and consistently. The few ground balls, fly balls, and throwing opportunities a player has in an average practice are not sufficient to develop the habit level the player needs.

The Simulation Drill should frequently be incorporated into practices, and coaches should encourage players to perform it on their own as well, as part of a home training program.

## SIMULATION DRILL
## FOR SPECIFIC BODY POSITIONS

*Purpose:* Provides players with an opportunity to develop good habits and a better feel and mental image of various fundamental skills.

*Equipment:* None necessary but can use glove and/or bat.

*Procedure:* Players spread out in the outfield and simulate the skill positions illustrated below. Players

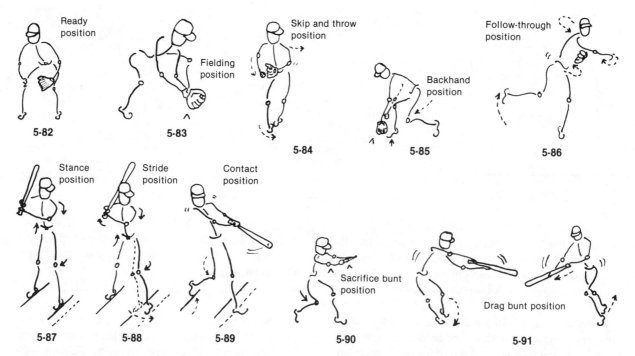

Ready position — 5-82

Fielding position — 5-83

Skip and throw position — 5-84

Backhand position — 5-85

Follow-through position — 5-86

Stance position — 5-87

Stride position — 5-88

Contact position — 5-89

Sacrifice bunt position — 5-90

Drag bunt position — 5-91

should repeat as many positions as possible in one minute, being careful to analyze and evaluate each of the positions (see Figs. 5-82 to 5-91).

Coaches should be alert for opportunities to positively reinforce players who perform the basic positions effectively, and to instruct those who need help.

The Shadow Drill has one player simulate, or shadow, while another player actually fields.

## SHADOW DRILL

*Purpose:* Creates a learning environment in which players can analyze and evaluate the fielding and throwing fundamentals of themselves and a peer.

*Equipment:* Gloves, ball, bat.

*Procedure:* One player stands about 12 feet behind a partner, and both assume a ready position. Both players react to the ground ball the coach or another player hits to them. The player in front fields the ball, while the player in back simulates all the correct fielding and throwing fundamentals for the same ground ball. After five ground balls, the players switch positions.

If both players perform properly, the player behind appears to be the "shadow" of the partner actually executing the play. The coach should encourage the players to perform the fundamentals simultaneously (see Figs. 5-92 to 5-96).

The Shadow Drill provides an excellent opportunity for the coach to instruct two players at once and to draw simulation and actual execution of a skill closer together.

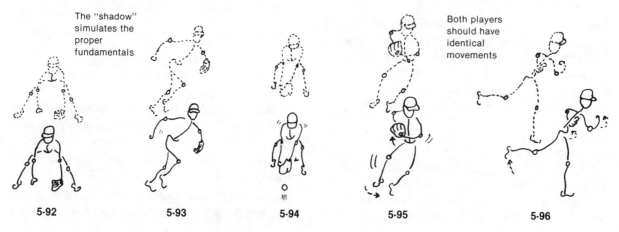

The "shadow" simulates the proper fundamentals

Both players should have identical movements

5-92    5-93    5-94    5-95    5-96

## Fielding and Throwing According to the Speed of the Runner and the Speed of the Ground Ball

Effective fielders make plays according to the speed of the runner and the speed of the ground ball. By watching opponents and studying scouting reports, players can learn which runners have good speed. A fast runner can get from the batter's box on the right side of the plate to a base 90 feet away in 4.2 seconds, and from the batter's box on the left side of the plate to the base in 3.9 seconds. These times are for players at high school, college, and professional levels. Times for players under age 14 are much slower.

Coaches can time players in their own leagues to get a better idea of speeds at their players' level. Coaches should time infielders as they field all types of ground balls in order to get a correct idea of how long it takes to make various plays as compared to the time it takes a runner to get to first base.

Fielding a ground ball gets particularly difficult when there are runners on first and third, and less than two outs. The infielder must make a split-second decision about whether to throw to the plate or try to get the double play. If the double play is started, the pivot player at second must decide whether to complete the double play or concentrate on the runner on third.

Teams need to practice fielding ground balls with runners on first and third, and to adjust their throws depending on the speed of the runner. These situations are often mishandled and lead to unnecessary runs for the other team. Developing basic fundamentals of fielding and throwing is not enough. Effective infielders must be aware of the *direction and speed of ground balls, location and speed of runners*, and must know the best way to deal with various situations as they develop during the game.

## Tagging Runners

Placing a tag on a runner sliding into a base is not difficult if a player understands how to do it. *Fielders need to let runners tag themselves out.* The infielder should not go looking for the runner, because the runner might then slide around or under the tag. The infielder should simply get behind the base and, after receiving the throw, quickly lay the glove down in front of the base, allowing the runner to slide into the tag (see Figs. 5-97 to 5-100).

Take throw with feet behind base    Place glove in front of base    Let runner tag himself out

5-97          5-98          5-99          5-100

# CHAPTER 6

# Positional Infield Skills

## First Baseman

### Qualifications

Effective first basemen should have quick reflexes, good glove action, and should be able to make split-second decisions. The player's throwing doesn't have to be exceptionally strong, but it should be accurate. Pure speed is not as important as agility and coordination. First basemen must be able to shift their feet quickly and gracefully, and know where and when to make the stretch for the ball. When one considers the number of throws that go to first base low, high, or wide, the importance of a sound defensive first baseman is easily appreciated.

### Fundamentals for Receiving Throws

*Footwork Around First Base.* The first baseman moves to the bag as soon as the ball is hit on the ground. Upon reaching the bag, the baseman faces the infielder making the throw to first. His heels should straddle the front of the base while waiting for the throw (see Figs. 6-1 to 6-3).

*Handling the Throw.* The first baseman waits until the last moment before starting the stretch for the ball. If the stretch is made too soon, he will not be able to adjust in time if the ball is thrown wildly (see Figs. 6-4 to 6-7).

In case of a poor throw, the first baseman's first priority is to catch the ball, even if it is necessary to leave the bag! Frequently, inexperienced first basemen keep their foot on the bag too long and end up letting a poor throw get by, which often allows runners to advance. An alert first baseman will know where the throw is going, and will then make the stretch to meet the ball.

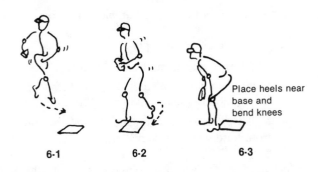

Place heels near base and bend knees

6-1          6-2          6-3

6-4

6-5

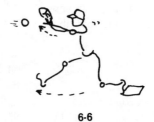

6-6

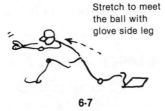

Stretch to meet the ball with glove side leg

6-7

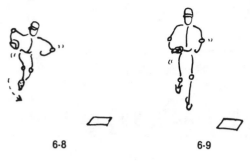

6-8                          6-9

6-10              6-11              6-12

Shift to foul side for throws on that side of base

6-13                          6-14

The stretch is made with the leg on the glove hand side. In other words, a right-handed first baseman stretches with the left foot, and a left-handed first baseman stretches with the right foot. This adds uniformity and coordination to the stretch.

Occasionally the first baseman will need to field a throw on the foul side of first base. Examples of such throws are those made by pitchers and catchers. In this situation, the first baseman should shift across the bag (see Figs. 6-8 to 6-14). Since the base runner will be coming quickly down the line, the first baseman should *never* reach across the bag for the throw, or a collision may result. If a throw pulls the first baseman off the bag toward home plate, he must make the catch and quickly lay the glove out in front of the base runner to try to get the runner to run into the tag.

First basemen should practice various shifts and stretches constantly to develop effective actions around the bag. They should practice both glove hand and backhand short hops from a stretch position frequently to establish proper timing and hand-eye coordination. This should be a major part of a first baseman's developmental system.

## Making Throws to Bases

A first baseman must be able to make the throw

1. to the *pitcher* covering first base,
2. to the *shortstop* to start a double play,
3. to the *third baseman* when a runner tries to go from second to third on a ground out, and
4. to the *plate* when a runner is trying to score from third with less than 2 outs.

Effective use of these throws helps create an effective defense. The throws require precise timing between players and need to be practiced throughout the season.

## Holding Runners on First

To hold a runner on first, the first baseman stands in a crouch with his eyes on the pitcher and the right

foot on the inside edge of the base (see Fig. 6-15). The first baseman needs to be alert for the attempted pick-off at first base, but immediately after the pitch is delivered to the plate, the first baseman moves off the bag into a ready position in case the ball is hit to that area (see Figs. 6-16 to 6-20).

6-15

Hold runners on first base

Break quickly away from first base following pitch

Assume a quality ready position

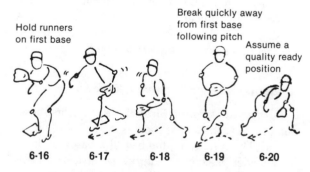

6-16        6-17        6-18        6-19        6-20

## Fielding Ground Balls

If the ball is hit to the first baseman's area, the baseman should instantly call for the pitcher to cover first. The first baseman may be able to make the play unassisted, but it is a good policy to remind the pitcher to cover first when the ball is hit to the right side of the infield. If the first baseman needs to throw to the pitcher covering first base, it should be with a skip and an underhand toss, since a skip and toss is easier to control than a sidearm or overarm throw. The first baseman should get the ball to the pitcher as soon as possible so that the pitcher has plenty of time to catch the ball, touch first, and get out of the way of the runner.

## Third Baseman

### Qualifications

Good third basemen should have a strong arm and be able to throw accurately. They should be quick on their feet, sure with their hands, and should be strong competitors.

### How to Play Third Base

A third baseman who masters these skills will be ready to play that position effectively.

1. A third baseman should be ready to *field balls which are hit far to his left*. The throw is much easier for a third baseman than for a shortstop on such balls.

2. A third baseman should try to *play most slow rollers down the third base line*. This will help the pitcher, who must also be ready to field this type of ball (see slow rollers, p. 58).

3. A third baseman should be ready to *knock down all balls that are hit down the foul line*. A ground ball hit down the foul line can be stretched into a double by a fast base runner. If necessary a third baseman should dive and knock the ball down in order to keep it in the infield. This type of play often saves games.

4. A third baseman should *play all left-handed hitters about even with the bag and slightly to the left of the normal position for right-handed hitters*. A third baseman must be alert for the drag bunt, not only from left-handers, but also from the leadoff hitter in each inning. He should observe opponents carefully to identify the potential drag bunters.

5. A third baseman should *field all pop flies on the third base side of the mound, and all those in foul territory from the plate to the dugout*. In general, he should field every pop fly within feasible reach on the third base side of the infield. This will relieve the pitcher and catcher of some pop fly responsibility.

6. A third baseman should *make as many of his throws as possible from an overarm position*. In this position the ball will travel on a straight line and will not dip, sink, or move to the right, as would be the case if the throw was made from a sidearm or underarm position. A sidearm sinking throw is much harder to catch; therefore, a third baseman should make every effort to use a straight overarm throw. However, if a ball is fielded in a manner that would require a sidearm delivery it would be advisable to make a sidearm throw to execute the play effectively.

7. A third baseman should try to *make chest-high throws to the second baseman when starting double plays*. This will make the double play quicker and assure the first out. Once again, the third baseman should strive for a straight throw which doesn't dip or sink; otherwise the second baseman will have to adjust to the quick change of direction of the throw and will be less likely to turn the double play.

8. A third baseman must *compete with all hard hits*. The ball does not have to be fielded in a picturesque manner, but simply knocked down or played off the chest, and followed by an accurate throw. This play requires determination and quick reflexes.

9. A third baseman needs to understand *fielding mechanics* (pp. 49-56), the *cutoff and relay system* (pp. 96-100), and *bunt coverage* (pp. 78-79) thoroughly, in order to understand his responsibilities and his part in the team's entire defensive effort.

## Second Basemen and Shortstops

The individual skills of second basemen and shortstops primarily involve the double play, so rather than dealing with these positions separately, they are discussed as a part of the execution of the double play. As do the first and third basemen, they also need to understand their responsibilities in bunt coverage, cutoffs and relays, and other situations which are discussed in Chapters 7 and 9.

### Turning Double Plays

There are several methods a shortstop or second baseman might use to try to turn a double play. The method they choose depends on where the ball was hit, how quickly the double play needs to be made, and the position of the runner sliding into second. Regardless of how the double play is made, the following points are important to remember:

1. The players must make sure of the out at second base.

2. All throws and tosses need to be accurate.

3. The player completing the double play should make a sidearm throw to first to force the runner to slide early.

4. The shortstop and second baseman need to be light on their feet in order to "roll" with a runner sliding in hard to second who is attempting to break up the double play.

5. Shortstops and second basemen should practice the proper footwork around the bag often so they will be relaxed and confident as they turn the double play quickly and accurately.

### Starting the Double Play—The Toss

The type of toss the shortstop or second baseman should use to start the double play depends on how the ball was hit. It is important that players understand that different tosses are best in different situations, because erratic throws can destroy potential double plays.

*Shortstop.* When *moving left* to play the ball, the shortstop should stay low, and after fielding the ball, should execute a *shuffle toss* to the second baseman. The shortstop keeps the hands well apart so that the ball is not hidden from the second baseman as it is released. The play should be completed with a smooth follow-through (see Figs. 6-21 to 6-26).

When fielding a ball *behind the bag*, the shortstop uses a *backhand toss* to the second baseman. Once again, he stays low and completes the play with a smooth follow-through (see Figs. 6-27 to 6-32).

When the ball is hit *straight at* the shortstop or *to the shortstop's right*, he executes a *sidearm toss*. The

toss should go to the second baseman's chest so that the second baseman can catch the ball and execute a quick, accurate throw to first base (see Figs. 6-33 to 6-38).

*Second Baseman.* When moving to the *right and toward second base*, the second baseman should make a *backhand toss* to the shortstop. This toss is generally most effective when made within 20 feet of second base, but second basemen should practice to find the distance at which they can make the toss most effectively (see Figs. 6-39 to 6-44).

If the second baseman fields the ball *behind second base*, the *glove shuffle toss* is the most effective throw. The entire movement is made with the glove hand, which should be kept low throughout the entire movement (see Figs. 6-45 to 6-50). It is a difficult play which players will need to practice frequently to master.

When the ball is hit either *at the second baseman* or *to his left* the second baseman should use a *sidearm toss*. He needs to make a half turn in order to get into an effective throwing position and should throw straight at the shortstop's chest at a speed the shortstop can handle easily (see Figs. 6-51 to 6-56).

### Completing the Double Play

Players must consider several factors before determining how to complete the double play: the *type of throw* starting the double play, the *position* of the

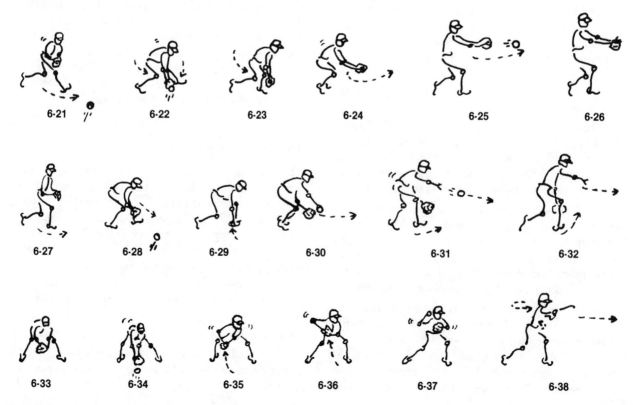

6-21    6-22    6-23    6-24    6-25    6-26

6-27    6-28    6-29    6-30    6-31    6-32

6-33    6-34    6-35    6-36    6-37    6-38

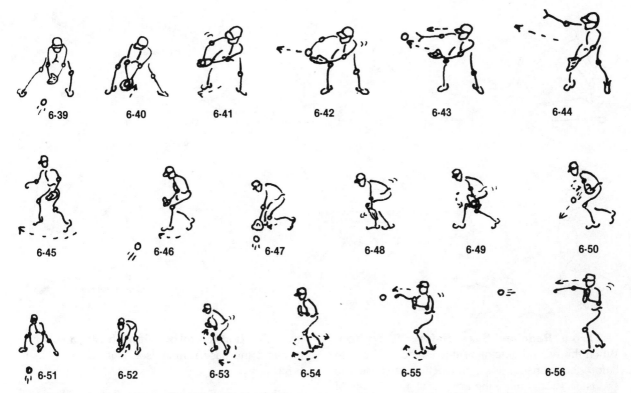

sliding base runner, and *how fast* the double play must be made. The shortstop or second baseman must consider these factors and make split-second decisions to figure out the most effective method of completing the double play.

When studying the following figures, pay special attention to the following points: (a) the manner in which the shortstop or second baseman receives the throw from behind the base, (b) the position of their feet as they reach the base, (c) the way the feet shift after they receive the throw, (d) the angle of their throwing arm as they make the throw, and (e) the

position of their feet after the follow-through, which should help prevent against injury from the sliding base runner.

***Shortstop Unassisted.*** When the ball is hit to the shortstop's left or near second base, the shortstop should make the play unassisted. In order to assure a quick double play, the shortstop should start the throwing motion while moving to the base, and be in the act of throwing as the left foot touches the base. The shortstop follows through with a little hop over the base to avoid the insliding base runner (see Figs. 6-57 to 6-67).

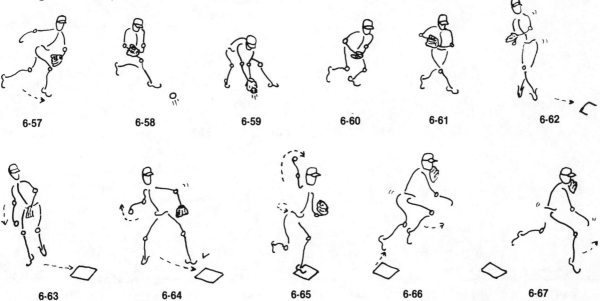

6-68    6-69    6-70    6-71    6-72

6-73    6-74    6-75    6-76    6-77

### Throw Reaches Base Before Shortstop.

When the second baseman's throw reaches the base before the shortstop does, on reaching the base, the shortstop should place the left foot along the side of the base while the right foot drags across the back edge (see Fig. 6-68). The shortstop receives the throw behind the base in case the throw is poor and the shortstop needs to make a split-second adjustment. If he comes across the base too quickly he may not be able to respond well to an erratic throw. The shortstop slides across the back of the bag and throws sidearm to first base (see Figs. 6-69 to 6-76). The sidearm throw will make the runner slide early without any chance to break up the double play. Once

again the shortstop follows through with a little hop to avoid the base runner (see Figs. 6-77; 6-78 to 6-84).

### Shortstop Reaches Base Before Throw.

If the shortstop receives the throw after reaching the base, he steps on the bag with the left foot, steps backward, and *throws from behind the base* (see Figs. 6-85 to 6-90). Since the throw was late, the shortstop will be able to avoid the insliding base runner more effectively by completing the double play from behind the base.

### Second Baseman Receives Throw Before Reaching Base.

If the second baseman receives the

6-78    6-79    6-80    6-81    6-82    6-83    6-84

6-85    6-86    6-87    6-88    6-89    6-90

throw before getting to the base, there are three ways to complete the double play.

1. The second baseman may place his left foot near the inside edge of the base, drag his right foot across the base, and then plant his right foot hard while throwing to first base. Just like the shortstop, the second baseman should follow through with a lit-

tle hop after the throw to avoid injury from the sliding base runner (see Figs. 6-91 to 6-103).

2. The second baseman can place his left foot in the center of the base and simply jump across the base. The player then lands on both feet and executes a quick throw to first base followed by the safety hop over the insliding base runner (see Figs. 6-104 to 6-115).

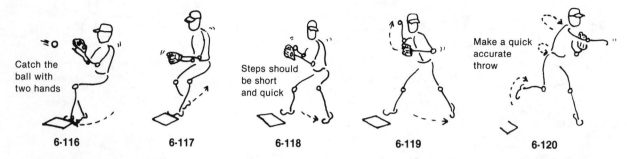

Catch the ball with two hands

**6-116**

**6-117**

Steps should be short and quick

**6-118**

**6-119**

Make a quick accurate throw

**6-120**

3. The second baseman can place his right foot on the inside of the base and use the base to shove off while throwing to first. The baseman will need to follow through with the hop since the base runner will be sliding directly at the baseman's feet.

***Second Baseman Reaches Base Before Throw.*** If the throw from the shortstop or third baseman is late and the second baseman has to wait for the ball, both feet should be placed behind the base. If the throw comes straight to the second baseman, he places his left foot on the base, and while using that foot to push backward, throws quickly to first base (see Figs. 6-116 to 6-120). If the throw comes to the second baseman's right, he should be in position behind the base ready to shift to the right, and should simultaneously tag the base with his left foot and throw. Likewise, if the throw is to the left, the second baseman should be ready to shift to the left, and should simultaneously tag the base with his right foot and throw to first.

Shortstops and second basemen should spend considerable time together practicing starting and completing every possible double-play situation to establish proper timing between them. The more repetition, the more effective their footwork, body positioning, and timing will be. The Receiving Tosses Drill and Ground Balls into Double Plays Drill will help the shortstop and second baseman develop their double play skills.

## RECEIVING TOSSES

*Age Group:* 8 and up.

*Purpose:* To practice receiving tosses near second base and making tosses from different areas using shortstop and second base positions.

*Equipment:* Ball, base, gloves.

*Procedure:* The shortstop gets in position near second base and receives tosses from the second baseman, who practices making throws from different areas of that position. Following 10 to 15 tosses, the second baseman stays near second base and receives

throws from the shortstop, who practices tosses from all the areas of that position. Each player strives to execute easy-to-handle, chest-high throws.

## GROUND BALLS INTO DOUBLE PLAYS

*Age Group:* 8 and up.

*Purpose:* Provides practice for performing double plays.

*Equipment:* First and second base, gloves, ball.

*Procedure:* One player stands near the pitcher's mound and throws a variety of ground balls and short hops to the shortstop and second baseman. Both infielders practice fielding the balls effectively, making the appropriate throw to start the double play, and executing the necessary pivot and throw to first base. A first baseman receives the final throw from the shortstop or second baseman.

The following two drills are effective methods for teaching and practicing double plays with other infielders as well as the second baseman and shortstop. The Double Play with Runners Drill puts extra pressure on infielders by having them make the play with runners on base.

## DOUBLE PLAY PRACTICE

*Age Group:* 10 and up; 8-9 (only shortstops and second basemen start double plays).

*Purpose:* To introduce, teach and practice double plays.

*Equipment:* Three bases, gloves, balls, bat.

*Procedure:* Place first and second base half their usual distance apart and an additional second base 10 feet behind. One third baseman, shortstop, and second baseman stand in their usual positions in relation to the bases. Additional third basemen, shortstops, and second basemen position themselves in relation to the additonal second base. One first baseman gets in position with regard to the shortened first base. Other first basemen back up throws to first base.

The coach tosses the ball to the first shortstop, who fields and throws to the appropriate second baseman, who catches and makes an easy throw to the first baseman. The second shortstop and second baseman simulate all the correct movements along with the players actually fielding. The coach then tosses the ball to the first third baseman, who fields and throws to the second baseman while the other third baseman and second baseman simulate movements. Actual fielders become simulators after fielding two balls. As play gets better, move first base progressively further away until it is at regulation distance from second base.

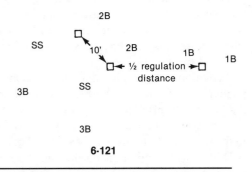

**6-121**

---

## DOUBLE PLAY PRACTICE WITH RUNNERS

*Age Group:* 10 and up; 8-9 (only shortstops and second basemen start double plays).

*Purpose:* To practice double plays in a game-like situation and to give players practice running.

*Equipment:* Infield setup, balls, bat, gloves, helmets.

*Procedure:* Third baseman, shortstop, second baseman, first baseman, catcher, and pitcher should go to their positions. All other players are runners and should wear helmets. One runner starts at first base and one runner starts in the batter's box. The coach hits a double play ball to one of the infielders. The runner at home plate simulates the swing with the coach and runs to first as the ball is hit. The runners run past first and, as they approach second, run to the side to avoid the throw. After running toward second, runners rejoin the line at home plate. Runners running past first base stay at first preparing to run to second. Players can be rotated so that fielders also practice running.

After some practice, points can be compiled. Fielders get a point for each out, and runners get a point for every base they reach safely.

---

## Pitcher's Fielding Responsibilities

After delivering the pitch, a pitcher becomes another infielder and must know how to fulfill that role in a variety of situations.

### Covering First Base

When the ball is hit to the pitcher's left and is past the mound, the pitcher immediately sprints to first base in order to be in the proper position to cover first in case the first baseman fields the ball. The pitcher should sprint to a point 6 feet down the line from first base, then turn down the line toward the base and be ready to take the throw. This should avoid a possible collision between the pitcher and the runner (see Fig. 6-122). Before reaching first base the pitcher should take short, choppy running strides to be prepared to respond quickly in case of a poor throw from the first baseman.

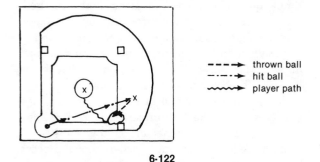

**6-122**

The pitcher receives the throw from the first baseman with two hands while advancing toward first base, and then quickly turns back into the infield toward second base after tagging first base and gets out of the way of the runner coming down the line. The pitcher also needs to be prepared to make any necessary throws.

If the pitcher happens to reach first base before the throw, he should behave as the first baseman ordinarily would by straddling the base, then stretching to meet the ball with the glove foot. This method is generally appropriate when the first baseman starts a double play and the pitcher needs to cover first base.

### Backing Up Home and Third

If there is a possible play at third base or home plate, the pitcher should sprint off the mound and stand halfway between third and home about 30 feet behind the foul line. The pitcher goes to the correct base after seeing where the throw is going, and thus assures proper defensive back-up coverage on all plays to home and third base (see Fig. 6-123).

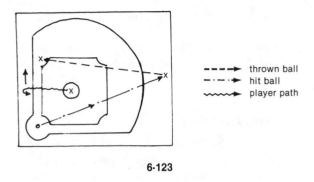

**6-123**

- - - → thrown ball
- · - · → hit ball
〰〰→ player path

## Pitcher Starting the Double Play

One of the fastest double plays in baseball is the one the pitcher starts by throwing to the shortstop. Because the ground ball reaches the pitcher faster than it reaches any other infielder, the pitcher can take a second longer to make the throw to second base. Thus, immediately after fielding the ball, the pitcher should quickly pivot and look at the shortstop. Then, with an accurate skip and throw, the pitcher should *lead* the shortstop carefully so that the shortstop has enough time to take the throw, tag second base, and throw to first base. The pitcher must *not* rush the throw or the ball may end up in center field.

If there are runners at first and third bases, the pitcher should fake the runner back to third after fielding the ball, then immediately throw to the shortstop for the force at second. Pitchers should practice both types of double plays often so that the coordination between pitcher and shortstop will be precise.

## Fielding Bunts

With a runner on first base and less than 2 outs, the pitcher must be alert for the bunt. As the pitcher approaches the ball, it is important that he listen to the catcher for directions in making the throw. However, the pitcher should be conscious of the fact that directions from the catcher are merely suggestions, not commands. The pitcher must know that he can definitely get the lead runner out; otherwise, *he should always get the sure out at first.*

For example, if there is a runner on first and the catcher yells for the throw to go to second base as the bunt is laid down, or if there are runners on first and second and the catcher yells for the throw to go to third base, the pitcher should be absolutely sure that he can get the lead runner out. If he has any doubts, he should immediately get the sure out at first base. If the pitcher doesn't get at least one out on a bunt, the rest of the defense will feel frustrated and let down. Also, the offense has been given a "free" base runner, and this can prove costly.

When approaching a bunted ball, a right-handed pitcher should straddle the ball, scoop the ball into the glove with his bare hand, turn his head to check the position of the lead runner, and decide whether to throw to first or to the lead base (see Figs. 6-124 to 6-128). A left-handed pitcher follows the same pattern but circles the bunt down the first base line so that he is facing toward the infield as he scoops the ball into the glove (see Figs. 6-129 to 6-134). From this position a left-hander can throw more quickly to first base.

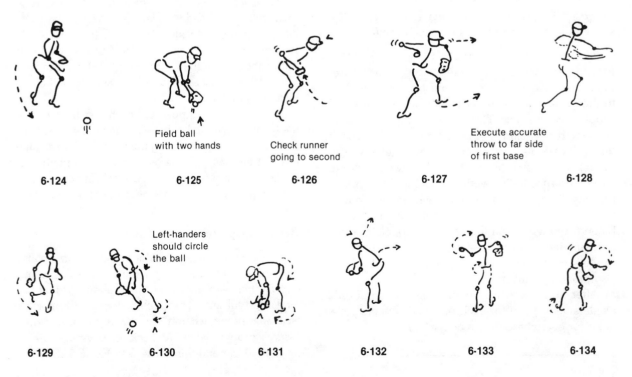

Field ball
with two hands

Check runner
going to second

Execute accurate
throw to far side
of first base

6-124          6-125          6-126          6-127          6-128

Left-handers
should circle
the ball

6-129          6-130          6-131          6-132          6-133          6-134

## Defensing the Squeeze Play

When there is a significant runner on third (the defense has a one-run lead, the score is tied, or the defense is behind) and there are less than 2 outs, the pitcher should pitch from the stretch and hold the runner close to third base by using an ordinary pick-off move to third base. The next pitch should be a pitchout that determines if the hitter is going to bunt. Prior to the next pitch, the pitcher should make his best pick-off move to third.

If either the hitter or base runner fails to demonstrate an intention to "squeeze," the pitcher must deliver his best pitches to the hitter, attempting to get a pop-up in case the hitter does try to bunt. If the pitcher sees the hitter square around to bunt, and if the runner breaks for the plate as the delivery starts on any of the succeeding pitches, the pitcher should throw a low or high fast ball to the third base side of the plate in order to push a right-handed hitter back and to create a difficult bunting position for the hitter. If the hitter fails to make contact with the ball, the catcher will be in a good position to receive the pitch and tag the runner out. If by chance the ball hits the batter, the runner will have to return to third base. However, if the hitter does lay the bunt down, the pitcher must move quickly off the mound, field the ball, and make a perfect underhand or backhand toss, low and to the catcher, depending on whether the ball is to the pitcher's right or left.

If either the pitcher or catcher suspects that the squeeze is on before a pitch, the catcher should signal for a pitchout. The defense must be mentally and physically ready for the possibility of the squeeze play when the game situation indicates its probability.

## Catcher's Fielding Responsibilities

### Qualifications

Catchers assume an extremely important position on the team. The catcher should be the stabilizer of the team, always trying to set an example of hustle, leadership, and desire. An alert, aggressive catcher, able to think on his feet, will be a tremendous asset to any team. Physically, catchers need superior agility and coordination to perform the necessary variety of tasks quickly and accurately.

### Pop Flies

Young, inexperienced catchers may find catching pop flies difficult to master. As with any difficult skill, the key to success is repetition using proper techniques. The more pop flies a catcher catches, the more efficient the catcher becomes.

As soon as a ball is popped up, a catcher should take the mask off and immediately spot the ball. After spotting the ball, the catcher should move in the direction of the ball and throw the mask in the *opposite direction* to make sure not to trip over it.

Catchers need to keep in mind that *balls popped up near home plate will have a spin that causes the ball to drift toward the infield* on the downward flight. Consequently, catchers should line up the ball so that it appears to be coming straight down on the catcher's nose. This position will permit any necessary last-second adjustments. Whenever possible, a catcher should circle the ball and make the catch with his back facing the infield so the ball will come towards the catcher instead of going away (see Figs. 6-135 to 6-143).

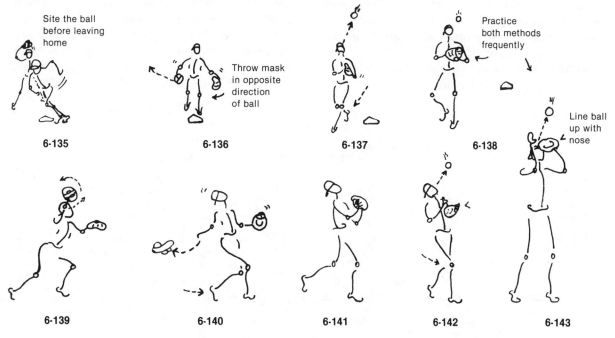

Site the ball before leaving home

Throw mask in opposite direction of ball

Practice both methods frequently

Line ball up with nose

6-135    6-136    6-137    6-138

6-139    6-140    6-141    6-142    6-143

Coaches can use the following drill to help catchers learn to catch pop-ups.

---

## POP-UPS FOR CATCHERS

*Age Group:* 8 and up.

*Purpose:* To give catchers practice on pop-ups.

*Equipment:* Catching equipment, bat, soft training balls, regular baseballs.

*Procedure:* The coach hits or throws pop-ups to one catcher in full gear, while other players either hit or throw pop-ups to each other.

---

### Steal and Pick-Off Situations

Among the catcher's most important responsibilities are to throw runners out as they try to steal and to pick runners off base. A catcher needs to try to keep a base runner's lead short, which helps eliminate steals. It is important for the first baseman to yell when the runner breaks for second base. This alerts the catcher to the attempted steal and allows the catcher to lean slightly toward the ball while catching, which helps place the catcher in a throwing position sooner. The catcher's throws don't need to be hard, but they need to be *quick and accurate.*

**The Throw.** When necessary, the catcher must get out of the stance quickly and execute a quick, accurate throw. Mastering quickness and accuracy requires considerable practice. A catcher needs to practice frequently moving quickly from the stance and then throwing. Catchers should perform between 10 and 15 stance and throws as part of their daily practice routine. Catchers must have confidence in their throwing ability because they face so many situations that require them to throw.

A catcher shouldn't waste any motion when throwing to second base. After receiving the pitch, the catcher simply shifts out of the stance, and starts concentrating on a target at second base, and throws. While pivoting into the throwing position, the catcher should take a short initial step with the throwing foot. To keep the throw on a straight line, he should keep the glove on the left side of his body and line up the glove side shoulder and hip with second base. In order to protect the arm and produce a harder throw, the catcher should shove hard with the back leg. This places the majority of the work load on the throwing shoulder and the back. The arm action should be quick and the throw should be straight overhand with the wrist perpendicular to the ground. This will help the ball hold a straight line after release (see Figs. 6-144 to 6-149). Catchers should review the discussion of pick-offs in the section on infield defensive play to get a more complete picture of the many possible pick-off moves (p. 79).

Catchers can use the following drill to work on moving quickly from the stance and getting off a quick, accurate throw.

---

## CATCHERS THROWING FROM THE STANCE

*Age Group:* 10 and up.

*Purpose:* To give catchers practice making throws to second base in order to throw out runners who are stealing.

*Equipment:* Home plate, second base, ball, gloves, catcher's mitt.

*Procedure:* Catchers should work in groups of three. If three catchers are not available, the coach may fill in as a pitcher. Also, second basemen and shortstops can cover second and practice tagging out imaginary runners going into second base. In each group of three, one player is the catcher, one the pitcher, and

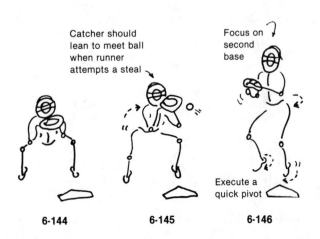

Catcher should lean to meet ball when runner attempts a steal

Focus on second base

Execute a quick pivot

6-144          6-145          6-146

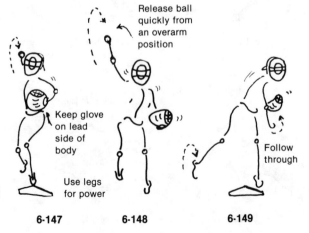

Release ball quickly from an overarm position

Keep glove on lead side of body

Use legs for power

Follow through

6-147          6-148          6-149

one the second baseman. Catchers need only wear masks for this drill since pitches should not be hard. The pitcher pitches to the catcher who throws to second base. Rotate players (within appropriate positions) after ten throws.

---

***Runners on First and Third.*** With runners on first and third bases, the runner on first might break for second as the pitcher throws to the plate. At this point, the first baseman should yell out to the catcher. As the catcher receives the pitch, he should jump quickly out of the stance and simultaneously look at the runner on third base. If the runner on third moves too far down the line, the catcher should make a realistic fake throw to second base, complete with follow-through, then pick the runner off third with a quick throw. If the runner on third holds tight at third, the catcher should execute an accurate throw to second base.

In summary, the catcher must think of two things in rapid succession: (a) preventing the runner on third from extending the lead too far and scoring on a throw to second, and (b) throwing out the runner breaking for second. This play is primarily the catcher's responsibility and should be practiced often. Catchers should review the discussions of first and third situations to understand more completely how they fit into the team's entire defensive effort (pp. 79-80).

### Tagging Runners Out at Home Plate

To tag a player out at the plate, the catcher rests the left foot on the front edge of home plate, which allows the runner to see the plate and slide into it. If the catcher stands in the third base line and blocks the plate, the runner has the right to run over the catcher. This is doubly important, for not only could this cause the catcher to drop the ball, but it might cause serious injury. When the runner sees the plate he is encouraged to slide.

As the runner starts the slide, the catcher should block the plate with the left foot and shin guard and make the tag with both hands. When making the tag, the catcher's entire throwing hand should be wrapped around the ball and placed in the glove pocket to prevent the runner from kicking the ball loose (see Figs. 6-150 to 6-154). After making the tag, the catcher should spring up and be ready to throw if necessary. The Catcher Making Tag Plays at Home Drill is one way for catchers to work on this skill.

---

## CATCHER MAKING TAG PLAYS AT HOME

*Age Group:* 8 and up.

*Purpose:* To teach the catcher to make the tag properly while preventing injury.

*Equipment:* Catching equipment, soft base.

*Procedure:* Place a loose soft base in a grassy area. The catcher wears full gear and assumes a position in front of the base as if it were home plate. The catcher's left foot should be placed on the front edge of the base so runners can see the back half of the base. Runners slide into this base (NO SPIKES). A player or coach throws a ball, timed to barely beat the runner, to the catcher. The catcher tries to tag the runner. After 10 tags catchers rotate.

---

### Backing Up First Base

The catcher should back up first base on ground outs when there are no runners on base. As soon as the batter hits a ground ball, the catcher should quickly move out of the stance and sprint to a place 30-40 feet behind first base in foul territory. From this position the catcher will be ready to prevent the hitter from advancing to second on an overthrow to first.

**6-150**

Allow runner to see home plate so he will slide

**6-151**

**6-152**

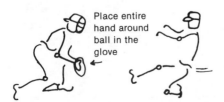

Place entire hand around ball in the glove

**6-153**

Block home plate with glove side foot, right shin guard, and glove

**6-154**

## Fielding Bunts

The catcher must be ready for all possible situations in a game, especially bunts, since the catcher is in the best position to *suggest* to the player fielding the bunt where to throw the ball. Whether the first baseman, third baseman, or pitcher fields the ball, the catcher should be looking at the runners and deciding where the throw should best go. The catcher must remember two points when making the decision: (a) always get one sure out, and (b) give the player fielding the ball ample time to execute the play effectively. Fielders shouldn't be off-balance when making the throw because they need to adjust their feet at the last moment. Therefore, just prior to fielding the ball, they should know where they are going to throw it. Ideally, fielders would like to get the lead runner out, but if the catcher has the slightest doubt about being able to get the lead runner, he should call for the throw to go to first base for the sure out.

If the catcher thinks the bunt will be fielded faster if he makes the play, the catcher should call for the ball quickly, spring out quickly in a fielding position, and make the play. The catcher approaches the ball in a low, crouched position with the belt buckle parallel to the foul line, scoops the ball into the glove, and skips and throws to first base (see Figs. 6-155 to 6-162). He should refrain from merely picking up the ball with one hand and making the throw. By scooping the ball with both hands, he insures a better play. After fielding the ball, he should make his throw to the fair side of first base. If his throw moves to the foul side of the base, the first baseman will have to compete with the runner coming down the base line, which means a more difficult movement is required by the first baseman to receive the throw. Therefore, the catcher should concentrate and attempt to execute a smooth follow-through, producing an accurate throw to the fair side of first base. Catchers should review all principles of bunt coverage so that they will understand all the infielders' actions (pp. 78-79).

## Cutoffs and Relays

Because the catcher is the primary participant in most cutoff and relay situations, catchers need to understand the entire cutoff and relay system thoroughly. See pages 96-100 for a complete discussion and series of illustrations. Every catcher should study this section carefully.

6-155          6-156          6-157          6-158          6-159

6-160                    6-161                    6-162

# CHAPTER 7

# Infield Play

This chapter deals with infield situations that require coordinated play among several infielders: run-downs, bunt coverage, pick-offs, first and third steal situations, and various play action for infielders.

## Run-Downs

Occasionally when infielders catch a runner in a rundown between two bases they let the runner get to the next base simply because they are disorganized. A run-down has an excellent chance of success if infielders follow these guidelines:

1. Infielders should *stay behind the bag while waiting for the next throw*.

2. Infielders should *go to meet the throw after it has been made*.

3. *All defensive participants should move out of the baseline after making the throw and should proceed to a position behind the next base.* If a runner hits a defensive player who is standing in the base path and doesn't have possession of the ball, defensive interference is called on the infielder and the runner is awarded the next base.

4. Each infielder should *sprint at the base runner*, in order to make the runner's momentum reach a peak about two-thirds of the distance to the next base. This is important because establishing maximum momentum in the runner and requiring each player to meet each throw reduces to a minimum the probability of mishandling the run-down.

5. Only *three or four fielders* are necessary and only *two or three throws* should be required to make the tag.

Teams can work on their performance in run-downs by doing the Run-Down Drill.

### RUN-DOWN DRILL

*Purpose:* To practice offensive and defensive run-down procedures.

*Equipment:* Bases (two for each group of eight players), balls, gloves.

*Procedure:* Place four players in one line behind a base and four in another line behind another base, with the bases regulation distance apart. Players keep their gloves on. The second player in one of the groups of four has the ball, and the first player acts as the base runner. The base runner gets 5 feet in front of the player with the ball who then yells "go." The player with the ball chases the runner. The lead player at the front of the other line stays behind the bag waiting for the throw but goes to meet the throw as soon as it is made. When the runner is 12 to 15 feet in front of the second line, the first player in that line, the tag player, yells "now" and the chaser tosses the ball to that player to make the tag. After the tag, the player gives the ball to the next player in line who becomes the base runner as the drill continues.

When the chaser yells "go," the chaser must get either to the inside or the outside of the base line, being sure to run on the glove side of the receiving player, and must run as hard as possible. The chaser should run using sprinting form, and when the tag player calls "now," he should release the ball with a firm, accurate toss. When the runner gets close enough (12 to 15 feet), the tag player yells "now" and at the same time takes a couple of controlled steps toward the runner, receives the ball and makes the tag.

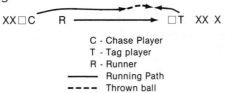

C - Chase Player
T - Tag player
R - Runner
———— Running Path
- - - - Thrown ball

T yells "now" and steps toward runner and makes the tag. After the run-down is completed and the tag is made, the tag player hands the ball to the player behind and then becomes the runner. Original chase player and runner continue to end of opposite line.

**7-1**

## Bunt Coverage

There are several methods for covering bunt situations, each of which has its strong points. *A team needs to settle on one system and learn to execute it effectively.* If a team can't cover bunts well, they will give away runs needlessly, so all infielders must learn their appropriate actions for bunt coverage and learn to perform them well. One method of coverage stresses the pitcher's role. This method is discussed below.

*The pitcher acts as an extra infielder when the hitter bunts.* If the hitter lays the ball down on the infield to the pitcher's left, the pitcher must decide instantly whether he or the first baseman should field the ball and then call the play accordingly. If the pitcher plays the ball, the first baseman goes back to the bag for the throw (see Fig. 7-2). If the first baseman fields the bunt, the second baseman and pitcher break to cover

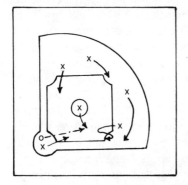

Key for Figures 7-2 through 7-5

—·—·— hit ball
———— player path
o hitter
x fielders

**7-2**

first base (see Fig. 7-3). The first baseman should make the throw either to the pitcher or to the second baseman depending on where he fields the bunt and on the position of the second baseman or pitcher when the first baseman starts the throw.

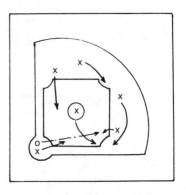

**7-3**

If the bunt is laid down to the pitcher's right, the pitcher and third baseman break for the ball and attempt to make the play. The *third baseman* must decide quickly if he or the pitcher should field the ball and should call the play instantly. The third baseman's decision depends largely on how hard the ball was bunted and on the ball's exact position on the infield. The player not fielding the ball immediately goes to cover third base in case the runner on first tries to advance all the way to third (see Figs. 7-4, 7-5).

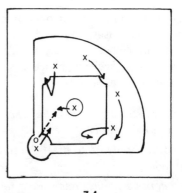

**7-4**

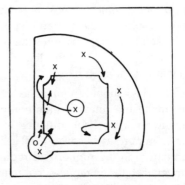

**7-5**

Other methods of bunt coverage include the first and third basemen charging the plate as soon as the hitter starts to bunt, or the catcher, rather than the pitcher, covering third base. A team should evaluate the options and adopt a system that utilizes the team's strong points.

## Pick-Offs

Pick-offs are attempted primarily for two reasons: (a) to try to throw a runner out who has a long lead, or (b) to reduce a runner's lead and cause a slow break to the next base if he attempts a steal. Many types of pick-off moves can be used; some of the most effective moves are listed here.

1. When a *runner is on first base*, the first baseman plays three to four steps behind the runner. The pitcher comes to the belt for the stretch and starts to count to three while turning his head away from first base. On the count of three, the pitcher executes a quick, snap throw to first base. The first baseman also counts as the pitcher touches his belt, and reaches the base at the same time the pitcher throws the ball.

Alternatively, the pitcher throws a pitchout and the first baseman breaks for the bag as the catcher makes the throw to first base.

2. After receiving the pitch, the catcher can make either a quick snap throw or a delayed throw to first. Either move can effectively keep runners close to the bag.

3. With a *runner on second base*, the shortstop can give a signal to the pitcher, such as touching his right ear. The pitcher will start to count when he comes to the belt during the stretch. The pitcher should then turn and look at home plate. At the count of three, the pitcher should turn and throw to second base, and the shortstop should be there at the right time to take the throw. If both the shortstop and the second baseman take a quick step further away from second base to encourage the runner to take a longer lead, this pick-off move will be even more effective. The shortstop needs to sprint to second and be there in time to take the throw.

The same move can be executed with the second baseman. The shortstop can still signal the pitcher using a different gesture than in the previous situation, such as touching the left ear, to indicate that the second baseman will receive the throw.

4. With *runners on second and third bases and less than 2 outs*, the shortstop should play in, near the runner, to cut off the run at the plate on a ground ball. The catcher first gives the pick-off sign, then the signal for the type of pitch to be thrown, and makes a target with his mitt. As soon as the catcher drops the mitt down to his side the pitcher turns and throws to second, where the shortstop takes the throw. The catcher should not lower the mitt until he sees the shortstop break toward second base. This move requires precise timing and needs to be practiced often.

Rather than having the pitcher make the pick-off throw, the catcher could make the throw after a pitchout in this situation.

5. One of the most effective pick-off moves, and the simplest to execute with a *runner on second*, is initiated by the shortstop moving in behind the runner at second base. After passing the runner's left arm, the shortstop quickly shows the palm of his glove to the pitcher. Once the pitcher sees the palm of the glove, the pitcher pivots and throws to second, where the shortstop takes the throw.

If infielders, pitchers, and catchers practice pick-off moves several times a week, these moves will be quite effective during the season.

## Defensing First and Third Steal Situations

When a team has runners on first and third bases, in many cases they will try to steal. The first and third steal situation has three basic variations each of which infielders must handle with precision

### Early First and Third Steal

During the early first and third steal, the runner breaks for second just as the pitcher comes to the belt in the stretch. In that case, the first baseman should yell that the runner is moving. The pitcher should then *step off the rubber* so he will not balk, fake the runner back to third, then turn and throw to the shortstop, who should be breaking in front of second base. The shortstop should then run the base runner back to first, being careful to watch the runner on third.

Many teams consider it unwise to make any other throws than this in attempting to tag out the runner from first base. If the defense chooses to develop a run-down to try to tag out the runner from first, they could easily throw the ball away or allow the runner from third to score because they were preoccupied with the run-down. In order to avoid this situation, many teams simply chase the runner all the way back to first base, call time out, and wait for the next pitch. If the runner on third breaks for the plate at any time, the shortstop should ignore the base runner from first, and throw to the plate in an attempt to throw out the base runner who is trying to score from third (see Fig. 7-6).

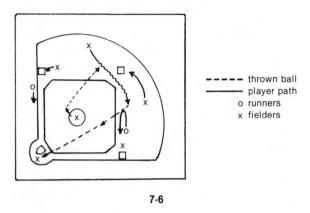

----- thrown ball
— player path
o runners
x fielders

**7-6**

### Regular First and Third Steal

During the regular first and third steal, the runner on first breaks for second base as the pitcher delivers the pitch to the plate. The first baseman should yell as the runner breaks. As the catcher receives the pitch, he jumps out of the stance quickly and simultaneously looks at the runner on third. If the runner on third moves down the line too far, the catcher should fake a throw to second base and pick the runner off third with a quick throw to third base. If, however, the runner on third holds tight, the catcher should execute an accurate throw to second base.

*The shortstop and second baseman need to predetermine who will back up second and who will cover in front of the base.* Usually this decision is based on what type of hitter is at the plate. For example, if a right-handed pull hitter is the batter, the second baseman covers one step in front of second. If a left-handed pull hitter is at the plate, the shortstop covers one step in front of second. Basing the decision on the type of hitter allows players to hold their positions slightly longer in case the hitter pulls the ball toward their positions.

When covering in front of second, the shortstop should watch the runner on third out of the corner of the eye as the throw is on its way. If the runner on third doesn't break for the plate, the shortstop takes the throw, takes one step back towards second base, and places the tag on the bag. If, however, the runner on third breaks as the catcher throws to second, the shortstop should go to meet the throw, cut the ball off, and throw home to try to throw out the runner (see Fig. 7-7). The same principle applies when the second baseman covers in front of second base.

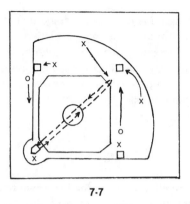

**7-7**

Another variation for the regular first and third steal defense is to have the catcher jump out of the stance as the runner breaks, and throw straight back to the pitcher, acting as if the throw was meant for second base. This may draw the runner off third base. The pitcher should cut off the throw and quickly throw to third to try to pick the runner off of third.

### Delay First and Third Steal

The delay first and third steal starts with the runner on first base breaking for second as the catcher starts to throw the ball back to the pitcher. Once again, the first baseman yells that the runner is moving. The pitcher receives the throw from the catcher and follows the same defensive moves he performed against the early first and third steal situation. The *pitcher fakes the runner back to third and throws to the shortstop, and the shortstop chases the runner back to first base.*

### In Sum . . .

Proper defensive behavior in a first and third steal requires precise timing and execution by every member of the infield. Teams need to practice these maneuvers until they establish a well coordinated effort among all the players. To formulate a method for the most effective defense in first and third steals it may be useful to review the section in Chapter 3 dealing with these and to develop a complete picture of how the offense tries to execute the play (pp. 36-37). The First and Third Steal Situation Drill is a good way to teach players and have them practice their responsibilities in these situations.

---

### FIRST AND THIRD STEAL SITUATION DRILL

*Age Group:* 10 and up.

*Purpose:* To teach infielders how to defense a first and third steal situation.

*Equipment:* Three bases, home plate, bat, balls, gloves, helmets.

*Procedure:* There should be a complete infield, a batter, and runners on first and third bases. Batters and runners should wear helmets. The batter may sometimes swing and sometimes not swing, but should not hit the ball.

1. Players practice defensive maneuvers for regular first and third steal. All possible situations should be explained and practiced several times.

2. Explain and practice early first and third steal maneuvers.

3. Explain and practice delayed first and third steal maneuvers.

Runners and fielders should be rotated often so all players understand their defensive responsibilities during the situations.

The Scramble Drill is a good way for infielders to work on many of their infield skills. With older players coaches can incorporate the Stuffed Glove Drill into this drill or others.

## SCRAMBLE DRILL

*Purpose:* Develops players' coordination and rhythm for fielding and throwing all types of ground balls, and helps develop players' reactions.

*Equipment:* Complete infield, four balls, gloves.

*Procedure:* All infielders report to their positions. If there are not at least two players at each infield position, pitchers or outfielders should take the vacant positions (see Fig. 7-8). The two players at each position should rotate after each has had an opportunity to execute a play. The coach should have four baseballs and should stand in front of home plate.

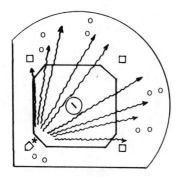

Key:
Coach ★
Players o
Ground balls ∿∿➤

**7-8**

The following should serve as a guide for administering the drill:

1. The coach starts the drill by rolling a ground ball to the throwing hand side of any infielder. After executing a proper crossover step and fielding the ball effectively, the infielder throws to first base. Players should get in front of each ball if possible and should only backhand balls which are so far to the right that they cannot get their bodies in front of them.

After receiving the throw, the first baseman throws the ball to the catcher, who hands the balls to the coach. The coach waits until the fielding infielder executes the throw to first base before rolling the next ball to a different infielder. Each infielder should have an opportunity to play a ball to the throwing hand side five times, which should only require a few minutes if the coach keeps the balls moving rapidly.

2. Next the coach rolls ground balls to each player's glove side and the drill procedes as described above. Each infielder should field about five balls.

3. Now all the infielders turn double plays. Each infielder must remain alert because one double play will be completed at about the same time the coach rolls another ground ball to start another double play. Each infielder should have about five opportunities to execute double plays.

4. The coach finishes the drill by rolling the ball directly at each infielder and requiring them to throw to home plate. Just as the infielder executes a throw to the plate, the coach rolls a slow roller somewhere near that player, and the infielder then fields that ball and throws to first base. After each player completes this sequence five times, the Scramble Drill is over.

The Scramble Drill is especially effective because it involves a large number of infielders in a short period of time and incorporates a wide variety of fielding and throwing opportunities for each player. If administered properly, this drill can help develop the fine quality of reactions and reflexes that reflect well on a defensive training program.

## STUFFED OR WOODEN GLOVE

*Age Group:* 10 and up.

*Purpose:* Develops "soft hands" in fielders by teaching them to cushion the ball.

*Equipment:* Stuffed or wooden glove (see Appendix B for instructions), other equipment depends on use.

## Infield Play Action Chart

| Situation | First Baseman | Second Baseman | Third Baseman | Shortstop |
|---|---|---|---|---|
| Outs: less than 2<br>Runners: 1st base<br>Score: any score<br>Type of ball hit: ground ball | If the ball is hit to the 1st baseman's right, he should throw to 2nd. The pitcher covers for the return throw from the shortstop. If the ball is hit to the 1st baseman's left and near the bag, he should step on the base and throw to the 2nd baseman who will tag the runner. | The 2nd baseman should try to turn the double play, but if the ball is hit far to his left, he should settle for one sure out at 1st. | The 3rd baseman should try to turn the double play, but if the ball is hit too slow, he should settle for the sure out at 1st. | Same as 3rd baseman. |

*Note: All slow hit balls should be played to first base. Get one out for sure.*

| Situation | First Baseman | Second Baseman | Third Baseman | Shortstop |
|---|---|---|---|---|
| Outs: less than 2<br>Runners: 1st and 2nd<br>Score: any score<br>Type of hit: ground ball | Same as above. The 1st baseman should *never* throw to 3rd. | Same as above. The 2nd baseman should *never* throw to 3rd. | Same as above. However, if the ball is hit to the 3rd baseman's right, he should step on 3rd and throw either to 2nd or 1st. | Same as above. However, if the ball is hit far to the shortstop's right, he should check 3rd for the possible force play. |
| Outs: less than 2<br>Runners: 1st and 3rd<br>Score: 1 run lead, tied, or behind<br>Type of hit: ground ball | The 1st baseman's primary concern is the runner on 3rd, since that represents an important run which should not be allowed to score. The player's secondary concern is to turn the double play or get one sure out at 1st. | Same as 1st baseman. | Same as 1st baseman. | Same as 1st baseman. |

*Note: If the defense is 2 or more runs ahead, they should let the run score and get the double play.*

| Situation | 1st Baseman | 2nd Baseman | 3rd Baseman | Shortstop |
|---|---|---|---|---|
| Outs: less than 2<br>Runners: 1st, 2nd, and 3rd<br>Score: 1 run lead, tied, or behind<br>Type of hit: ground ball | Same as 1st baseman. | The primary concern is to get the easiest double play. The direction of the ball will determine the type of double play at 2nd; otherwise, the play is to home plate. | The primary concern is to get the easiest double play. The direction in which the ball is hit will determine how to perform the double play. If the ball is hit to the 3rd baseman's far left, his play is at 2nd; otherwise, the play is to home. If the ball is hit close to the bag, the 3rd baseman could tag 3rd and throw to 1st. If there are *no* outs, after tagging 3rd, he should get the runner from 3rd in a rundown, thus preventing the runner from scoring, and assuring the double play. | Same as 3rd baseman. An additional option for the shortstop is to throw to 3rd, if the ball is hit far to his right. |
| Outs: less than 2<br>Runners: 2nd and 3rd, or only 3rd<br>Score: 1 run lead, tied, or behind<br>Type of hit: ground ball | The primary concern is the runner on 3rd. After fielding the ball, the 1st baseman should check the runner at 3rd and get the sure out at 1st. The 1st baseman's ready position should be even with 1st base. | Same as 1st baseman. The 2nd baseman's ready position should be two strides behind the base line between 1st and 2nd. | Same as 1st baseman. The 3rd baseman's ready position should be even with 3rd base. | Same as 1st baseman. The shortstop's ready position should be two strides behind the base line between 2nd and 3rd. |

*Note: If the defense is 2 or more runs ahead, all infielders should play at their regular depth. Let the run score and get the sure out at 1st base.*

| Situation | 1st Baseman | 2nd Baseman | 3rd Baseman | Shortstop |
|---|---|---|---|---|
| Outs: less than 2<br>Runners: 2nd base<br>Score: any score<br>Type of hit: ground ball | The runner will be moving to 3rd as the ball is hit if it goes to the right side of the infield, so the only play is to 1st. The pitcher should cover 1st. | Same as 1st baseman. The 2nd baseman will also need to cover 2nd when the ball is hit to either the shortstop or 3rd baseman in order to force the runner back to the bag. | As the 3rd baseman plays the ball, he should force the runner to go back to 2nd, then make the throw to 1st for the sure out. | If the ball is hit to the shortstop's left, the runner will probably be able to advance to 3rd, so the only play is to 1st. If the ball is hit to the shortstop's right or straight at him, he should check the runner and throw to 1st. If the runner tries to advance, the shortstop should throw the runner out at 3rd. |
| Outs: less than 2<br>Runners: none<br>Score: 1 run lead, tied, or behind<br>Type of hit: any kind | Be ready for any type of ground ball or pop fly. Watch for the drag bunt with no outs and a runner with good speed at the plate. | | Same as 1st baseman. The 3rd baseman should play in a little for left-handed hitters. | Same as 3rd baseman. |

*Procedure:* Fielders practice fielding with the stuffed glove. A good fielder fields the ball with two hands and absorbs the impact. A poor fielder will have the ball rebound off the glove. Fielders will miss many balls while using this glove, so they can practice "staying with" the ball and moving quickly to throw the runner out.

Catchers can use the glove to emphasize the use of two hands when catching. This glove is also very beneficial for teaching shortstops and second basemen to turn the double play pivot quickly.

## Play Action

The correct defensive action of each infielder depends on several variables, each of which must be considered carefully before the ball is hit. The *number of outs*, the *position of the runners* and their *speed*, the *score*, and the *type of ball hit* all have a bearing on how fielders should play the ball and where they should throw it. Players' choices of play action during a game often separates outstanding infielders from mediocre ones. Experience is usually the best teacher for this phase of infield play. By remaining mentally aware of appropriate defensive actions in various situations and by anticipating many possible situations, players will be prepared to handle successfully any situation that occurs during games. The Play Action Chart is a summary of a variety of different batted ball situations and of proper play action choice for the four primary infielders: the first baseman, the second baseman, the third baseman, and the shortstop.

# CHAPTER 8

# Outfield Play

Quite often coaches minimize the importance of sound defensive outfield play. The majority of practice and preparation time seems to revolve around pitchers, catchers, and infielders. Coaches sometimes forget, however, that a ball misplayed in the outfield can cost the team runs rather than an extra base. An outstanding catch or a misjudged fly ball can often change the entire tempo of a tight pitching duel. An outfielder does not execute great catches by mere chance. He must diligently practice intricate details which will help him to make outstanding defensive plays.

This chapter on outfield play is presented with the intent of making the outfielder and the coach more aware of the total responsibilities of each outfielder and his obligations toward his teammates, as well as stimulating an inquiry into the basic mechanics of his position. It should be emphasized that repetition is a key to success; therefore, an outfielder who aspires to become more efficient at his position should constantly strive to put into practice the insights discussed here.

## Qualifications

Successful outfielders generally possess better than average speed and quickness. They should be able to throw with power and accuracy, be competitive and alert, and have sound judgement and determination. A successful outfielder eagerly awaits opportunities to make a challenging play—catching the low liner or, a long drive hit overhead, or throwing out a base runner attempting to advance.

The center fielder should be the best outfielder of the three. A center fielder needs good speed in order to be able to cover a large area of ground. He needs a strong, accurate arm, and needs to be a leader. Like all fielders, he needs to be keyed up on every pitch in order to get the "jump" on every ball.

## Ready Stance and Getting "The Jump" on the Ball

In the ready position the outfielder's *weight is on the front part of his feet, the center of gravity is low, the elbows are loose, and the eyes are fixed on the hitter's bat* (see Fig. 8-1). An outfielder should be able to get the best jump on all balls from this position. He should get into a ready position before each pitch regardless of the length of the game or the number of pitches thrown. Outfielders have no way of knowing when the ball will be hit towards them, so they must be ready on every pitch!

8-1

Mentally the outfielder should be eager to play the next ball. He should hope for an opportunity to display his skills and to assist his ball club. He does not know until the ball comes off the bat whether he will have to come in on a sinking liner, go back on a line drive, or challenge the fence in his attempt to make the play. Consequently, he must be mentally keyed to respond instantly to each situation as it develops.

## Sun and Wind

All outfielders must contend with the sun and wind. By throwing grass into the air between pitches they can remain aware of the wind's direction and velocity. Outfielders should use their gloves as a sun shield to keep the sun from getting in their eyes on a play (see Fig. 8-8).

## Fly Balls Overhead

When the ball is hit over an outfielder's head, he should perform a quick crossover step as soon as the ball makes contact with the bat. The player should be moving at *top speed* after the first two strides and should concentrate visually on the flight of the ball to enable the outfielder to adjust more effectively to changes in the flight of the ball. Some outfielders prefer instead to perform the crossover step, sprint to a spot, and then pick up the flight of the ball; this can give an outfielder greater speed to the ball. Whichever method they use, outfielders should run on the balls of their feet so their eyes remain steady while

they chase the ball. Running on the heels may cause the eyes to jerk and will hinder an outfielder's ability to track the ball.

Outfielders must *sprint* to the ball, no matter how far they have to run. An effective outfielder will sprint and then wait for the ball. This way outfielders can make any adjustments necessary to catch a ball that might have been misjudged or caught by the wind.

Outfielders should catch with *two hands*. By catching with two hands they increase the probability of a successful catch and can get off a faster, more coordinated throw after the catch (see Figs. 8-2 to 8-11.)

Coaches can use the Toe-Running Drill to help teach players to run on their toes in order to keep their heads and eyes still while catching a fly ball.

### TOE-RUNNING DRILL

*Purpose:* To teach outfielders to keep their heads level when running for fly balls.

*Equipment:* Six balls, gloves.

*Procedure:* Outfielders line up outside the right field foul line facing the infield. When the coach yells "go" the first outfielder sprints to the right, catches a ball that the coach throws, immediately returns to the left to catch the second ball, and then immediately sprints back to the right for a long throw. As outfielders catch each ball, they toss it back towards the coach's helper who puts the ball in a container. After catching the last ball, the player returns to the foul line.

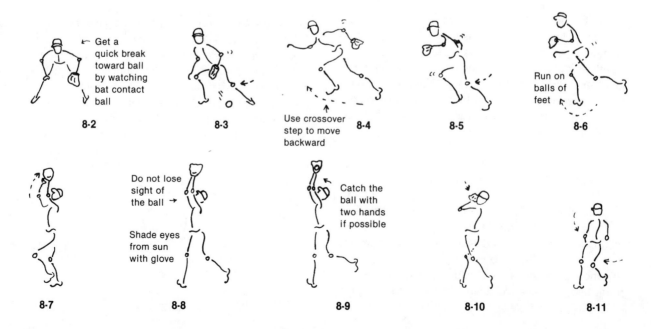

8-2  8-3  8-4  8-5  8-6  8-7  8-8  8-9  8-10  8-11

Players should run on their toes, not on their heels. Players should pick a point head high and concentrate on that point before looking for the thrown ball. Players should turn their heads only to look for the ball, not their entire bodies.

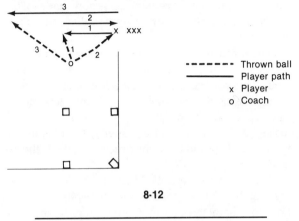

**8-12**

## Circling Fly Balls

When a high fly ball is hit with runners on base, outfielders should circle around the ball and come straight into it as they make the catch. This maneuver will insure maximum power when they throw back into the infield. The most critical time to circle a fly ball is when an outfielder needs to throw out a runner attempting to tag up and advance. Figures 8-13 to 8-24 provide a detailed study of an outfielder circling a fly ball.

## Fielding Ground Balls

Outfielders should field ground balls in basically the same way as infielders. Figure 8-25 shows the basic fielding position; outfielders should also review the basic mechanics of fielding discussed with infield skills (pp. 49-56). When outfielders don't have to make an important throw after catching the ball they can use one of the two alternative fielding positions shown in figure 8-26. These positions put the outfielder's body in a better position to block the ball, but make it more difficult to get off a quick throw.

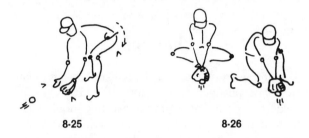

**8-25**    **8-26**

If an important runner is attempting to advance from first to third or attempting to score from second on a hit, outfielders should field the ball and get the throw in as quickly as possible. In this case, they need to charge the ball hard, field the ball, and throw to the cutoff person. Outfielders need to field the ball with the glove foot back in order to establish proper rhythm and timing for the crow-hop and throw. In order to get the most power and accuracy, they should shove hard with the throwing-side leg and

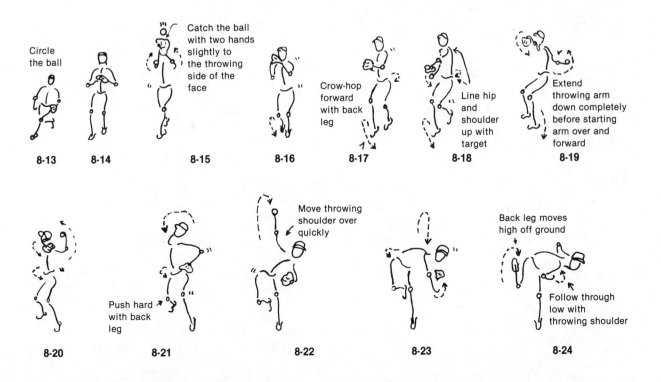

**8-13**    **8-14**    **8-15**    **8-16**    **8-17**    **8-18**    **8-19**

**8-20**    **8-21**    **8-22**    **8-23**    **8-24**

continue running after releasing the ball (see Figs. 8-27 to 8-35).

Regardless of the method an outfielder uses to field a ball, he must make sure not to bobble it or let it get by him. An outfielder's mistake could allow a runner to advance one or more bases and allow the opponents unnecessary runs. Outfielders need to practice coming in on ground balls, using proper fielding mechanics, and throwing correctly to appropriate bases. Through repetition and analysis of fundamentals outfielders should become familiar with various speeds of ground balls and how fast to charge the balls in order to throw out runners at any base.

## Throwing

The throw from the outfield is very similar to an overhand pitcher's delivery (pp. 105-110). As outfielders play a fly ball or ground ball they should build their momentum into the throw by performing a little "crow-hop" which distributes the weight on the back leg and allows them to put the full force of the body into the throw. In this move the elbow is relaxed as it extends backwards during the throw, and the glove hand points toward the throwing target. As the weight comes forward, the outfielder should release the ball from an overhand position and follow through low with the throwing shoulder (see Figs. 8-36 to 8-43).

The throw from the outfield must be *overhand* so that it stays on a straight line as it comes into the infield. If the ball has the slightest side-spin it will kick to one side as it hits the infield grass. Outfielders should develop a strong downward wrist snap as they release the ball, to impart the proper spin and to insure that the ball goes in the right direction as it hits the infield grass.

Throws from the outfield should be kept low. A high, arching throw doesn't have the speed or direction that characterizes a low throw. In order to throw low, an outfielder should be certain not to drag the throwing shoulder. The throwing shoulder must reach a higher plane than the lead shoulder does as

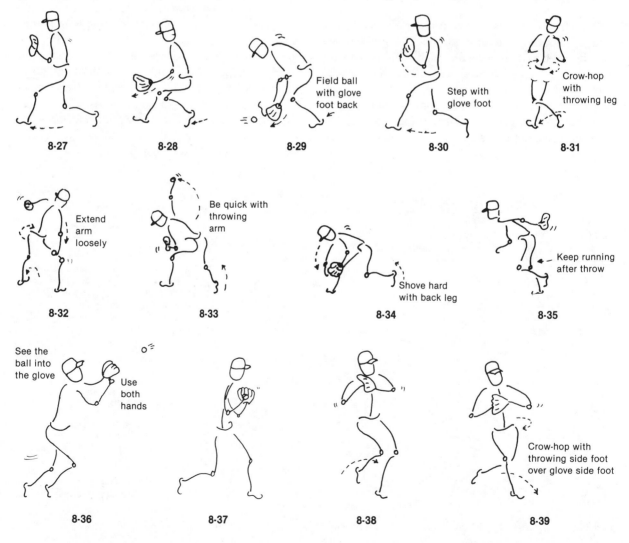

8-27

8-28

8-29   Field ball with glove foot back

8-30   Step with glove foot

8-31   Crow-hop with throwing leg

8-32   Extend arm loosely

8-33   Be quick with throwing arm

8-34   Shove hard with back leg

8-35   Keep running after throw

8-36   See the ball into the glove / Use both hands

8-37

8-38

8-39   Crow-hop with throwing side foot over glove side foot

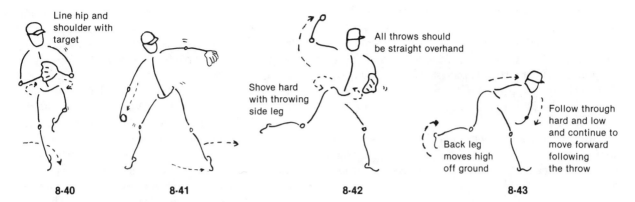

Line hip and shoulder with target

Shove hard with throwing side leg

All throws should be straight overhand

Back leg moves high off ground

Follow through hard and low and continue to move forward following the throw

**8-40**          **8-41**                    **8-42**                    **8-43**

the throwing arm starts forward to release the ball. The outfielder must get "on top" of the throw with the upper part of the body, otherwise the throw will sail off with a high, ineffective arch.

To be effective, outfielders should learn to hit specific targets. They should practice throwing to second base, third base, and home plate, always trying to hit the base on a *low, one-bounce throw*. They should practice "hitting" the cutoff and relay people in the chest from various distances on direct throws. If an outfielder's throwing is sound mechanically and he is mentally alert, he can be invaluable to his team.

The Outfield Ground Ball—Fly Ball Drill is an excellent way for outfielders to practice their fielding and throwing.

## OUTFIELD GROUND BALL— FLY BALL DRILL

*Purpose:* To work on outfielding fundamentals.

*Equipment:* Four balls, gloves, bat.

*Procedure:* A coach stands on the right field foul line about 30 feet behind first base. Three players stand in left-center field. One player acts as the catcher, feeding the coach balls, and another stands closer to the outfielders and acts as a relay person. The coach hits a variety of ground balls and fly balls to players in the outfield. They throw to the relay who throws to the catcher (see Fig. 8-44). The coach should hit balls fairly continuously. Players rotate periodically.

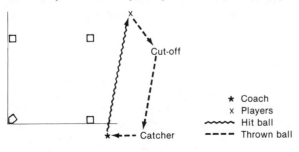

Cut-off

★ Coach
x Players
∿ Hit ball
--- Thrown ball

Catcher

**8-44**

A variation of this drill can be performed by having only one outfielder field the batted balls at a time. After fielding a ball, the outfielder throws the ball to a cutoff man and promptly assumes another ready position. The coach then hits another type of ball to the outfielder. Each outfielder fields 20 balls, then a new outfielder begins.

## Playing Balls Off or At the Fence

Outfielders need to know how to play balls that land near or bounce off the outfield fence. Coaches can use the following two drills to teach and develop these skills.

## BALLS LYING AT THE FENCE

*Purpose:* To teach outfielders how to play balls lying at the fence.

*Equipment:* Four balls per group, fence, gloves.

*Procedure:* Have outfielders work in threes—two players act as outfielders and one as a relay man. Place four balls at the fence for each pair. Have balls about 5 feet apart and leave 10 feet between groups. Outfielders start 25 feet away from the fence, and relay men stand about 75 feet from the fence. The first outfielder approaches the ball from various angles and throws to the relay man (see Fig. 8-45).

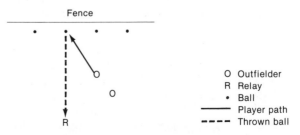

Fence

O Outfielder
R Relay
• Ball
— Player path
--- Thrown ball

R

**8-45**

Right-handers should pick up the ball with their right foot on the right side of the ball. Left-handers should pick up the ball with their left foot on the left side of the ball without straddling it. Outfielders should begin their throws at precisely the point where they pick up the ball, and as quickly as possible. (Remember—an average runner takes 4-5 strides per second.)

After throwing, the first outfielder retreats to the starting point and the second outfielder runs to pick up the next ball. Players rotate after retrieving four balls.

## BALLS HIT OFF THE FENCE

*Purpose:* To teach outfielders how to play balls which bounce off the fence.

*Equipment:* Balls, fence, gloves.

*Procedure:* The coach hits or throws balls against the fence at different angles. The outfielders play the balls off the fence and throw to the relay.

## Playing Line Drives

Hard shots or line drives to the outfield can be difficult to field because of the direction and spin of the ball. The ball will often sink, take off, move up, or sail as it travels into the outfield. An outfielder should know some general rules which can make it easier to play a line drive. If the ball is hit on a line to the opposite field, such as a left-hander hitting to left field or a right-hander hitting to right field, the ball might have a tendency to drift toward that foul line and sink slightly, especially if the wind is blowing into the hitter's face. As he sprints to the ball, an outfielder needs to carefully watch line drives which sink in front of him or take off and move over his head. Occasionally the additional concentration will allow an outfielder to make last-second adjustments and may lead to an outstanding catch.

## Know the Hitter and the Pitch

If outfielders know the hitter's *bat action, power, and speed,* they will be better able to determine the depth and direction they should play the hitter. A slight adjustment before each hitter's appearance at the plate might make the difference in a successful catch. Scouting reports and watching each hitter's habits throughout the game are good ways to obtain valuable information.

The shortstop and second baseman can also signal the next pitch to the outfielders inconspicuously. Many such signals are possible from this position. For example, if the next pitch will be a fast ball, the shortstop could hit his glove once, or if the next pitch is a curve or change-up, the second baseman might touch his right or left thigh. Outfielders can't see the finger signs the catcher gives the pitcher, so they must rely on infielders to convey that information. This information can help outfielders get a better jump on the ball, since the hitter is more likely to pull a curve or change-up, than a fast ball, and knowing the pitch helps the outfielder to prepare. The outfielder's slight mental adjustment could make a difference between a successful catch and a base hit.

## Backing Up Plays

An outfielder should back up as many plays as possible. He should concentrate on plays as they develop and determine how he can best assist in backing up both the primary play and the secondary plays in his area of the field. He should strive to be in the right place at the right time when wild throws or missed balls occur. Also, by looking for the pick-off signs he should be aware of when his team is about to attempt a pick-off. In case of a mix-up in the infield or a poor throw from the catcher or pitcher, he should try to keep the base runner from advancing by backing up the play quickly. Qualities such as alertness and attentiveness should help an outfielder perform defensive backup services for his team.

## Play Action

The correct defensive action of each outfielder depends on several variables, each of which must be considered carefully before the ball is hit. The *number of outs,* the *position of the runners and their speed,* the *score,* and the *type of ball hit* all have a bearing on how outfielders should play the ball and where they should throw it. Outfielders' choices of play action during a game often separate outstanding players from mediocre ones. Experience is usually the best teacher for this phase of outfield play, but by studying appropriate defensive actions in various situations and by staying mentally alert, players will be more prepared to deal with various game situations. The Outfield Play Action Chart summarizes a variety of different situations, and proper play action choice for the outfielders. It includes some information on cutoff and relay situations, which will be covered more completely in Team Defense, Chapter 9.

## Outfield Play Action Chart

| Situation | Left Field | Center Field | Right Field |
|---|---|---|---|
| Outs: any number<br>Runners: none<br>Score: any score<br>Type of hit: single to any field | The ball should be fielded and thrown to 2nd base. | Same as left field action. | Same as left and center field action. |
| Outs: any number<br>Runners: 1st base<br>Score: any score<br>Type of hit: single to left center or right center | The first outfielder to reach the ball checks the runner rounding 2nd. The primary throw is to 3rd, but depending on the runner a throw to 2nd might be feasible. | Same as left field action. | Same as left and center field action. |
| Outs: any number<br>Runners: any number<br>Score: any score<br>Type of hit: double to left center or center | The first outfielder to reach the ball should field the ball and throw to the shortstop, who is the relay man in shallow left center. | Same as left and right field action. | The first outfielder to reach the ball should field the ball and throw to the 2nd baseman, who is the relay man in shallow right center field. |
| | *Note: Same defensive coverage regardless of outs, runners, or score.* | | |
| Outs: any number<br>Runners: any number<br>Score: any score<br>Type of hit: double in the left or right field corner | The ball should be fielded quickly and thrown to the shortstop, who is the relay man near the left field foul line. | Encourage the outfielder playing the ball to make an accurate throw to the relay man. | The ball should be fielded quickly and thrown to the 2nd baseman, who is the relay man near the shallow right field foul line. |
| | *Note: Same defensive coverage regardless of outs, runners, or score.* | | |
| Outs: any number<br>Runners: 1st and 2nd<br>Score: 1 run lead, tied, or behind<br>Type of hit: single to any field | The ball should be fielded quickly and thrown home. The 3rd baseman is the cutoff. | The ball should be fielded quickly and thrown home. The 1st baseman is the cutoff. | Same as center field. |
| | *Note: If the defensive team is 3 or more runs ahead, fielders should consider a secondary throw to 3rd base to keep the runner from 1st base from going any further than 2nd.* | | |

## Outfield Play Action Chart (cont.)

| Situation | Left Field | Center Field | Right Field |
|---|---|---|---|
| Outs: less than 2<br>Runners: 1st, 2nd, and 3rd<br>Score: 1 run lead, tied, or behind<br>Type of hit: fly ball | The fielder should circle, catch, and throw the ball home. If the ball is deep, the throw should go to 3rd to keep the runner on 2nd from advancing to 3rd. | The fielder should circle, catch, and throw the ball home. If the ball is deep, the throw should go either to 3rd or 2nd, depending on which is more feasible. | Same as center field. |
| Outs: any number<br>Runners: 1st, 2nd, and 3rd<br>Score: 1 run lead, tied, or behind<br>Type of hit: single to any field | The ball should be fielded and thrown home. The 3rd baseman is the cutoff. If it appears that a throw to home would be too late, the throw should go to 3rd. | Same as left field. | Same as left and center fields. (A secondary throw should go to 2nd base.) |
| Outs: any number<br>Runners: 1st and 3rd<br>Score: 1 run lead, tied, or behind<br>Type of hit: single to any field | The left fielder should field the ball quickly and throw to 3rd base. He should check the runner rounding 2nd base. | Same as left field. | Same as left and center fields. |
| Outs: less than 2<br>Runners: 2nd and 3rd<br>Score: 1 or more runs ahead<br>Type of hit: fly ball to any field | The left fielder should circle, catch, and throw the ball home. The 3rd baseman is the cutoff man. If the ball is hit deep, the throw should go to 3rd to try to keep the runner at 2nd from advancing. | Same as left field. The 1st baseman is the cutoff man. The decision of whether to throw home or to 3rd depends on how deep the ball is hit. | Same as left and center fields. |
| Outs: less than 2<br>Runners: 1st and 3rd<br>Score: 1 run lead, tied, or behind<br>Type of hit: fly ball | The left fielder should circle, catch, and throw the ball home. If the fly ball is too deep, he should throw to 2nd to hold the runner at 1st. | Same as left field. | Same as left and center fields. |

While studying the chart, note that nearly all of an outfielder's actions can be governed by two rules: (a) *the safest throw is to the base in front of the base runner at the moment the outfielder plays the ball*, and (b) *an outfielder's primary concern is the most significant base runner at that particular moment in the game*. Outfielders must continually remain sensitive to these points throughout each game.

## Outfield Communication

Outfielders must communicate with one another. Often an outfielder must turn his back on the infield to retrieve a ball, and is therefore unaware of where to throw the ball after fielding it. He needs to focus all his attention on executing the play. Other outfielders should observe the locations of the base runners and tell the fielder where to throw. The Outfield Teamwork Drill forces players to rely on one another, teaching them to communicate and to work together.

## OUTFIELD TEAMWORK DRILL

*Purpose:* To teach outfielders to work together.

*Equipment:* Balls, gloves, bat, bases.

*Procedure:* Place one set of outfielders in defensive positions and place extra outfielders in the infield to receive throws. Tell them that an imaginary runner is on base. The outfielder who will play the ball is not told where the runner is. The outfielder turns away while the coach signals the other outfielders where the runner is stationed. The coach tells all outfielders the number of outs and the score. There can be more than one runner on base.

The coach hits balls to outfielders from behind second base. The outfielder nearest the fielder catching the ball tells that player where to throw it just before the fielder catches the ball.

# CHAPTER 9

# Team Defensive Play

This chapter covers pop fly and fly ball coverage and the cutoff and relay system. These two areas require that the entire defense understand some general rules concerning their responsibilities and coordinate their efforts with those of several other fielders.

## Pop Fly and Fly Ball Coverage

Fielders must constantly be ready to go back or come in on fly balls. Fielders need to be in the ready stance to make sure they get the best possible jump on the ball. When a ball is hit over an outfielder's head, he should take a quick crossover step to go back for the ball.

Players should *always call for a fly ball* to avoid any collisions, but they should wait to call for the ball until it reaches its peak height to make sure they know where the ball is going. The wind might catch the ball and may change the ball's flight considerably before it comes down. Players must also call for the ball before it reaches a halfway point on its downward path in order to eliminate last second collisions.

The best method for insuring maximum coverage for all types of fly balls is to establish policies for catching them. In general, the center fielder has the right-of-way over the other fielders. All outfielders have the right-of-way over all infielders since they have a better angle on the ball. The first baseman, second baseman, third baseman, and shortstop have the right-of-way over the pitcher and catcher. The second baseman should play balls hit behind first base into shallow right field, and the shortstop should

play balls hit behind third base into shallow left field. They are in the best position to catch such pop flies on their side of the field and should make every effort to do so. The first or third baseman should field high pop flies hit near the pitcher's mound and first and third base dugouts. Infielders should do everything possible to take the responsibility of catching pop flies off the pitcher and the catcher, and should call them off pop flies whenever possible. All players should pursue a fly ball until they hear someone with the right-of-way call them off.

The following summary is presented to try to make pop fly and fly ball responsibilities as clear as possible. Following these guidelines should assure maximum coverage and safety.

1. *The center fielder has priority over everyone else and can recall any fly ball at any time even though someone else calls for the ball first.* The center fielder must realize that even though another ball player calls for the ball he can recall it and make the catch if he can get to the ball. This helps prevent collisions that often occur between outfielders.

2. *All outfielders have priority over all infielders, and if necessary, should recall infielders off any pop fly.* This will reduce the collisions between infielders and outfielders which occasionally cause serious injury and allow unearned runs. It is much easier for outfielders to come in on pop flies than it is for infielders to go back. Of course, if an infielder never hears the outfielder call for the ball, he should go all out for the catch.

Outfielders should never call for the ball at the last second, since this could lead to a collision. Calls should be made before the ball is halfway down.

3. *Infielders have priority over catchers and pitchers.* Every infielder should follow the flight of the ball off the bat. As soon as the ball reaches its peak in the air, an infielder should call for the ball. The remaining infielders should back away and encourage the player to make the catch while they cover a base.

The first and third basemen should make all catches near the mound, in front of home plate, down the base lines, and near the dugouts in order to take the pressure of catching pop flies off the pitcher and catcher. The second basemen should try to make all catches down the right field foul line and behind first base, since he has a much better angle than the first baseman. The same is true for the shortstop making catches behind third base and down the left field foul line. He has a much better angle than the third baseman.

4. *The catcher should handle only pop flies that other infielders can't easily reach.* If the catcher calls for the ball, and while moving toward the ball hears an infielder recall the ball, the catcher should step out of the way and let the infielder make the play. This will eliminate collisions and dropped balls.

5. Finally, *pitchers shouldn't try to catch pop flies unless it is absolutely necessary.* The pitcher should step out of the way and encourage infielders to make the catch. There are a few occasions, however, when a pitcher should make the catch. The pitcher is responsible for pop bunts and weak pop-ups in front of and behind the mound which occasionally come off the bat handle. As a rule, it is much easier for the pitcher to leave the high towering pop flies to the more experienced infielders. However, if the pitcher is one of the best athletes on the team, the coach may want the pitcher to catch *all* pop flies near the mound.

## Cutoff and Relay System

Every fielder must have a clear picture of the cutoff and relay system so that game situations are handled with maximum efficiency. The following illustrations and descriptions clearly depict proper action in all cutoff and relay situations.

### Situation: Runners at Second; First and Second; or First, Second, and Third; Less Than 2 Outs

If the ball is a base hit to *left-center, center or right field, the first baseman* is the cutoff. If the ball is a

base hit to *left or down the left field foul line, the third baseman* is the cutoff. The first and third basemen must talk to each other in this situation to insure that there is proper coverage. The cutoff man should hold up both hands and yell at the outfielder to "hit me," so the outfielder will have no difficulty spotting him. Figures 9-1 and 9-2 show the proper position of the cutoff man when the fielder is throwing to the plate.

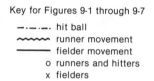

Key for Figures 9-1 through 9-7

—·—·— hit ball
〰〰 runner movement
———— fielder movement
o runners and hitters
x fielders

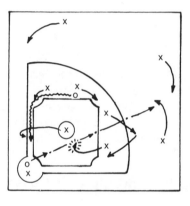

**9-1**

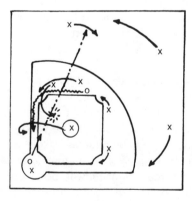

**9-2**

The catcher needs to help the cutoff man quickly find a position on a straight line between home plate and the outfielder playing the ball. Then the catcher must let the cutoff man know in plenty of time whether to: (a) cut the ball off and throw it home, (b) cut the ball off and throw to another base to catch another runner rounding a base too far, or (c) simply not cut off the ball.

## Situation: Runners at First and Second; or First, Second, and Third

*If a base hit is driven into center or right field and the outfielder decides to throw to third base instead of home plate, the shortstop is the cutoff man.* The third baseman now does the same thing the catcher does on throws to the plate; he lines up the shortstop on the straight line between third base and the outfielder fielding the ball and tells the shortstop either to let the ball go through or to cut it off and throw to third or another base (see Fig. 9-3).

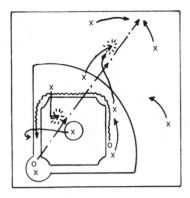

9-4

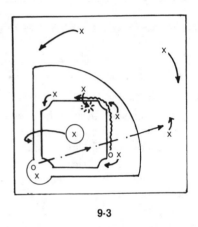

9-3

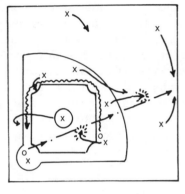

9-5

## Situation: Sure Doubles to Left-Center Field, Center Field, or Right-Center Field

*On all sure doubles to left-center, center, or right-center, the shortstop and second baseman should trail each other out into the outfield to become relay men.* This is especially important if there is a runner on first base. Occasionally the outfielder will hurry the throw and miss the relay man. Since left-center, right-center, and straight-away center are the deepest parts of a ball park, a poor throw that misses the first relay man might allow base runners to advance one or more bases. By sending two relay men out about 30 feet apart, an effective relay is assured. The second relay man must tell the first where to throw the ball *before* the first receives the ball from the outfielder. If the relay man knows where the throw is going, he will not have to hesitate when receiving the ball. This will assure a faster, smoother relay into the infield.

The first baseman should follow the hitter down to second base and cover the bag. This will keep the runner from rounding second too far (see Fig. 9-4). The first baseman can't do this when there is a runner on first and the ball is hit to right or center field, since he would then be the cutoff in the middle of the infield (see Fig. 9-5).

## Situation: Sure Doubles in the Left Field Corner or Right Field Corner

If a ball is hit into the *left field corner, the shortstop moves out on the left field line to be the relay man, and the third baseman serves as the cutoff man* (see Fig. 9-6). If the ball is hit to the *right field corner, the second baseman moves to the right field line and serves as the relay man, and the first baseman serves as the cutoff man* (see Fig. 9-7).

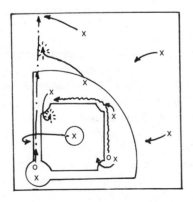

9-6

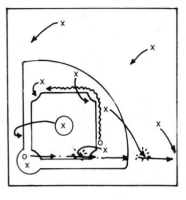

**9-7**

When the second baseman or shortstop is the relay man, the other should cover second base. It is important that these two infielders communicate effectively during each of these situations to insure that throws are made to the correct places.

When cutoff and relay men receive throws, they should position their bodies so that they will be able to make the quickest possible relay throw. The Five Player Cutoff and Relay Drill helps players practice this skill.

## FIVE PLAYER CUTOFF AND RELAY DRILL

*Purpose:* To develop quickness, precision, and correct body position in relay throws.

*Equipment:* Gloves, balls.

*Procedure:* Players work in groups of five. The players arrange themselves in a straight line with the furthest players about 250 feet apart, depending on the age of the players (see Fig. 9-8). Players who act as relays and cutoffs most often should be in middle positions.

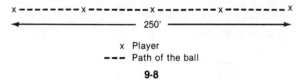

x  Player
- - -  Path of the ball
**9-8**

The first player executes a strong, accurate throw to the second player who executes a similar throw to the third player. Once the last player in line catches the ball, the process starts again in the opposite direction. Before receiving the relay throw, players should line up their glove shoulder with the next throwing target. Regardless of the ball's path as it comes to cutoff players, they should always adjust their body position so that they can simply catch the ball and throw immediately with maximum velocity and accuracy.

The coach can time each cycle of the drill, or arrange two groups to compete against one another to get the team working as intensely as possible.

---

The Cutoff and Relay System Drill is designed to involve a maximum number of players for a minimum amount of time in the proper mechanics of cutoff and relay situations. The entire drill should only take 15 minutes.

---

## CUTOFF AND RELAY SYSTEM DRILL

*Purpose:* To work on the proper mechanics of all cutoff and relay situations.

*Equipment:* Balls, gloves, infield bases.

*Procedure:* Players take their defensive positions. Each infielder (except the pitcher and catcher) has a ball. The coach stands in shallow outfield to instruct both the infielders and outfielders. The coach starts by calling out the number of runners on base. Then each infielder, one at a time, calls the number of outs and makes any type of throw, ranging from singles and doubles to sure outs, to an outfielder. The effectiveness of the drill depends largely on the variety of throws the infielders make to the outfielders. The coach uses every baserunning situation possible to cover the complete spectrum of cutoff and relay circumstances.

The third baseman should start the drill as soon as the coach calls the baserunning situation. Other infielders wait until the previous cutoff or relay play is complete before calling the number of outs and making the throw. Each outfielder should have an opportunity to make at least one throw during each baserunning situation. The *catcher* should direct the cutoff men to their positions and call the play. The *pitcher* should back up either third base or home plate.

The coach should check each infielder and outfielder carefully, not only for mechanics of throwing, catching, and fielding, but also for proper choice of where to make the throw.

The drill can be visualized by studying Figure 9-9 and the possible sequence of events shown in the chart.

1.  Each infielder has a ball.

2.  The coach stands in the shallow portion of the outfield.

3.  The coach starts the drill by calling out the number of runners on base.

4. Infielders alternate calling the number of outs and throwing to outfielders.

5. Each infielder waits until the previous cutoff or relay play is over before calling the next situation and making the throw.

6. After every infielder throws a ball to an outfielder, the coach calls the next situation.

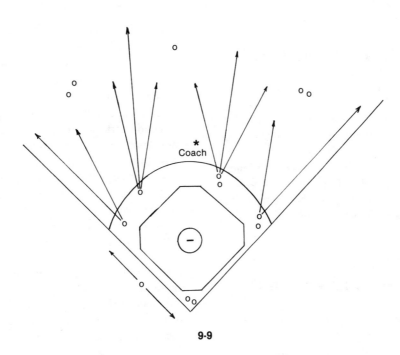

**9-9**

## Cutoff and Relay System Drill

| Coach | Third Baseman | Shortstop | Second Baseman | First Baseman |
|---|---|---|---|---|
| 1. Shouts, "No runners on base." | Next, the 3rd baseman shouts the number of outs and throws a fly ball or ground ball in the area from the left field foul line to left-center. | Next, the shortstop shouts the number of outs, and throws a fly ball or ground ball in the area from left-center field to straight-away center field. | Next, the 2nd baseman shouts the number of outs and throws a fly ball or ground ball in the area from straight center to right-center field. | Next, the 1st baseman shouts the number of outs and throws a fly ball or ground ball in the area from right-center to the right field foul line. |
| 2. Shouts, "Runner on 1st only." | Same | Same | Same | Same |
| 3. Shouts, "Runners on 1st and 2nd." | Same | Same | Same | Same |
| 4. Shouts, "Runners on 1st, 2nd, and 3rd." | Same | Same | Same | Same |
| 5. Shouts, "Runners on 1st and 3rd." | Same | Same | Same | Same |
| 6. Shouts, "Runners on 2nd and 3rd." | Same | Same | Same | Same |
| 7. Shouts, "Runner on 3rd only." | Same | Same | Same | Same |
| 8. Shouts, "Runner on 2nd only." | Same | Same | Same | Same |

The Cutoff and Relay System Drill involves many of the skills included in Chapters 5 through 9 including (a) cutoffs and relays, (b) pitchers backing up home or third, (c) catchers calling cutoffs, (d) throwing from the outfield, and (e) the skip and throw by infielders. Coaches should have a clear understanding of all these areas before teaching this drill.

## Other Drills and Suggestions

The rest of this chapter includes drills which incorporate several skills discussed in Chapters 5 through 9. Coaches can use the Throwing for Points Drill to get the whole team in fielding positions working on throwing accuracy in a fun drill, and can use the Three Player Drill to continue to perfect players' fielding and throwing skills. The Three Player Drill can be adapted for many purposes by changing the distance between players and the type of balls they throw to one another.

### TEAM THROWING FOR POINTS

*Purpose:* To develop throwing skills in each member of the team.

*Equipment:* Gloves, baseballs, infield setup.

*Procedure:* The coach assigns a player to each position on the field. The coach teaches the players the number of their positions as in the numbering system in the official scorebook (Pitcher-1, Catcher-2, First baseman-3, Second baseman-4, Third baseman-5, Shortstop-6, Left fielder-7, Center fielder-8, Right fielder-9).

The pitcher (1) starts the drill by executing a skip and throw to the player whose number the coach calls. The coach calls a different number after each throw. The players continue to throw to the player at the position the coach calls.

The team earns points as in the Skip and Throw for Points Drill by throwing to specific spots on the other players' bodies—the chest earns 5 points, the head 3 points, the arms and legs 1 point each, and away from the body takes a point away from the total score. The team keeps an account of the points they earn and the number of throws they make. The team's objective is to use a minimum number of throws to earn 50 points. Each time the team practices this drill, they should try to establish a "team record" for fewest throws required to reach 50 points. (The goal for players 9 years old and younger should be 25 points.)

### THREE PLAYER DRILL

*Purpose:* To practice all the fundamentals of fielding, throwing, and catching the ball under various structured conditions.

*Equipment:* Balls (one for every three players), gloves.

*Procedure:* Players arrange themselves in a triangle as illustrated in Figure 9-10. One player rolls various types of ground balls and fly balls to the other two players. Ground balls should vary from fast ground balls and short hops to slow rollers and balls requiring considerable range to either side of the fielder. Fly balls could be line drives or high pop flies.

The player fielding the ball executes a quick snap throw to the fielding partner. The partner catches the ball with two hands and executes a proper skip and throw to the player rolling the balls. The player who rolls the ball receives each return throw with two hands while stretching out with the glove side foot to meet the throw, as if executing a force play. Players rotate positions every tenth ground ball.

Coaches should remain alert for opportunities to instruct weaker players on fundamentals and should positively reinforce players properly executing the skills.

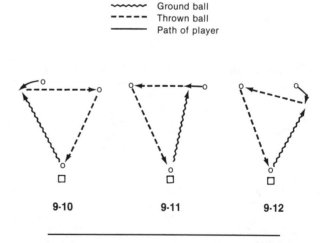

Key:
〰〰〰 Ground ball
- - - - Thrown ball
───── Path of player

9-10                9-11                9-12

The Short Base Situations Drill is a good way to introduce players to their responsibilities in various defensive situations. Rather than having players spread out in their usual positions, they are placed close enough together so that everyone can hear the coach easily. Players go through plays, learning where throws should go, and where they need to be without having to worry about performing other skills.

## SHORT BASE SITUATIONS

*Purpose:* To explain specifics of baseball in a modified setting.

*Equipment:* Three bases, home plate, balls, gloves.

*Procedure:* Set up an infield with bases only 30 feet apart. Players take positions on the field. Some players stay at home plate to be walkers (rather than runners). Coach sets up situations with the walkers to explain proper play. The coach throws balls to the infielders, who field them appropriately. All throws should be lobs. Rotate players periodically.

Once players understand the specific responsibilities of their position, they can develop the skills unique to that position by performing the Individual Position Drill. After they understand their responsibilities and how to execute the skills necessary to perform them, players can help achieve consistent performance by developing their mental image and feel for each skill through the repetition done in the Game Situation Drill.

## INDIVIDUAL POSITION DRILL

*Purpose:* Provides players with an opportunity to work on skills specific to their defensive positions.

*Equipment:* Gloves, balls.

*Procedure:* Players report to their defensive positions and perform the following skills specific to their position:

*Catchers:*
1. Practice shifting on low pitches in the dirt
2. Practice stance and throws to all bases
3. Practice fielding bunts and pop flies
4. Practice cutoff and relays
5. Practice tagging runners out

*Pitchers:*
1. Practice covering first base
2. Practice starting various double plays
3. Practice bunt coverage
4. Practice pick-off moves to all bases

*First basemen:*
1. Practice shifting around the bag
2. Practice receiving various types of throws
3. Practice starting double plays
4. Practice bunt coverage
5. Practice cutoff and relays
6. Practice pitchers covering first

*Second basemen and Shortstops:*
1. Practice starting and finishing double plays
2. Practice cutoffs and relays
3. Practice fielding slow rollers
4. Practice fielding all types of ground balls
5. Practice pick-off plays

*Third basemen:*
1. Practice moving to the right and left
2. Practice slow rollers
3. Practice cutoff and relays
4. Practice bunt coverage
5. Practice starting double plays

*Outfielders:*
1. Practice fielding line drives over their heads
2. Practice fielding ground balls and executing throws to cutoff
3. Practice circling high fly balls

Players should practice in groups to assist one another by rolling various types of ground balls, throwing short hops, line drives, or fly balls. Coaches will have many opportunities to instruct those players needing help and to positively reinforce players performing well.

## GAME SITUATION DRILL (SIMULATION)

*Purpose:* Provides players with an opportunity to work on skills specific to their defensive positions.

*Equipment:* None necessary, but can use gloves.

*Procedure:* Players go to their defensive positions and simulate all the various defensive requirements of the position. After each simulation, players should assume another ready position, imagine another type of game situation, and proceed to execute the play successfully. Each player should have ample opportunity to execute imaginary cutoff and relay plays, pick-offs, first and third steals, bunt coverage, and double plays, as well as various types of ground balls and fly balls.

Players should invent their own typical game situations and exhibit a disciplined approach toward the proper execution of each play. During a 5-minute period, the coach will have ample opportunities to instruct players who need help.

Coaches should stress the importance of *repetition* and *simulation of skills*. As players practice they will become aware of the relationship between meaningful repetition and successful performance in a game and should become even more motivated to pursue a disciplined individualized program of simulation.

The Formal Infield and Outfield Drill is an effective drill for reviewing many fielding and throwing conditions in a short period of time. Every team should use a drill like this as a pregame warm-up and as a general review during practice.

## FORMAL INFIELD AND OUTFIELD DRILL

*Purpose:* Effective pregame defensive warm-up.

*Equipment:* Complete field, balls, gloves, bat, catcher's equipment.

*Procedure:* All players assume their defensive positions except the pitcher, who is warming up in the bullpen. Coaches can design any sequence of events necessary for their team. The following is one possible method.

*1. Outfield Phase:* The coach hits two fly balls and two ground balls to each outfielder. The left fielder makes two throws to second base and two throws to home plate. The center and right fielders make two throws to third base and two throws to home plate.

The last ball hit to each outfielder should be a ground ball which the outfielder must charge quickly. They then execute a correct overhand throw to the cutoff man. Before hitting the last ball to the outfielders, the coach instructs them to imagine the potential winning run on second base and to pretend that the runner will attempt to score on the next ground ball into the outfield.

This situation is one of an outfielder's most difficult plays. The outfielder must charge the ball quickly, field the ball slightly to the glove side, and hit the cutoff man with a powerful, accurate throw. The fielding fundamentals on this play are different from those in the infield, since the outfielder must sprint to the ball, field it while running, crow hop, and throw overhand to the cutoff man in the infield. In order to develop control and coordination throughout the play, the outfielder must practice it often.

*2. Infield Phase:* Each infielder fields a ground ball and throws to first base. The first baseman skips and throws to the catcher who then executes a throw to the infielder who fielded the ball and is now covering the base nearest to his position. The infielder promptly skips and throws back to the catcher.

*3. Double Play Phase:* The procedure continues as described above, but now the infielders *turn double plays*. The return throw from the catcher goes to the infielder who initially fielded the ball. That fielder promptly throws to another baseman who then returns the ball back to the catcher. The cycle continues until every infielder has an equal opportunity.

*4. Throws Home:* The coach hits a final ground ball to each infielder which the infielder fields and throws to home plate. The catcher instantly rolls the ball back to the infielder, who charges the ball and executes a proper throw to first base. Then the infielder hustles off the field.

*5. Completion:* The coach concludes the drill by hitting a pop-up to the catcher.

# CHAPTER 10

# Pitching

It has often been said that pitching is 75% of a team's defense. Without a strong pitching staff, a ball club is definitely at a disadvantage. All pitchers should realize their importance to the team and their responsibility to their teammates. The pitcher's fielding responsibilities have already been discussed with other infield positional skills. This chapter is devoted entirely to pitching.

Realizing the major role they play in the success of their team, pitchers should devote themselves to a program of total preparation both physically and mentally. They should maintain a high-level program of physical fitness and coordination designed to develop and refine their pitching delivery and specific pitches. By carefully studying the subject matter and illustrations in this chapter, pitchers can gain the insights necessary to be successful in all areas of pitching, but knowledge alone does not guarantee success. Pitchers must spend many hours meaningfully practicing through the insights they have gained to obtain successful results.

## Physical Conditioning

More than any other player, a pitcher needs to engage in a complete physical fitness program. Every year, many young pitchers injure their arms just because they failed to realize the value of a conditioning program before and during the season. If pitchers condition themselves properly and use the proper mechanics in their delivery, they will rarely have arm trouble.

Before throwing a ball in the early spring, pitchers should run or jump rope as much as possible in order to gain stamina and to condition the whole body. They should also perform stretching exercises and agility drills. Running and stretching should continue throughout the season because a pitcher's legs, back, and shoulders all play a significant role in developing a sound rhythmical delivery. If the legs are in top condition and a pitcher remains flexible, his arm should also remain strong.

The amount of running and conditioning necessary varies with individual pitchers. Body weight, structure, natural aptitudes, and other such factors all influence an individual's general conditioning. For example, as a rule slender pitchers need to run less than heavier pitchers.

Pitchers can maintain a superior physical condition by pursuing a fitness program and pitching regularly. They should do most of their running in early spring, followed by a lot of stretching and lighter running once games have started. Since many athletes get bored with running, coaches could have pitchers perform the conditioning drills presented in Appendix A, Baseball Conditioning.

The system of calisthenics in Appendix A should also be part of a pitcher's total fitness program throughout the year. When anyone engages in a solid fitness program, *strength, coordination,* and *endurance* increase, which will help a player become more proficient at baseball skills. This is especially critical for pitchers, who must be highly conditioned athletes. A lack of conditioning will negatively affect a pitcher's developmental program.

During the winter or off-season, pitchers can get stronger by engaging in periodic workouts with light weight and dumbbells. Once the season starts and pitchers begin to throw, they should discontinue any heavy weight program.

## Mental Aspects of Pitching

Pitching is not all physical. Pitchers' control of their pitches and general effectiveness frequently is directly related to their mental and emotional stability. In order to be successful a pitcher must be able to concentrate on specific targets, basic mechanics, hitters' weaknesses, choice of pitches, execution of pitches, pick-offs and fielding fundamentals. The most effective pitchers are often the ones who can concentrate consistently.

By concentrating, pitchers can become more successful and success tends to build confidence, an attribute so important to a pitcher's success. Pitchers are most effective when they believe they can get out any hitter they face. If pitchers aren't confident, they won't challenge hitters properly and generally won't be able to get them out. Self-confidence and a positive self-image are essential for consistent success.

In addition to confidence, pitchers should have a strong desire to compete. They should be aggressive and eager to meet a challenge. They should have no thoughts of inferiority, anxiety, or passivity as they go to the mound each inning. Determination, kindled with a strong desire to excel, should characterize a pitcher's total performance. Pitchers should put all their effort into each inning, aware that past success, even though it tends to build confidence, does not guarantee future success. Just like each game, each inning is a new occasion and requires the pitcher's total attention.

## Two Basic Tenets of Pitching— Throw Strikes and Get the Leadoff Hitter Out

*Effective pitchers get ahead of hitters in the count.* If the pitcher throws strikes most of the time, the fielders will be more alert and the umpire will subconsciously favor the pitcher on close pitches. If a pitcher consistently falls behind, going to 1-0, 2-0, or 3-1 with the hitter, he is at a disadvantage in several ways. First of all, the pitcher is throwing too many pitches and may tire early. Second, it allows the hitter to examine the pitcher's assortment of pitches more readily. Hitters will be able to wait on their pitch more often, since they assume that the pitcher will have to throw the fast ball for strikes eventually.

*Pitchers who are consistent winners get the leadoff batter out in most innings.* If the leadoff hitter gets on base, not only will the pitcher have to work from the stretch but the entire ball club will have to play the inning under added pressure, which may lead to costly mistakes. Pitchers who fall behind in the count and allow leadoff players to get on base are seldom effective.

## Warming Up

Pitchers need to run and stretch before every practice and every game in order to warm up, loosen muscles, and promote joint flexibility so that they won't be as likely to strain and pull muscles when they start throwing. Jumping jacks, three point stretch, sit ups, leg rolls, jack knives, rise on toes, arm rollers, squat jumps, squat thrust, bunny hops, and scissor claps, which are all detailed in Appendix A, are good exercises to use before a workout. If done lightly, these exercises are also an excellent warm-up before games. Pitchers soon will realize that using these exercises in a systematic warm-up before practices and games will help them perform smoothly and with more coordination early in the practice or game. Once pitchers warm up, they need to conserve the elevated body temperature and not cool off. This will help prevent muscle pulls and strains. The same exercises may also be used to develop strength and endurance by increasing the number of repetitions of each exercise.

*Key Point:* Warm up to throw—never throw to warm up.

## Pregame Warm-Up

Inexperienced pitchers often lose games before delivering the first pitch because they don't know how to warm up before the game. Pitchers will learn through experience some aspects of warming up, but several factors are detailed below that pitchers should keep in mind while they prepare to deliver the first pitch of the game.

1. *Stretch and warm up muscles.* Pitchers should stretch and do some light running before they throw in order to promote proper rhythm in their pitching motion. They will need to throw fewer pitches to finish warming up and they won't be as likely to strain muscles.

2. *Consider the temperature and humidity.* Pitchers should throw more in warm-up when the

weather is cool and dry, as opposed to hot and humid.

3. *Consider the pitcher's body build.* Slender, wiry pitchers usually require fewer warm-up pitches than heavy, burly pitchers. Neither should ever enter a game without being thoroughly loose and warm.

4. *Consider the time.* Pitchers should begin their warm-up tosses with enough time to allow themselves to get completely loose, work on their assortment of pitches, and take at least a 3-minute break before stepping on the mound to deliver the first pitch of the game. It should be the pitcher's responsibility to check the time; the coach should not have to remind him constantly.

5. *Pitch some from the stretch.* Wise pitchers will throw about one-third of their warm-up pitches from the stretch so their timing and coordination will be fine-tuned in case the leadoff hitter gets on base.

6. *Do not press an issue.* If a certain type of pitch is not working properly in the warm-up, a pitcher shouldn't keep throwing it to try to get it to work. After checking his pitching mechanics, such as the motion, the release of the ball, and other fundamentals, if the pitch still fails to work properly the pitcher must acknowledge that the pitch is ineffective and should use other pitches more at the start of the game.

Some inexperienced pitchers keep trying to force a pitch to work after the game begins. If unable to get the pitch to work properly, they often continue to throw it primarily from habit. This usually leads to failure. In this situation pitchers should start the game by throwing pitches that are working properly, making sure to keep the ball low and changing the speed of the pitches and, occasionally, the angle of delivery. The pitcher can use the pitch that is not working properly as a "waste pitch," and the player may find that the situation reverses as the game continues. The pitcher's best pitch, which previously had not been working, may suddenly start to work and the pitcher can then go back to his regular routine. Pitchers must be aware of this possibility and know how to deal with it.

7. *Concentrate on the mental as well as the physical.* Pitchers should be relaxed and free from any emotional disturbance that could interfere with their concentration. It is essential that pitchers develop a positive, aggressive state of mind before delivering the first pitch.

8. *Conserve heat obtained from warming up.* Pitchers must try to keep their muscles warm once they are warmed up. They should wear a windbreaker every time they stop throwing. If the pitcher's

team is at bat for over 10 minutes, the pitcher should stand up and do some stretching exercises and even take a few warm-up pitches before the next inning.

## The Pitcher's Motion

A pitcher's motion or rhythm is extremely important for overall effectiveness. Pitchers must practice diligently to master a rhythmical, coordinated move toward the plate. In a perfect pitching motion, every portion of the body works harmoniously.

No two pitcher's delivery will be the same, but there are some common denominators among all effective pitchers. One such factor is the ability to hide the ball effectively throughout the delivery. The entire hand and part of the wrist should be placed in the glove, either at the start of the motion or as the hands swing over the head (see Figs. 10-1 to 10-5).

After the pivot foot slides in front of and parallel with the pitching rubber, the front shoulder and hip should rotate so that both are directly in line with the catcher's mitt. This part of the motion should be slow and deliberate in order to prevent the pitcher's body from drifting too far forward during the initial phase of the motion. The pitcher should try to complete the full pivot of the hips and shoulders before starting the move to the plate. Not only will this help hide the ball during the delivery, it will also help to build power into the pitch (see Figs. 10-6 to 10-8).

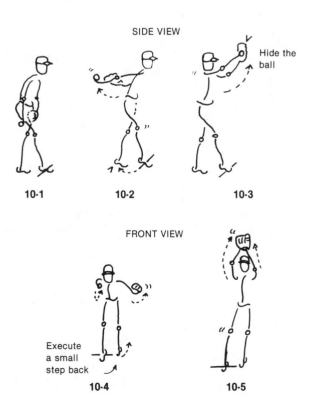

SIDE VIEW

Hide the ball

10-1          10-2          10-3

FRONT VIEW

Execute a small step back

10-4          10-5

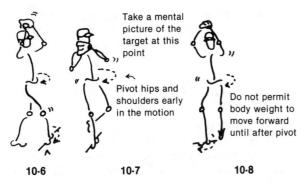

Take a mental
picture of the
target at this
point

Pivot hips and
shoulders early
in the motion

Do not permit
body weight to
move forward
until after pivot

**10-6**          **10-7**          **10-8**

The pitcher can make the motion more powerful through proper hip rotation and also by slightly collapsing the back leg and getting a hard, firm shove off the pitching rubber. This is the primary reason why running is so important for a pitcher. If the legs stay in top condition, the arm will probably remain strong throughout the season. Smart pitchers place most of the load of the pitching motion on their legs and back rather than their arm, thus decreasing the probability of a sore arm (see Figs. 10-9 to 10-14).

To complete a coordinated motion, the pitcher should land on the front flat portion of the stride foot—not the heel. Landing on the heel of the stride foot encourages a lazy back shoulder and increases the chance of pitches going high. Landing on the flat portion of the foot helps direct the throwing shoulder into proper position at the top of the delivery (see Figs. 10-15, 10-16).

The stride foot should land so that the pitcher's hips can open toward home plate. An overarm pitcher's stride foot should land slightly to the glove side of an imaginary straight line stretching from his pivot foot to home plate. This promotes better control and effectiveness for each pitch (see Figs 10-17, 10-18). At the moment the pitcher releases the ball, the throwing arm should be extended (see Fig. 10-19).

Pitchers will have better control and effectiveness if they allow their throwing arm to extend freely. A loose arm will also increase power in pitches and place the work load on the body rather than the arm. The throwing side foot should push off the rubber and pivot upward (see Figs. 10-15, 10-16). As the ball is released, the throwing side foot leaves the ground to enable the throwing shoulder to move over the top of the delivery and follow through properly (see Figs. 10-17; 10-20 to 10-23).

As the pitcher actually releases the ball, the weight is thrusting forward while the stride foot remains firm. The wrist snaps firmly as the throwing shoulder follows through low toward home plate (see Figs. 10-20 to 10-23).

The pitcher's eyes should focus sharply on specific targets throughout the entire motion in order to facilitate control and accuracy. The body must function as an *integrated whole* during the entire motion. Finally, after completing the delivery, the pitcher must quickly prepare to field the position as effectively as possible.

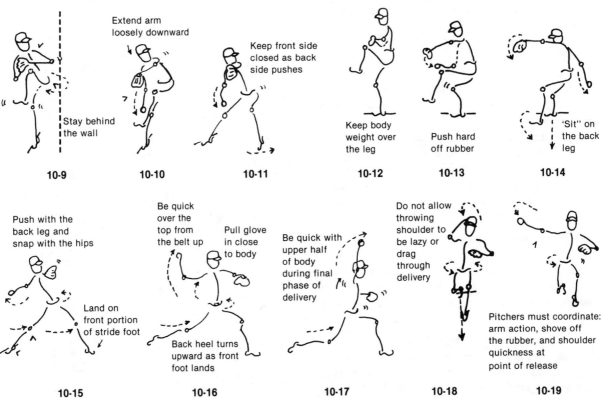

Extend arm
loosely downward

Keep front side
closed as back
side pushes

Stay behind
the wall

Keep body
weight over
the leg

Push hard
off rubber

'Sit" on
the back
leg

**10-9**        **10-10**        **10-11**        **10-12**        **10-13**        **10-14**

Push with the
back leg and
snap with the hips

Be quick
over the
top from
the belt up

Pull glove
in close
to body

Be quick with
upper half
of body
during final
phase of
delivery

Do not allow
throwing
shoulder to
be lazy or
drag
through
delivery

Land on
front portion
of stride foot

Back heel turns
upward as front
foot lands

Pitchers must coordinate:
arm action, shove off
the rubber, and shoulder
quickness at
point of release

**10-15**          **10-16**          **10-17**          **10-18**          **10-19**

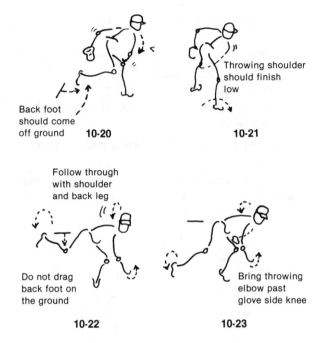

Back foot should come off ground    **10-20**

Throwing shoulder should finish low    **10-21**

Follow through with shoulder and back leg

Do not drag back foot on the ground    **10-22**

Bring throwing elbow past glove side knee    **10-23**

## Common Denominators of All Effective Pitchers

• A pitcher should hide the ball from the hitter by placing the entire throwing hand in the glove.

• The first half of the motion should be slow and the second half much quicker.

• The pivot foot should slide diagonally or parallel to the front edge of the pitching rubber before the back foot comes off the ground.

• The glove side shoulder and hip should rotate to form a straight line with home plate.

• As the glove side knee starts down, the throwing hand should separate from the glove.

• Following the break from the glove, the throwing arm should extend completely and quickly and the shove leg should collapse slightly in order to generate power in the motion.

• The pitcher should get a maximum shove off the rubber and a maximum snap of the hips.

• The throwing shoulder shouldn't drag through the delivery; the pitcher should strive for quickness, getting the upper body "over the top" of the motion by the time the glove side foot lands.

• The pitcher should land on the flat portion of the stride foot, never on his heel.

• The stride foot should land so that it promotes maximum force from hips and shoulders to produce more power and control in the delivery (see p. 109).

• The throwing arm should be extended as the pitcher releases the ball.

• The throwing shoulder should follow through low and hard.

• The pitcher should take a mental picture of the target before making the delivery, and his eyes should concentrate on specific targets throughout the delivery.

• Most of the work load of the delivery should be placed on the legs and back, not on the arm.

• The pitcher's delivery should be smooth, coordinated, and properly synchronized into a perfectly timed series of body movements. Every movement should be the same on each pitch unless the angle of delivery changes.

## Five Phases of the Pitcher's Motion

The progression of the pitcher's motion can be better understood by being divided into five phases. The important elements of each phase are noted and several views of the pitcher's body position during each phase are illustrated.

### Phase I (see Figs. 10-24, 10-25)

• Turn the back of the glove toward the catcher.

• Hide the entire ball in the glove.

• Step only a few inches back with the glove side foot.

• Take a mental picture of the target.

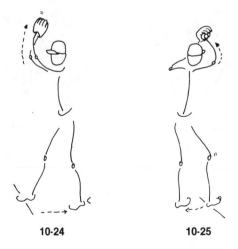

**10-24**    **10-25**

### Phase II (see Figs. 10-26 to 10-29)

• Slide the pivot foot in front of the pitching rubber.

- Turn the glove side hip and shoulder toward the catcher.

- Maintain exact balance.

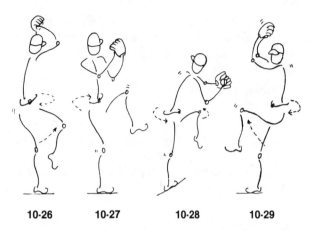

10-26        10-27        10-28        10-29

*Key Point:* Phases I and II are slow and relaxed, while Phases III, IV, and V are quick and explosive.

## Phase III (see Figs. 10-30 to 10-32)

- Completely extend and relax the throwing arm.

- Slightly collapse the throwing side leg.

- Remove the ball from the glove as the front knee starts down.

- Point the front shoulder in the direction that complements the angle of release (see p. 109).

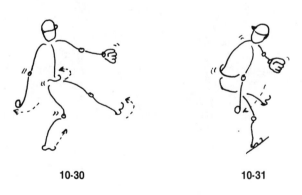

10-30                      10-31

10-32

## Phase IV (see Figs. 10-33 to 10-35)

- Firmly shove off the pitching rubber.

- Quick, smooth arm action should follow extension and release point.

- Thrust the throwing shoulder quickly over the top of the motion.

- Completely extend the throwing arm during release.

- Land on the flat portion of the glove side foot and in the proper location to complement the angle of release (see p. 109).

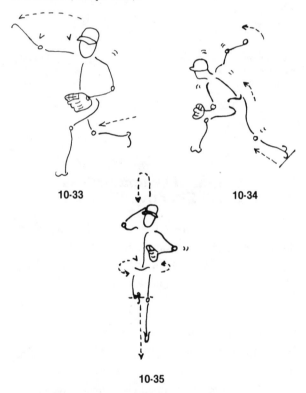

10-33                      10-34

10-35

## Phase V (see Figs. 10-36 to 10-38)

- Follow through quickly and low with throwing shoulder and elbow.

- Lift the throwing side foot high off the ground to aid a correct follow-through.

- Be ready to respond defensively if the ball is hit.

10-36

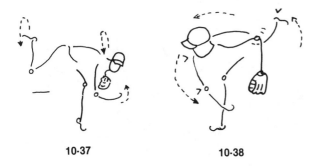

**10-37**              **10-38**

## Angle of Delivery

Developing an effective delivery requires attention to several variables. The angle of the arm and position of the stride foot during the release, and the position of the front shoulder during the last phases of the motion, are important factors to consider when trying to develop a delivery that has balance, power, rhythm, timing, control, and produces movement of the ball. The following illustrations focus on these fundamental mechanics and their interrelationship.

A pitcher must determine the most effective angle for his delivery. To do so, he should experiment with various arm release points and observe the action of the ball. He can learn more about his primary release point by executing long throws from the outfield. Usually the glove side foot will land in the same place during every throw and the arm will flow through a path that feels natural. A pitcher may want to incorporate some of these same mechanics into his pitching delivery.

In designing their delivery, pitchers should pretend there is a clock behind the catcher. During Phases III-IIIa of the delivery, a right-handed pitcher's glove side shoulder should point to 1 hour earlier than the angle of his arm at the point of release. Also, the right-hander's glove side foot should land at a spot 1 hour earlier than the release point (see Figs. 10-39, 10-40). A left-handed pitcher's glove side shoulder and foot should point to

a spot 1 hour later than the point of release. This positioning permits the legs, hips, and shoulders to help generate the power he needs to deliver good pitches and also prevents arm injury. If a right-handed pitcher is out of position, for example, by stepping at 1 o'clock and throwing from 12 o'clock or stepping at 10 o'clock and throwing from 3 o'clock, the result is often arm strain, poor control, lack of velocity, and poor quality of movement. A pitcher should follow this procedure:

*Right-handed pitcher:*
Step at 11 o'clock, throw at 12 o'clock.
Step at 12 o'clock, throw at 1 o'clock.
Step at 1 o'clock, throw at 2 o'clock.
Step at 2 o'clock, throw at 3 o'clock.

*Left-handed pitcher* (opposite pattern from right-handers):
Step at 1 o'clock, throw at 12 o'clock.
Step at 12 o'clock, throw at 11 o'clock.
Step at 11 o'clock, throw at 10 o'clock.
Step at 10 o'clock, throw at 9 o'clock.

Pitchers also need to design the path of the throwing arm behind the body during Phase III of the delivery. If a right-handed pitcher plans to throw from a 2-3 o'clock release point, the arm should extend further to the back and side of the body than if he releases the ball from a 12-1 o'clock angle. A release point of 12-1 o'clock requires the pitcher to extend the throwing arm almost straight down so that he can get the arm over the top of the delivery faster. If the arm doesn't follow the proper path, during Phase III of the delivery the pitcher may experience arm strain, poor velocity, lack of control, and poor movement quality, and poor quality pitches will occur (see Figs. 10-41 to 10-43).

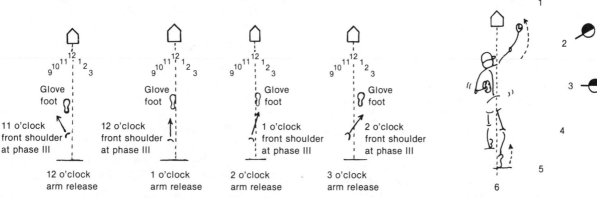

Glove foot — 11 o'clock front shoulder at phase III — 12 o'clock arm release

Glove foot — 12 o'clock front shoulder at phase III — 1 o'clock arm release

Glove foot — 1 o'clock front shoulder at phase III — 2 o'clock arm release

Glove foot — 2 o'clock front shoulder at phase III — 3 o'clock arm release

**10-39**                                                           **10-40**

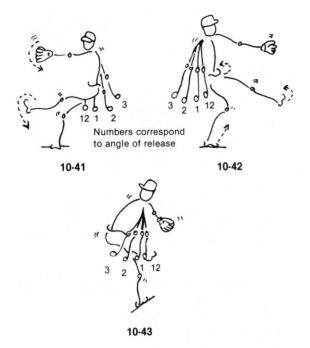

Numbers correspond
to angle of release

**10-41**                              **10-42**

**10-43**

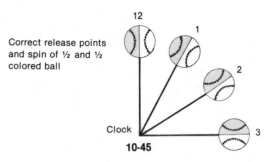

Correct release points
and spin of ½ and ½
colored ball

Clock

**10-45**

## Key Points for a Pitcher's Delivery

1. The hips and shoulders should pivot early in the motion, before the body weight starts driving toward the plate. The pitcher should be able to stay behind an imaginary wall 1 foot in front of the pitching rubber as his hips and shoulders turn. This will help keep the body weight over the leg, which generates power in the delivery through the legs and hips and helps protect the arm. This is the essence of Phases I and II.

2. The glove side knee should trigger the ball to separate from the glove. When the glove side knee starts down, the arm action of Phase III begins. This will keep the pitcher from overstriding and being late with the throwing shoulder.

3. To promote power from the hips and legs the pitcher should keep the glove side (shoulder, hip, and knee) closed while the throwing arm extends and the back leg bends, as the pitcher pushes off the rubber. As he shoves toward the plate he should feel half the drive coming from the back leg and half from the hip pop. The hips and knees should snap quickly toward home plate once the throwing side elbow extends behind the body. This places the throwing side shoulder and arm in the proper release position, thus completing Phases III and IV.

Coaches can use a colored baseball to determine if the pitcher's wrist and finger position aligns properly with the release point. The ball should be divided in half and colored two colors (see Appendix B). Pitchers should hold the ball exactly in the center, with the thumb and first two fingers placed on the center line so they can see the spin of the ball (see Fig. 10-44). This will help pitchers evaluate whether there is correct movement on the ball.

4. If the pitcher starts to shove toward home plate before executing the hip pivot, the throwing shoulder will be late. The arm will not have time to catch up with the rest of the body. The pitcher's back leg will be straight because the body will already be out in front, so there will not be any push from the leg. High pitches and arm strain can result because the hips will not snap on time and the throwing shoulder will be late.

5. There is a cause and effect relationship in all five phases of the pitcher's motion. If early phases are too fast, a negative effect will be experienced in later phases. Therefore, constant simulation of all five phases of the motion are essential to promote effective development of rhythm and timing.

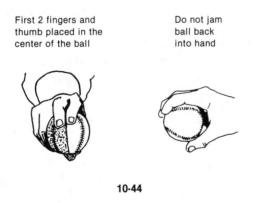

First 2 fingers and
thumb placed in the
center of the ball

Do not jam
ball back
into hand

**10-44**

If a pitcher holds the ball properly and snaps his wrist correctly, the ball will spin so that the center line separating the two colors appears to match the angle of the pitcher's release point. One color of the ball will stay on one side of the release point and the other will stay on the other side (see Fig. 10-45). Inexperienced pitchers often hold the ball wrong or turn the wrist incorrectly at the point of release, which can contribute to loss of velocity, lack of control, poor movement quality, and arm strain.

Figures 10-46 through 10-69 show the total movement of pitching.

Front view: Figures 10-46 through 10-55

**10-46**

**10-47**

**10-48**

**10-49**

**10-50**

Do not start to turn hips and knees toward plate until throwing elbow extends downward

**10-51**

Land flat on glove side foot

**10-52**

Throwing side heel turns upward as glove side foot lands

**10-53**

**10-54**

Back leg comes off ground and rolls over to the ground

**10-55**

Side View: Figures 10-56 through 10-69

Step back only a few inches from rubber

**10-56**

Hide wrist and hand in glove

**10-57**

**10-58**

Concentrate on target

Pivot foot slides in front of rubber

**10-59**

Turn shoulder early

**15-60**

Start hip and shoulder turn before glove side foot leaves the ground

**10-61**

Stay behind a "wall" 1 foot in front of rubber

Maintain balance at top of motion

**10-62**

Extend throwing arm down completely as glove knee starts down

Bend throwing side knee in order to build power

**10-63**

Keep glove side shoulder closed and point shoulder at correct position*

Keep front knee closed

**10-64**

Develop smooth continuous, full arm action in the correct path*

Shove hard off rubber

**10-65**

Throwing side shoulder should reach a peak as glove side foot lands

Push with the throwing side leg and twist hips quickly

**10-66**

Move throwing shoulder over the top quickly

Place stride foot in correct position*

**10-67**

Extend throwing arm at release

Land on flat portion of glove side foot

Follow through low with throwing shoulder and elbow

**10-68**

**10-69**

*Refer to Figures 10-39 and 10-40.

All pitchers should experiment with the general principles of pitching to see how these relate to their own delivery. They should remain sensitive to any slight adjustment while developing their own delivery to make it more effective.

A pitcher should simulate at least 50 motions daily, concentrating on each phase of his motion. He should practice the simulations in front of a mirror and pretend to be throwing into a mitt. Not only should he analyze and evaluate his motion, but he should also concentrate on throwing to spots in a strike zone. This can be accomplished by placing pieces of tape on a mirror to outline a typical strike zone.

Another good way for pitchers to practice their delivery is to simulate pitching against a hitter who simulates swings. Both players should imagine they are competing in an actual game. The pitcher should tell the hitter which simulated pitch he is about to deliver, as well as the location of the pitch. This will give both players practice in game skills.

The Pitcher's Bunny Hop Drill helps players coordinate their pitching motion.

## PITCHER'S BUNNY HOP DRILL

*Purpose:* To develop the proper timing between Phases II, III, IV, and V of a pitcher's delivery and to establish length of stride, weight distribution, and balance.

*Equipment:* Gloves.

*Procedure:* First the pitcher must be able to perform the regular bunny hops and scissor clap exercises (see p. 146). Pitcher's bunny hops are a combination of these two exercises interwoven into Phases II, III, IV, and V of a pitcher's delivery.

The pitcher should assume the Phase II position of the delivery. When completely balanced, the pitcher starts Phase III by letting the glove knee start down as the hands separate. The pitcher should then push firmly with the throwing side leg (similar to the regular bunny hop exercise) and proceed to snap the hips quickly. While landing, the pitcher bends the glove side leg (similar to the scissor clap exercise), and proceeds to touch the throwing side elbow to the glove side knee. The pitcher remains in this position for a few seconds, balancing on the glove side leg. The throwing side leg should not touch the ground. Once balanced in that Phase V position, the pitcher should then firmly push back to the Phase II position.

This drill can help develop a pitcher's strength, balance, timing, rhythm, and coordination of the delivery. Pitchers should be encouraged to make 50 repetitions a part of their daily practice program along with the calisthenics found in Appendix A.

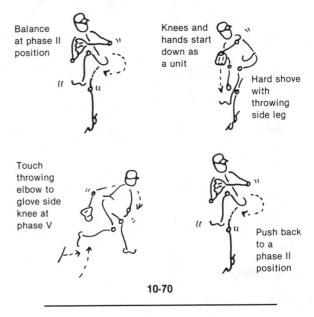

Balance at phase II position

Knees and hands start down as a unit

Hard shove with throwing side leg

Touch throwing elbow to glove side knee at phase V

Push back to a phase II position

**10-70**

## Coaches' Analysis and Evaluation of Pitchers

Coaches should continually analyze and evaluate the following elements in their pitchers. If mistakes occur, the coach and the player should be able to diagnose the weaknesses and substitute correct movements. Hundreds of simulated deliveries each week should be a major part of a pitcher's training program. This checklist should be part of a daily routine as a pitcher simulates his delivery in front of a mirror. This mental and physical review is essential if a smooth, coordinated, precise delivery is to be developed and maintained.

### Phase I (see Fig. 10-71)

1. During the full delivery does the pitcher bring hands and arms over the head or simply start from the belt? Pitchers should use the method that helps them stay back in the delivery best.

2. Is the pitcher stepping back only a few inches so that his concentration is on timing, not lunging toward the plate?

**10-71**

## Phase Ia (see Figs. 10-72, 10-73)

3. Are the ball and the pitcher's wrist well hidden in the glove, and is the back of the glove facing the catcher?

4. Is the pitcher starting the shoulder and hip turn before the back foot clears the ground?

5. Does the pitcher slide the throwing side foot in front of the pitching rubber?

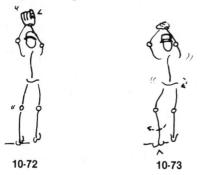

**10-72**          **10-73**

## Phase II (see Fig. 10-74)

6. Is the pitcher keeping the ball and glove in a position that will produce optimal arm action? (The loop formed by the pitcher's arms and hands can be over the knee or behind the knee.)

7. Does the size of the pitcher's loop complement the type of arm action used? (The loop can either remain close to the body or extend away from the body.)

8. Is the pitcher keeping the leg strength under the body weight?

9. Is the pitcher remaining behind an imaginary wall 1 foot in front of the pitching rubber? (If the body weight passes in front of the wall before the full hip, shoulder, and knee turn, the entire delivery will be late and lazy, resulting in arm strain and high pitches.)

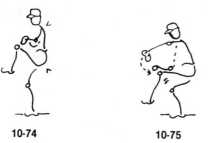

**10-74**          **10-75**

## Phase IIa (see Fig. 10-75)

10. Is the pitcher separating the hands the instant the glove side knee starts down? (Separating later in the delivery causes the arm to drag through Phase IV.)

11. Is the pitcher bending the back knee slightly in order to develop power and place the load of the delivery on the legs, back, and hips?

## Phase III (see Fig. 10-76)

12. Is the pitcher's wrist following a path that will keep the ball pointing downward once it separates from the glove? (The arm should be quick and smooth, and should follow a path that complements the pitcher's release point.)

13. Do the pitcher's glove side knee, shoulder, and hip remain closed until the throwing elbow extends? (Pitchers lose power if they open earlier.)

14. Is the pitcher developing the feeling of the hips and knees snapping quickly toward home plate once the throwing elbow extends at the point of release?

15. Is the pitcher developing the feeling of 50% push with the back leg and 50% snap of the hips during Phases III and IV?

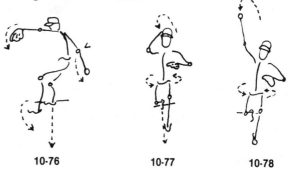

**10-76**          **10-77**          **10-78**

## Phases IIIa to IV (see Fig. 10-77)

16. Is the pitcher's glove side foot landing flat and the throwing side heel turning upward simultaneously during phase IV?

17. Is the pitcher developing a feel for a quick thrust of the throwing shoulder over the top of the delivery? (If the throwing shoulder is slow, pitches will go high.)

18. Does the position of the pitcher's feet and legs during Phase IV match the position in the scissor clap exercise? (See Fig. A-17.)

## Phase IV (see Fig. 10-78)

19. Does the throwing arm reach total extension and the wrist snap hard at the release point?

20. Is the pitcher's glove tucked close into the body during Phases IV and V? (This will help the throwing shoulder move over the top quickly.)

**Phases IVa to V (see Fig. 10-79)**

21.  Is the pitcher developing the feeling that the belt buckle snaps directly toward home plate at the moment the glove side foot lands flat on the ground during the stride?

22.  Is the pitcher releasing the throwing side foot to travel "up and over" during Phase V? (Dragging the foot off the rubber restricts the follow-through.)

23.  Is the pitcher's throwing elbow finishing low and near the glove side knee, and is the throwing shoulder following through low and toward the plate?

**Phase V (see Fig. 10-80)**

24.  Is the pitcher ready to field following the pitch?

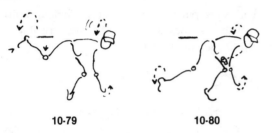

10-79                    10-80

## Different Pitches

### Fast Ball

To throw a fast ball, an overhand pitcher holds the fingers close together with the tips of the fingers across a seam to help produce movement on the ball (see Figs. 10-81 to 10-83). Some pitchers prefer to hold the ball across the narrow seams (see Figs. 10-81, 10-82) and others across the wide or broad seams (see Fig. 10-83). Sidearm pitchers often find that the ball sinks more if they place their fingers *with* the narrow seams (see Fig. 10-84) rather than across them. Pitchers need to experiment with finger placement to find what works best for them.

The fast ball is most effective when the pitcher has a hard shove off the rubber, his hips snap quickly, he moves quickly with his throwing shoulder over the top at the point of release, and his wrist snaps strongly. It is important that the pitcher doesn't jam the ball back into the hand (see Figs. 10-82, 10-84). The fingers must be placed to maximize the wrist snap and assure a smooth release. The pitcher must remain aware of the wrist position at the point of release. For example, the pitcher should be aware that the wrist should be perpendicular to the ground

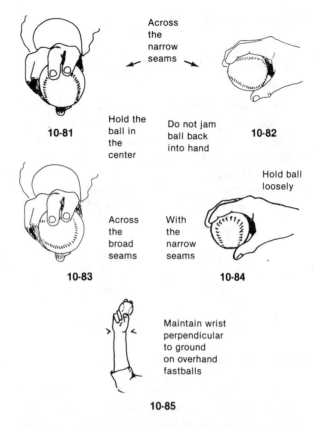

Across the narrow seams

**10-81**    Hold the ball in the center

Do not jam ball back into hand    **10-82**

**10-83**    Across the broad seams

With the narrow seams    **10-84**    Hold ball loosely

Maintain wrist perpendicular to ground on overhand fastballs

**10-85**

as the pitcher releases the ball in order for the ball to "jump" (see Fig. 10-85). If the wrist is turned to the inside, the ball may slide or sail. If the wrist is turned to the outside, the ball may sink.

Pitchers should throw the fast ball either low in the strike zone near the knees, or high inside near the hitter's chest. Pitchers will want to keep all pitches out of the belt area of the hitter's strike zone because this is where hitters can hit the ball best.

### Curve Ball

In order for the curve ball to be effective, it must have a sufficient amount of spin and rotation. Spin and rotation are not possible without proper finger pressure and arm action. The pitcher should place the middle finger in the exact center of the ball, next to the broad seam and in a straight line with the thumb; the first finger should go next to the middle finger. The ball should touch only the fingers, *not* the hand (see Figs. 10-86, 10-87). If the middle finger is off center, the

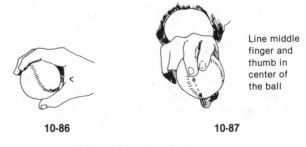

Line middle finger and thumb in center of the ball

**10-86**                    **10-87**

Wrist should face inward at point of release

Force hand down in karate fashion with knuckles facing catcher

**10-88**

pitcher won't be able to apply proper rotation to the ball.

Once pitchers understand proper finger position and pressure, they must work on the position of the arm as they deliver the pitch. The inside flat portion of the wrist should face the pitcher's cap as the arm comes over the top of the delivery, and the elbow should point toward home plate. Then the pitcher should come straight down as if executing a judo chop, simultaneously applying maximum finger pressure on the ball. The pitcher's knuckles should face the catcher's mitt immediately after the pitcher releases the ball (see Fig. 10-88). If the pitch is thrown properly, it will have an end-over-end rotation and will break down.

*Warning:* Occasionally, young pitchers try to make the ball curve using the same wrist position as they would for a fast ball. Then they compound the problem by applying a quick snap with the wrist and elbow, trying to produce enough spin to cause the ball to break. This does *not* produce enough rotation speed to cause a good curve ball and can seriously injure a young pitcher's arm. *Young pitchers should not be allowed to throw this kind of curve ball.*

Throwing a curve ball with an end-over-end rotation usually will not harm a pitcher's arm because it requires very little wrist snap or pressure on the elbow. When the pitcher turns the flat part of the wrist toward the cap as the arm comes over the top of the delivery, the primary work load is on the legs and back. With a hard shove off the rubber, a quick movement over the top with the throwing shoulder and arm, proper finger pressure, and a firm follow-through, the ball should break straight down and away from the hitter's vision. Pitchers should learn how to throw this pitch with at least two speeds, fast (about 85 m.p.h.) and slow (about 10-15 m.p.h. slower).

In order to throw a flat curve that breaks straight away from the hitter, the pitcher only needs to alter the motion slightly. By slanting the upper body down and to the side while executing his delivery toward the plate, the angle of the arm drops down slightly.

Again the leg strength, shoulder quickness, finger pressure, and follow-through should supply the necessary spin to get the ball to break straight away from the hitter when a right-handed pitcher throws to a right-handed batter, or a left-handed pitcher faces a left-handed hitter.

Pitchers should practice throwing curve balls using only the middle finger and thumb to help develop proper finger control and spin (see Fig. 10-89). This is an excellent drill for pitchers who are having trouble perfecting their curve ball.

Pitchers need to develop various speeds on the curve ball and must have complete control over the pitch. Since most hitters look for a fast ball when the count is 2-0, 3-1, or 3-2, pitchers can help themselves tremendously by learning to keep the ball down and to throw the curve for strikes when they are behind in the count. After missing the strike zone with a regular curve, it is effective to throw a change-up curve. The hitter is generally looking for a fast ball at this point and will be off balance on the change-up curve.

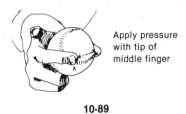

Apply pressure with tip of middle finger

**10-89**

### Change-Up

There are several different ways to throw the change-up pitch. The primary purpose of the pitch is to take speed off the pitch so the hitter is off balance with his hitting mechanics. Some pitchers "jam" the ball back between the thumb and first finger to reduce wrist snap during the release, which limits the speed of the pitch. Some pitchers prefer the "palm ball," thrown with all four fingers close together. While releasing the palm ball, the pitcher might try to twist the wrist out or in to make the ball move slightly in either direction. One of the simplest methods for young pitchers is to throw a "half fast ball." They simply reduce the fast ball to an optimal speed, which generally results in a smooth, well controlled change-up.

Regardless of how the ball is held or thrown, pitchers should keep several points in mind when throwing a change-up: (a) *Show the hitter a regular motion,* just as though the pitch is going to be a fast ball; (b) *Keep the ball low;* (c) The change is most effective against strong, *power hitters,* rather than punch hitters; (d) The change is more effective when the pitcher is *even* or *behind* in the count; (e) Have *confidence* in the change-up; it will make other pitches more effective because the hitter's timing will be destroyed by the changes of pitch speeds. A well disguised change-up is extremely valuable for a young pitcher to develop.

Pitchers can perform the 50 Pitch Change-Up Drill to practice this facet of their pitching.

## 50 PITCH CHANGE-UP DRILL

*Age Group:* 10 and up.

*Purpose:* Develops a pitcher's off-speed pitches and promotes better fundamentals in the pitching motion.

*Equipment:* Ball, gloves.

*Procedure:* Following warm-up exercises and light running, a pitcher should pair up with another pitcher or a catcher and pitch a combination of 50 change-up fast balls and change-up curve balls. The pitches should be thrown at 75% of the regulation distance. Half the pitches should be delivered from the stretch position with imaginary runners on base. Pitchers should concentrate on keeping each pitch *low*. Since the pitchers are throwing only change-ups and curves, they can perform this drill daily.

Pitchers can work on their control using the following three drills.

## TARP TARGET

*Age Group:* 10 and up.

*Purpose:* To help pitchers develop better control.

*Equipment:* Tarp target (see Appendix B for instructions), three-colored home plate, 20 balls.

*Procedure:* Place three-colored home plate in front of the strike zone. Pitchers practice delivering pitches to various spots on the tarp. After throwing 20 balls, they collect the balls and start over. Pitchers may pitch from two-thirds or regulation distance. They should deliver half the pitches from the stretch. Pitchers get points for pitches delivered in the crotch to knee area. Pitchers may also work on pick-off moves into the tarp.

## HIT THE SPOT PITCHING DRILL

*Age Group:* 10 and up.

*Purpose:* To develop a pitcher's ability to throw at specific targets.

*Equipment:* Three-colored home plate (see Appendix B for instructions), catching gear, ball, glove.

*Procedure:* Pitchers and catchers get into position at a regulation distance from one another, catchers get behind home plate. The pitcher throws at the catcher's left and right shoulders, left and right knees, at the catcher's chest, and at the catcher's glove. Catchers can keep track of the pitchers' hits and misses. A catcher should wear full gear for this drill.

Pitchers can also benefit by executing this drill from two-thirds their normal distance and throwing pitches at only two-thirds normal speed. If done at two-thirds speed, catchers may prefer using only a mask.

## PITCHER'S CONTROL DRILL

*Age Group:* 10 and up.

*Purpose:* To help the pitcher develop good awareness of the strike zone.

*Equipment:* Bat, three-colored home plate (see Appendix B for instructions), catching gear, ball, glove, helmets.

*Procedure:* Have pitchers and catchers in position at a regulation distance from one another. The catcher is behind home plate and a batter stands at the plate. The batter alternates between a left- and right-handed batting stance but does not swing. Catchers act as umpires, calling balls and strikes.

The catcher should wear full gear for this drill and the batter should wear a batting helmet.

Hitters can also practice their initial stride and call the proper contact point (1, 2, or 3—see p. 11). This will help them develop their visual tracking system. They should see the ball as it leaves the pitcher's fingers and carefully track the ball as it travels to the plate. Hitters need to remain sensitive to the speed and spin of each pitch as well as the contact point in order to hit well.

## Pitching Strategies

### Changing Angles

The angle of the pitcher's arm largely determines the way the ball will move. A straight overhand fast ball, thrown at maximum speed, should have a tendency to jump or move up slightly, provided the first two fingers on the ball are *not* tilted to the side. A three-quarter, overhand fast ball from a right-hander should move up and in on a right-handed hitter, while a sidearm fast ball should sink or move into a hitter.

The same concepts apply to the curve ball. An overhand curve should break down if the emphasis of the finger pressure is a downward action. A three-quarter overhand curve from a right-handed pitcher should break down and away from a right-handed hitter, while a sidearm curve should break away on a flat plane from the hitter.

All pitchers should experiment with different angles to discover which angles give them maximum velocity, movement, and control. The most effective angle is usually the one at which the pitcher reaches maximum leverage and arm extension at the point of release.

By changing the angle of the arm occasionally, pitchers add to their assortment of pitches and thus are less likely to be charted and "typed" by the hitters. All good hitters constantly evaluate the pitcher, and they become less certain about a pitcher who sometimes changes his arm and body angles. By doing this, a mediocre pitcher can become a more effective pitcher. If a pitcher has a good fast ball, curve, and change-up from one angle, he should use that angle most of the time.

## Waste and Purpose Pitches

In some cases a pitcher should "waste" a pitch to set up a hitter for the next pitch. Following are some examples.

1. If the pitcher uses 2 fast balls in order to get 2 consecutive strikes on a hitter, the next pitch might be a curve ball, low and out of the strike zone, to set up the hitter for a fast ball on the next pitch.

2. If the pitcher throws a fast ball and then a curve ball for strikes, the third pitch might be a high, inside, fast ball, followed by another curve ball.

3. If the pitcher has only a mediocre fast ball, that pitch should be kept low and on the corners and should be used to set up the curve ball or change-up, especially when the pitcher is facing a strong hitter. In this case the pitcher must have complete control of the curve and must be very careful not to throw the fast ball in the middle of the hitter's strike zone.

4. If the pitcher has only a mediocre curve ball, it should be kept low and away from the hitter. The pitcher should use the fast ball most of the time, attempting to change speeds and angles occasionally. The pitcher should try to throw the fast ball high inside, low inside, and outside, within the strike zone, trying to avoid delivering the same pitch with the same speed in the same area.

5. One of the most effective times to throw the change-up or the off-speed curve is when the pitcher is even or behind in the count. Hitters usually look for a fast ball in this situation, so their timing may be off and they may pop-up or ground out.

6. If the hitter pulls a fast ball foul, the next pitch might be a change-up. The hitter's timing generally will be altered, and as a result the hitter may pop-up, ground out, or strike out.

7. Occasionally, a right-handed pitcher can be effective with a left-handed batter by throwing a fast ball low and inside very close to the hitter's knees, followed by another fast ball on the outside corner. The same holds true for a left-handed pitcher facing a right-handed batter.

8. Pitchers must be sensitive to the quality of their pitches in order to be effective. During each inning a pitcher should identify which pitch is working best. He should strive to get ahead in the count with that pitch, and use the other pitches to set up the most effective pitch. The pitcher must be aware that the quality of various pitches may change over the course of a game, and the choice of pitch should change accordingly.

## Hitters' Weaknesses

Most hitters have some weakness or flaw in their hitting style. Pitchers must be able to detect and remember these weaknesses. The following are some general rules about certain types of hitters.

1. Hitters who crowd the plate could be thrown fast balls or sinker balls in on the hands.

2. Hitters who stand well away from the plate could be thrown sliders and overhand curves on the outside corner.

3. Hitters with narrow stances and long strides usually have difficulty hitting off-speed pitches, overhand curve balls, and high inside fast balls.

4. Hitters with wide stances usually have difficulty with high inside fast balls.

5. Hitters who pull the stride foot back in order to pull the ball more could be thrown curve balls and off-speed pitches on the outside corner.

6. Hitters with upright stances should be pitched low, while hitters with a crouch should be pitched high.

7. Off-speed pitches can be effective against the second, third, fourth, or fifth batters in the line-up, since they generally hit the fast ball well.

8. Good fast balls and quick curve balls should be thrown to the seventh, eighth, or ninth hitters, since

they are usually weaker hitters who hit off-speed pitches well.

In general, pitchers should get ahead of the hitters and try to vary the speed and types of pitches. They should move the ball up, down, inside, and outside within the strike zone, change the angle of delivery occasionally, and use their best pitch most of the time. Most successful pitchers learn to keep their pitches low because most hitters have trouble with pitches at knee level. There will be exceptions to such general rules, but they will be obvious and attentive pitchers can easily adjust for them.

## Pitching Out of Trouble

One of the most difficult situations for a pitcher is to have to pitch himself and his teammates out of trouble. Obviously, if a team never lets runners get on base they never have to face this problem. If a pitcher does not walk hitters, and if he keeps the base hits down to a minimum, he usually can control the tempo of the game—assuming his teammates don't make any errors.

But, as usually happens at one time or another, situations develop and suddenly a pitcher is in trouble with the bases loaded and no one out. At this point the pitcher must focus all his energies into practically every aspect of pitching. Even though the situation may appear hopeless, there are still several possible courses of action. A pitcher working with runners on base should consider the following points carefully:

1. Keep the ball *low and away* from the hitter's vision to try to get the hitter to hit a ground ball. A double play is essential in this situation. High pitches often result in base hits and fly balls that produce runs.

2. *Change speeds* and keep the hitter off balance. Pitches should be varied so that the hitter won't see the same pitch with the same speed in the same location.

3. Throw *breaking pitches*, such as sinkers, curves, and sliders instead of fast balls, unless the fast ball is moving with tremendous speed.

4. *Push the hitter away from the plate* with an occasional high, tight, fast ball to make the breaking pitches even more effective.

5. The pitcher must be relaxed and confident, yet compete even harder, because the ball game might be decided on a single pitch.

6. Occasionally after missing with a fast ball or curve ball, the pitcher should deliver the *same pitch at reduced speed*. The change of speeds often results in pop-ups and ground outs.

7. The pitcher may *try several pick-offs*, being careful not to throw the ball away. The pick-off attempts will disrupt the base runner's timing; it will also make the hitter wait longer for the next pitch, thus disturbing his concentration.

## Pitching With Runners on Base

A pitcher's effectiveness often is determined by how well he pitches with runners on base. The entire tempo of his performance may change with runners on base. Pitchers must be concerned not only about how to pitch to the hitters, but must also be aware of the potential activity of the runners.

The pitcher must not allow runners to get extended leads. Otherwise they may steal bases and execute hit-and-run plays, because runners will be able to get a maximum jump off the pitcher. In order to protect against the extended lead, the pitcher must know how to pitch from the stretch and develop good pick-off moves.

Although pitchers must be concerned about the activity of the base runners, it is more important for them to concentrate on the control of the pitches while working against each hitter. Pitchers must focus on the catcher's target before delivering each pitch, otherwise they may start losing control of the pitches. The pitcher should keep the ball low in the strike zone and near the hitter's knee height. If the pitch is aimed right and moves well, the hitter probably will hit the ball into the ground and give the infielders an opportunity to turn the double play. Good pitches to throw in these situations are strong, sinking fast balls and curve balls that break down.

## Pitching From the Stretch

When pitching from the stretch, pitchers start the motion at Phase Ia. The throwing side foot starts in front of the rubber, and the lead shoulder points toward the catcher. If the pitcher is right-handed, and there is a runner on first base, the lead shoulder and hip should be open slightly (turned a little more toward the base line between home and first base) so the pitcher can keep better watch on the runner's activity. The pitcher must still keep the ball and hand hidden in the glove before the delivery as in the full motion (see Figs. 10-88; 10-93, 10-98).

Pitchers must vary the amount of hesitation before the pitch. The hesitation should vary from 1 to 10 seconds so runners can't time the pitcher's delivery and get a better jump. The hesitation must vary regardless of the position of the base runners.

Pitchers must also vary the number of times they look at a runner on second base so the runner will not be able to steal third. If pitchers always look at the runner the same number of times, the runner can time his jump and easily steal third.

When pitching from the stretch, a right-handed pitcher shouldn't pick the left foot up more than a few inches while delivering the pitch to the plate. However, if a right-handed pitcher is capable of picking his left foot up high and setting it down quickly, he should be permitted to do so. Some pitchers lose a major source of power by failing to pick their legs up naturally. They should realize, however, that the longer it takes to deliver the pitch, the better jump a runner at first base can get. Therefore, a right-handed pitcher must get the pitch on its way to the plate in the shortest time possible, regardless of how high the leg goes as the pitch is delivered. Left-handers must be more concerned about the finesse of the move rather than its quickness, since their high, right leg kick should help make the move toward first base more deceptive.

When pitching from the stretch, pitchers must also be able to stay "behind the wall" as they get to the pitching position of Phase II before delivering the pitch to the plate (see Fig. 10-62). If a pitcher thrusts his body past the wall while picking up the glove side leg, the weight will not be distributed properly throughout the delivery. Thrusting the weight beyond the wall before the hands separate is one of the

major causes of arm strain, loss of velocity, lack of control, and poor movement on the ball.

When pitching from the stretch, pitchers should get to Phase II as quickly as possible without going past the wall, and then execute Phases III, IV, and V at their regular tempo. Pitchers need to be equally effective from the stretch and the full motion, so they must divide their mental and physical preparation between the two types of delivery.

**Pick-Off Moves**

If the base runner appears to have too much of a lead, the pitcher should try to pick him off base. The best pick-off move should be saved for tight situations. A *right-hander's* pick-off move to first and second base must be quick and precise. As pitchers start the move, they should pivot quickly and make a quick snap throw to the base. They shouldn't extend the throwing arm to perform this pick-off, because it will require too much time. A proper pick-off move requires quick feet and quick arm action. This move requires considerable practice because the pitcher should strive to eliminate full elbow extension when throwing to the bases. The bent arm snap throw makes a much quicker pick-off compared to the full arm extension throw used to deliver a pitch to the plate. A left-handed pitcher uses the same move to pick off a runner at second or third base (see Figs. 10-90 to 10-99).

| 10-90 | 10-91 | 10-92 | 10-93 | 10-94 |

Do not pause at belt for same number of seconds

Pivot feet quickly

Do not extend throwing arm

Execute quick throw to low, inside corner of first base

| 10-95 | 10-96 | 10-97 | 10-98 | 10-99 |

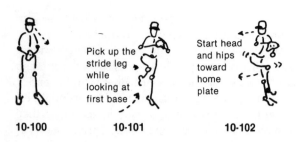

10-100   10-101   10-102

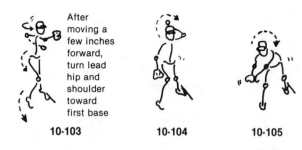

10-103   10-104   10-105

The *left-handed pitcher's* pick-off move to first requires precise head, leg, and hip movement. He should keep his head facing the runner at first base while picking up the stride leg. At this point the pitcher turns the head to the plate while starting a slight move toward the plate. After continuing forward for about 2 or 3 inches, the pitcher bends the front shoulder back toward first and delivers a sidearm throw to first. The success of this pick-off depends on deception and timing, not quickness. This is the same type of move that a right-hander uses to pick a runner off third base (see Figs. 10-100 to 10-105).

The Pick-Off Drill is a good way for pitchers to practice their moves to all the bases.

## PICK-OFF DRILL

*Age Group:* 10 and up.

*Purpose:* To work on pick-off plays.

*Equipment:* Infield setup (home plate not needed), gloves, three balls, helmets.

*Procedure:* Three pitchers stand around the mound and execute pick-off moves to the closest base. After two throws they rotate clockwise and make pick-off throws to the next base. Infielders practice receiving the pick-off throws and baserunners can practice their leads and reaction back to the base. Runners should wear helmets.

### Balk

There are so many variations and interpretations of the balk rule that it would be wise for every pitcher to read carefully the balk rules in the baseball rule book. All pitchers should keep in mind a few general rules when pitching with runners on base.

1. As long as the pivot foot is not in contact with the rubber, a pitcher can't balk. For example, if there are runners on first and third, and the runner at first breaks for second as the pitcher goes into the stretch, the pitcher should calmly step back off the rubber, bluff the runner back to third base, and throw to the shortstop who should be covering second base and who will tag out the runner coming from first, or run him back to first base.

2. Once there is a stop in the stretch, the pitcher must not move at all. Even a small movement of the glove is considered a balk.

3. A pitcher must step in the general direction of first base or third base when attempting a pick-off at that base. If the umpire thinks the pitcher stepped at an angle closer to home plate than to the base, the umpire will call a balk.

4. The umpire will call a balk if a pitcher throws to an unoccupied base without first stepping off the rubber.

### Signs and Shake-Offs

The signs between the pitcher and the catcher should be as simple as possible, yet difficult for base coaches and runners to decode or steal. One system highlights a series of signs that compose a key. The catcher could touch a part of his gear as a key, then give finger signs, each of which is activated by the key. For example, the catcher's mask could be the key for the first finger sign, the chest protector could be the key for the second finger sign, and the shin guard could be the key for the third finger sign. The catcher could touch all three keys but only the first key touched would be the "live" key. The finger signs could be as follows: one finger for a fast ball, two fingers for a curve, and three fingers for a change. So if the catcher touched the mask and then gave a series of three finger signs such as 2-1-2, the pitch would be a curve. However, if the catcher first touched the chest protector and gave 2-1-2 finger signs, the pitch would be a fast ball.

A simpler system consists of two sets of finger signs only, the first of which is a key. A catcher could give an initial finger sign of 1, 2, 3 or 4, which would indicate to the pitcher which sign is "live" in the next set of signs. After the initial finger sign and key the catcher should pause, then proceed to give four different finger signs, one of which is the live sign corresponding to the initial key. For example, 1/1, 2, 3, 4 is a fast ball; 2/1, 2, 3, 4 is a curve; 3/2, 2, 1, 4 is a fast ball; 2/4, 3, 2, 2 is a change.

These are examples of how a pitcher and catcher can keep a base runner or coach from stealing their signs and conveying the information to the hitter. With a little practice, a pitcher and catcher may never have their signs stolen.

The dummy shake-off is another effective maneuver the pitcher can use. Suppose the pitcher doesn't want to throw a certain pitch that the catcher calls. The pitcher could shake his head to ask for another sign. But if the pitcher wants to get the hitter guessing about the next pitch, he can wiggle his glove. Each time the pitcher wiggles the glove, he should pause as though the catcher is giving another sign, when actually the pitcher is keeping the original sign the catcher gave. The purpose of this maneuver is to divert the hitter's concentration.

## Statistics

Pitchers will find it helpful to keep precise statistics on their performances. They tend to serve as a stimulus to greater success. A pitcher's strike outs, walks, base hits, earned runs, and won-loss or save records should become important and meaningful to him. Pitchers should set goals for each game of the season and strive to meet those goals.

A pitcher's earned-run average is the most important statistic. A pitcher's true effectiveness is often deceiving when he has a poor win-loss record. He might have been a victim of poor defensive play by his teammates, or maybe his team produced insufficient runs for him to establish a victory. Therefore, all pitchers should consider carefully their earned-run average (E.R.A.) mark as the season progresses. It can be calculated by adding up the earned runs he allowed, multiplying the sum by nine (innings) and dividing that total by the innings he pitched.

$$\text{E.R.A.} = \text{earned runs} \times 9 \div \text{innings pitched}$$

## Pitching Charts

In Chapter 1 pitching charts were used to help hitters discover what kind of pitches the pitcher threw (see p. 17). The same chart should be kept for the pitcher's use. The chart will help pitchers become more aware of the percentage of strikes they throw for each type of pitch, how many innings they successfully get the lead batter out, what type of pitch each hitter hit, and what happened to the hitter. Charts should be kept on file so that pitchers can track their progress as the season continues. This procedure tends to encourage pitchers to set standards of excellence for themselves for each game, such as delivering 70% strikes, getting the leadoff batter out 70% of the time, and allowing few hits each game. If pitchers combine these statistics with their bases-on-balls total and E.R.A., soon they will be able to figure out just how well they are pitching.

Every pitch should be recorded on the pitching chart. After a few innings, the chart will begin to show certain information about the pitcher. It will reveal how consistently the pitcher throws strikes, the percentage of strikes for each type of pitch, and which pitch the pitcher prefers to throw. Pitchers and coaches can use this information to discover pitchers' trends, characteristics, and pitching effectiveness.

# CHAPTER 11

# Catching as It Relates to Pitching

The catcher's fielding responsibilities and qualifications have been discussed with other infield positional skills. This chapter is devoted entirely to the catcher's reponsibilities that relate to pitching. Throughout this chapter the emphasis will be not only on the proper physical mechanics of catching, but on the mental aspects of the position as well. It has often been said that the primary objective of the catcher is to do everything possible to help the pitcher. If one regards catching from this standpoint, a catcher should learn as much about pitching as possible. Because the catcher should think like a pitcher, on several occasions in the following discussion specific references are made to proper pitching techniques in various game conditions. As a catcher accumulates knowledge of pitching, his value to both the pitching staff and to the team will increase considerably. Each catcher and coach should be aware of the importance of assimilating the information presented earlier in the pitching segment. Without a thorough understanding of the fundamentals, concepts, ideas, and strategies necessary for effective pitching, a catcher severely limits himself as a source of assistance to his pitcher.

## Catching Position

### Giving Signs

When catchers give signs to pitchers, they should place the glove just off the left knee to keep the third base coach from stealing the sign. The feet should be kept about 10-12 inches apart and the sign should be given well back in the crotch (see Fig. 11-1). From this position, base coaches won't be able to steal signs.

Keep feet
12" apart

12"

**11-1**

### Giving the Pitcher a Target

When giving a target, catchers should place the glove just above the hitter's knees. The catcher's toes should point straight ahead and be slightly wider apart than his shoulders (see Fig. 11-2).

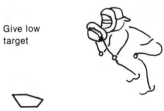

Give low
target

**11-2**

*The catcher must do everything possible to help the pitcher concentrate on each pitch*, not only for the good of the pitcher but for the whole team. Catchers should encourage pitchers to concentrate and should give them a quick target, while reminding them to take a mental picture of the target before the delivery. A pitcher could use the catcher's knees, shoulders, or mask as well as the mitt for a target. If a catcher gets into position quickly following the sign, it gives the pitcher more time to concentrate on a target and take a good mental picture. Unless a pitcher reduces his concentration to a specific point, his pitches will tend to be off the desired mark and he is likely to issue more bases-on-balls and give up more base hits.

If there are no runners on base, the catcher can assume a different catching position to relax his legs. The catcher may rest on his left knee while stretching his right leg out to the side (see Fig. 11-3). When there are runners on base, he should not use this position, because it restricts shifting and throwing movements.

**11-3**

### Shifting on Low Pitches

Catchers can use several methods to shift for pitches in the dirt. Whatever method catchers choose, they must *keep the ball in front of them* and try to "smother" the ball with their body (see Figs. 11-4 to 11-7).

The catcher's primary responsibility is not to catch the ball, but simply to drop to one or both knees and play the ball off some piece of his equipment in order to keep the ball from getting past him. Runners will advance if a catcher doesn't smother the ball. Some catchers try to backhand the pitch to their right, or "short hop" the ball off the bounce to speed up the play when a runner is stealing. This practice is unwise because it is not likely that a catcher can throw out a runner when the pitch is in the dirt; and if the ball happens to get past the catcher, the runner may be able to advance another base. The best policy on pitches in the dirt is to block the ball with one or both knees and keep it in front where a catcher can play the ball easily, especially when there is a runner on third base.

Shifting on low pitches must be an automatic response for catchers, so they must practice it often. Catchers should not let a workout pass without having a teammate or coach throw them pitches in the dirt. The Shift Drill will help them develop the proper movements.

### SHIFT DRILL

*Purpose:* To help catchers learn to shift on pitches in the dirt.

*Equipment:* Full catcher's equipment, or sometimes no equipment.

*Procedure:* Catchers learn to use their body to block the pitch by keeping their hands behind their backs. Another player or coach can throw balls at the catchers if they are wearing equipment. This drill can be done without equipment by the catchers' imagining a pitch coming at them in the dirt and blocking the imaginary pitch (see Figs. 11-8 to 11-12). Catchers should repeat this drill 20-30 times daily in order to establish proper habits.

Slide knees to ground quickly to block pitches in the dirt

Smother the ball with entire body

**11-4**          **11-5**          **11-6**          **11-7**

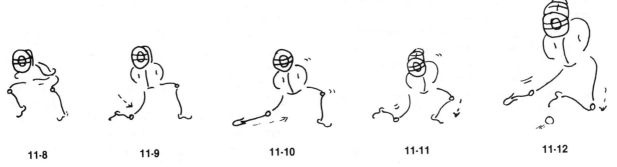

|      |      |       |       |       |
|:----:|:----:|:-----:|:-----:|:-----:|
| **11-8** | **11-9** | **11-10** | **11-11** | **11-12** |

Shift Drill: Practice shifting with hands held behind the back.

## Communication Between Catchers and Pitchers

### Helping the Pitcher Establish Mental and Emotional Control

Frequently a pitcher's effectiveness is directly related to his mental and emotional state. This is where the catcher can be of the greatest assistance by doing everything possible to help the pitcher maintain a positive mental and emotional state. This will help the pitcher concentrate at the highest possible level, which is an essential component of effective pitching.

A pitcher needs to concentrate on specific targets, to be aware of his basic mechanics, to notice which pitches are working best, to be sensitive to selecting effective pitches for different hitters, to be perceptive to hitters' weaknesses, and to be ready to field his position effectively. A catcher needs to encourage the pitcher to concentrate on these areas and, by thus helping the pitcher, the catcher helps the whole team. If a pitcher breaks down in any of those areas it can seriously affect the team since pitching is a major part of the defense.

A pitcher's mental state should be one of confidence and positive thoughts, stimulated by a burning desire to compete. He should be aggressive and eager to meet a challenge, and should have no thoughts of inferiority, fear, or passiveness as he walks out to the mound each inning. Determination, kindled with a strong confident attitude, should be so active within the pitcher that it will direct his total performance. It is the catcher's responsibility to look for signs of breakdown in any of these psychological areas and to make appropriate suggestions or comments to the pitcher when necessary. In order to fulfill this duty successfully, the catcher should study the pitcher closely, not only while he is on the mound, but also while he is sitting on the bench between innings.

The catcher should remind the pitcher that each inning is a brand new opportunity that requires renewal of the pitcher's full attention. Both the pitcher and catcher should pour all their efforts into each inning, being aware that previous success does not guarantee future success and that past failure does not doom one to more failure.

A catcher should encourage the pitcher to get ahead of hitters in the count. If the pitcher consistently falls behind in the count, such as 1-0, 2-0, or 3-1, he will be hindering himself in several ways. First, delivering too many pitches may result in early fatigue. Second, this allows hitters to "type" him more readily, since they have a chance to look at more pitches and thus to better determine what type of pitches the pitcher is bringing to the plate. Consequently, the hitter is able to wait on his pitch more often, assuming that when he is consistently behind in the count the pitcher must deliver his fast ball for strikes. Therefore, the catcher should continually emphasize to the pitcher the importance of getting ahead of each hitter.

Pitchers who are consistently successful, usually get the leadoff man out. If the pitcher is throwing strikes most of the time, his teammates will be more alert in their defensive efforts, and the umpire will subconsciously favor him on close pitches. The catcher should remember that if the lead man in any given inning reaches base, not only will the pitcher have to work from the stretch, but also the entire club will have to play the inning under added pressure, which often leads to costly mistakes. For these reasons, at the start of each inning the catcher should remind the pitcher to try extra hard to get the first man out.

### Recognizing Weaknesses in Hitters

Most hitters have some weakness or flaw in their hitting style. The catcher and pitcher should detect and remember the weaknesses. A summary of various weaknesses of different types of hitters was outlined in the chapter on pitching (see pp. 117-118). Catchers should memorize those weaknesses to be of greater assistance to the pitchers.

In general, the pitcher should get ahead in the count on each hitter, try to vary the speed and types of pitches, change the angle of delivery occasionally, move the ball around in the strike zone, and use his best pitch most of the time. Since most hitters have trouble hitting pitches around knee level, the catcher should give a low target and encourage the pitcher to throw to the mitt.

## Helpful Hints From a Catcher To a Pitcher

A catcher can assist the pitcher in many ways. An intelligent, alert catcher is invaluable to a team. Following are some helpful suggestions a catcher should keep in mind.

1. The catcher should encourage the pitcher to start his warm-up plenty of time before the start of the game. Catchers should review conditions affecting a pitcher's warm-up, such as physical build of the pitcher, temperature, wind conditions, and other factors discussed in Chapter 10. A catcher should also make certain that the pitcher does not throw too much during pregame warm-up. The pitcher must be totally ready when he brings the first pitch down; therefore, a catcher should be mindful of how much warm-up each pitcher needs in order to be ready.

2. The catcher should remind the pitcher to back up third base and home plate on all base hits with runners on base, in order to save needless runs on overthrows.

3. With runners on base, the catcher should review the situation with the pitcher and alert him to the most advantageous play if the ball is hit back to the mound. For example, with runners on first and third bases with less than 2 outs, when the ground ball is hit back to the mound, the pitcher should field the ball, "look" the runner back to third, and throw to second. The catcher should call the pitcher's attention to this sort of situation before the ball is hit back to the mound.

4. As soon as the ball is hit to the pitcher's left, the catcher should shout for the pitcher to cover first base. An instant reminder like this may determine successful coverage rather than late movement.

5. Just before the ball reaches the pitcher, when he is fielding a bunt, the catcher should suggest where the pitcher should throw. The pitcher may then approach the ball properly, anticipating a specific play.

6. If the pitcher comes off the mound and sits for more than 10 minutes while his team is at bat, the catcher should remind him to toss some pitches so his arm will not cool off.

7. When the pitcher is pitching with men on base, the catcher should remind him to vary how long he pauses in his stretch so that runners will not be able to get an added "jump" off the motion. The catcher should also remind him to eye the target before starting each delivery from the stretch. Many inexperienced pitchers will pay too much attention to the runners and fail to concentrate on the target.

## The Catcher's Analysis of the Pitcher's Motion

Catchers can be very helpful to pitchers when they are having trouble with control or cannot get various pitches to work correctly. Occasionally a catcher may recognize a slight flaw in the pitcher's motion or minor error in finger pressure on the ball as the cause of the difficulty. Every catcher should thoroughly understand every aspect of pitching in order to best assist the pitcher in maintaining a consistent, successful performance (see Chapter 10).

## Waste and Purpose Pitches

On some occasions a pitcher will want to waste a pitch to set up a hitter for the next pitch. The catcher must signal the purpose pitches at the appropriate times. Every catcher should memorize the section on Waste and Purpose Pitches in Chapter 10, Pitching. Using purpose pitches correctly can disrupt a hitter's timing and lead to outs.

## Helping the Pitcher out of Trouble

One of the most difficult situations a pitcher encounters is having to pitch his team out of a jam. The catcher should assume a major role in assisting the pitcher to pitch the team out of trouble. The catcher should motivate the pitcher to keep the bases-on-balls down to a minimum and give up only a limited amount of hits; this can help keep problems from materializing.

However, sudden, unfortunate situations can develop which require the pitcher's and the catcher's total awareness. Even though a situation may appear impossible, the pitcher and the catcher still have several courses of action to pursue in their attempt to get out of trouble. These steps are carefully outlined in Chapter 10. Every catcher should learn this phase of pitching in order to think as one with the pitcher during those periods when the outcome of a game may be riding on each pitch.

# PART III

## PLANNING

Coaches need to do more than understand the mechanics of offensive and defensive skills. They also must organize constructive practices and determine offensive and defensive strategies for their team. The final chapter of this book helps coaches incorporate the skills and drills discussed previously into effective practices by organizing several drills into a system of simultaneously conducted drills, and by combining several skills into one drill. Guidelines are presented which will help coaches learn how to create a practice environment which is conducive to learning. Methods for determining appropriate game strategies for various game situations are discussed, as well as how to assess another team's strengths and weaknesses.

# CHAPTER 12

# Drill Systems, Multipurpose Drills, and Strategies

## Practices

A team's success usually is largely related to the amount of meaningful practice the team has. A disciplined, well-drilled team will perform more effectively and be more consistent than a poorly prepared team.

Workouts should be interesting and varied, never ordinary and monotonous. Players should have fun while practicing, and one way to ensure this is to put competitive elements into drills. Coaches must also keep workouts organized. All players should understand that meaningful practice can help them play their best and can help them develop positive personal qualities.

It is vital that coaches use imagination and ingenuity when planning practices. Practice plans should be based on available facilities, the season's schedule, weather conditions, practice time, and the players' needs. Players should be moving constructively throughout the practice period. If they stand idle, talk, or waste time, players will eventually become bored and will not get much out of practice. Coaches need to prepare programs that are beneficial and enjoyable.

## Creating a Learning Environment

The players' state of mind can affect their interest in practice. Coaches can't control the multitude of variables that affect whether a program captures and maintains all the players' interest throughout the season, but a coach who is sensitive to each player's

needs will be able to create a good learning environment most of the time. Some of the players' more stable characteristics, such as their need to achieve, their aspirations, goals, abilities, maturity level, personality, health status, and personal living habits are just a few factors that affect their level of interest in practice and baseball. Other less constant factors—their mood that day, whether they are sick, or what the weather is—also influence the players' attention and enthusiasm for practice.

Coaches must maintain a lot of enthusiasm by properly reinforcing and encouraging their players. If players and coaches remain committed to the program throughout the season, they are likely to meet their goals and gain a sense of achievement through an enjoyable experience.

Considering the maze of factors that affect a program's effectiveness, coaches are continually challenged to develop innovative methods to capture each player's interest. The following recommendations should help give coaches a base from which to construct their practice sessions. No single recommendation is more important than any other. Each concept, method, and procedure has helped individuals learn motor skills. (For further information on these aspects of coaching, see *Coaching Young Athletes* by Martens et al., Human Kinetics Publishers, Inc., Champaign, IL, 1981.)

Coaches should use the following principles to help create an effective training program.

1. Players need to review their physical skills frequently, not only to improve but also to maintain quality performance once it has been developed.

Players can benefit from an individualized daily program that supplements the organized team drills. Coaches could give players a personal comprehensive drill system that they can go through during batting practice. A player's individual daily drill system should include all the skills he may have to perform during a game. Any drill system should approach each skill through several different drills so players don't get bored repeating the same drill.

2. Players need to understand how it feels to perform a skill correctly (a kinesthetic awareness), and should have a mental image of the skill in order to perform consistently. Thus, players should perform both physical and mental practice daily. Simulation and mental practice away from and during organized practice helps players develop physical skills.

3. Coaches should help players understand the components of skills, how the components relate to the players' performance of these skills, and how the players use the skills at their positions.

4. Coaches should encourage players to analyze and evaluate their performance daily. Players should get adequate feedback to knowledgeably modify their performance in order to perform at their peak. If players are highly attentive to body parts and proper body positions, simulating fundamental skills in front of a mirror will help develop players' analytical and evaluative skills. Players must be especially aware of the toes, heels, knees, hips, hands, elbows, shoulders, and head. While analyzing movement, players also must work on their visual discipline in order to concentrate on the ball.

5. Coaches need to understand how to use positive reinforcement. If they use too much or not enough, players' development can be slowed. If coaches find it necessary to use negative reinforcement or punishment, they should reward or positively reinforce at the next opportunity. When players show good reactions, reflexes, quickness, speed, hustle, or skillful execution of any fundamental, coaches should praise them alone or in the team's presence. Proper reinforcement facilitates learning and helps develop a closer rapport between coaches and players.

6. The reason for practice is to improve. Since the primary objective of practice is to make the team successful, workouts should be planned with the games in mind. Drills should be designed to develop game skills such as cutoffs and relays, first and third steals, pick-offs, bunt coverage, pop-up and fly ball coverage, bunting and stealing, and hit-and-run situations. Players should perform a complete system of individual fundamentals as well as team drills.

7. Players must "overlearn" in order to perform successfully consistently. To be able to perform

under pressure, players must repeat skills over and over and must concentrate on the skill the entire time. Because baseball skills generally require players to react instantly, they must make the reactions habits and retain those habits throughout the season.

8. Players learn best by *doing*, not by watching or listening. Even though demonstrations, films, drawings, and discussion often enhance meaning, players must actually perform the skills to learn how to do them. Workouts should be designed around activity.

9. Identifying the components of the skills facilitates learning them. Players should write about the skills, talk about their components, evaluate teammates, and simulate components in front of a mirror. This will help them develop a complete mental picture of the skills and perform the skills consistently.

10. Practicing a skill three times during a practice for 10 minutes each time is more effective than practicing the skill once for 30 minutes. Coaches should develop a seasonal plan and workout schedule to make sure that all necessary skills are being covered each week. Coaches could distribute a similar guide to players and encourage them to pursue a self-directed developmental program by cycling through a system of game situations and individual drills.

11. Drills that strengthen weaknesses in separate parts of skills become whole learning experiences when players mentally fill in the rest of the skill. Every mechanical fundamental of hitting, bunting, baserunning, pitching, catching, and infield and outfield play should be an integral part of a drill system.

12. Practices should be organized, systematic, competitive, challenging, innovative, and interesting. Players should perform many movements during each practice and gets considerable feedback. When players are standing in the outfield watching batting practice, they aren't learning.

13. At advanced levels, serious errors tend to be constant errors and players may be unaware of their cause. The error must be brought to the player's attention, the correct part substituted, and the new part practiced within the whole unit until it is an automatic part of the performance. Demonstration, discussion, analysis of self and others, manipulation by coaches, films of the player, and indicating the differences between the desired movement and the erroneous movement all help correct faults.

14. Players must be inspired by their coaches to develop their skills and be ready for every game. Players' psychological and physical preparation are directly related to their enthusiasm and self-motivation. One of a coach's primary concerns should be to motivate players to strive to reach their full potential. This pursuit is one way that baseball can most benefit its participants.

## Drill Systems and Multipurpose Drills

Following are a series of drill systems and multi-purpose drills which coaches can use to help organize effective practices.

### Station Drill System

The station drill system is designed to give each player, regardless of position, a review of the common denominators of basic skills in a rather short period of time. Players pair up and go through the entire drill system that way, with each player executing each skill five times. The drill begins with at least one pair at each station. The complete drill system should take about 45 minutes. The coach should move among stations, correcting faults and keeping the players hustling between stations (see Fig. 12-1).

The drills that players perform at each station are listed below, with corresponding page numbers for easy reference to the drill and/or skill involved.

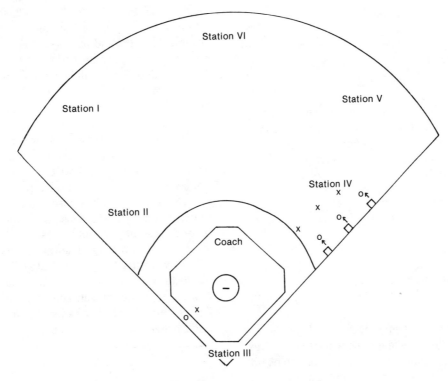

**Figure 12-1** Organization: Players get in pairs. Each player performs each skill five times (except for pepper station). Each pair hustles from station to station. Coaches correct flaws at each station.

|         Station I          |      |
| Drill                      | Page |
| -------------------------- | ---- |
| Skip and Throw for Points  | 55   |
| Rhythm Drill               | 56   |
| Short Hop Drill            | 56   |
| Backhand Drill             | 57   |
| Fly Balls Overhead         | 57   |

*Key Suggestion:* To get maximum benefit from Station I drills, players should make their partners practice hard by giving them difficult balls to field. These basic defensive drills form the foundation for all defensive skills. They should therefore be practiced during every workout throughout the season.

|         Station II              |      |
| Drill                           | Page |
| ------------------------------- | ---- |
| Simulated Swings Drill          | 15   |
| Hip Turner Drill                | 8    |
| Wrist Roller Drill              | 9    |
| Throwing Bats Drill             | 9    |
| Lead and Follow Hands Swings Drill | 10 |
| Bat Press Drill                 | 10   |

*Key Suggestion:* During bat drills, players should help their partners correct flaws in their swings by carefully analyzing the swing and making suggestions.

### Station III

| Drill | Page |
|---|---|
| Sacrifice Bunt | 25 |
| Drag Bunt | 26 |

*Key Suggestion:* Players should pitch to their partners from the stretch to provide a more realistic bunting situation. Pitches should be accurate and firm.

### Station IV

| Drill | Page |
|---|---|
| Sacrifice Bunt Lead | 32 |
| Offensive Lead | 32 |
| Walking Lead | 32 |

*Key Suggestion:* One member of each pair serves as the pitcher while the other works on leads. After five repetitions of each lead, players alternate. Each player should pretend to be both a left-handed and right-handed pitcher.

### Station V

| Drill | Page |
|---|---|
| Stand-up Slide | 41 |
| Stand-up Slide and Advance | 41 |
| Sliding Around a Tag (Decoy Slide) | 42 |
| Hook Slide | 42 |

*Key Suggestion:* One member of each pair acts as a baseman ready to make the tag while the other executes the proper slides. If there isn't something soft to slide on, players should walk through the slides. Players sliding on grass should remove their shoes to prevent injury.

### Station VI

| Drill | Page |
|---|---|
| Three Person Pepper Games | 135 |
| Contact Point Drills with Lead Hand | 14 |
| Contact Point Drills with Follow Hand | 14 |

*Key Suggestion:* Each player should pepper with only the lead hand, then with the follow hand, in order to establish better bat control with either hand. The hitter should turn and face his partner so that his hips are open as he hits each pitch. The fielder should work on his fielding mechanics. Try 25 repetitions for this drill.

## Fungo Stations

The primary purpose of the fungo stations is to give each infielder and outfielder as many opportunities as possible to field various types of ground balls. Coaches should carefully examine basic mechanics of both fielding and throwing. Each player should field between 20 and 30 balls.

There should be four fungo stations. At Stations I and IV a coach or player hits fly balls, line drives, and ground balls to the outfield, and at Stations II and III a coach or player hits a variety of ground balls to the infield (see Fig. 12-2). The drill should last 20 minutes. For the first 10 minutes the fungo hitter at Station II hits ground balls to the right and to the left of the second baseman and first baseman, while the fungo hitter at Station III hits ground balls to the right and left of the third baseman and shortstop. All infielders should make their throws back to the fungo catchers.

During the last 10 minutes the fungo hitter at Station II hits slow rollers to the third baseman and first baseman, while the fungo hitter at Station III hits double play balls to the shortstop and second baseman. The third and first basemen should make their throws to each other's bases, while the shortstop and second baseman should make their double play tosses to second base. The outfielders should make all throws to the fungo cutoff players.

Pitchers and catchers help the coaches by hitting the fungos. Other players can alternate hitting fungos if necessary. The skills used in the fungo stations are listed below for easy reference.

| Skill | Page |
|---|---|
| Basic fielding mechanics | 49 |
| Fielding the ball on the backhand side | 57 |
| Fielding slow rollers | 58 |
| Turning double plays | 65 |
| Shifting at first | 63 |
| Circling fly balls | 87 |
| Going back on line drives | 86 |

## Pick-Offs – Bunt Coverage – Covering First Base

This multipurpose drill reviews a great deal of baseball in a short time. The field is divided in half. One group of pitchers with one catcher works on pick-offs with the shortstop and second baseman, while another group of pitchers with another catcher works with the first and third basemen and the coach. Both groups work on bunt coverage, pitchers covering first base, pitchers starting double plays,

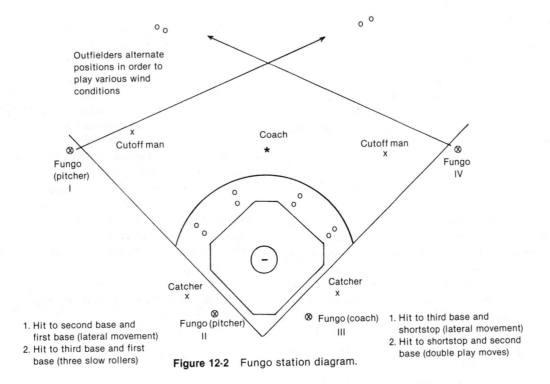

1. Hit to second base and first base (lateral movement)
2. Hit to third base and first base (three slow rollers)

1. Hit to third base and shortstop (lateral movement)
2. Hit to shortstop and second base (double play moves)

**Figure 12-2** Fungo station diagram.

and pick-offs to all bases. Pitchers should periodically alternate groups. Outfielders serve as base runners at first, second, and third. Once all the players learn the basic components of the drill, they will have had an excellent review of these critical game condition skills. Runners should wear helmets.

Each ball player should execute several moves with each group. These infield situations require precise timing among all the players involved, so it is a good drill to do often. The drill should take no more than 15 minutes. The skills used in the drill are listed below for easy reference.

| Skill | Page |
| --- | --- |
| Pick-offs | 79 |
| Bunt coverage | 78 |
| Pitchers covering first | 71 |
| Pitchers starting double plays | 72 |

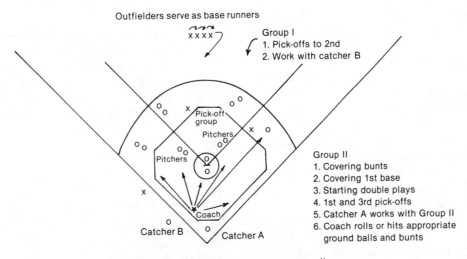

**Figure 12-3** Pick-off and bunt coverage diagram.

## Batting Practice

Batting practice should mean much more to a team practice than simply having each hitter take 5 or 6 swings before going to the outfield to shag balls. Each player must be fully occupied throughout batting practice. Every team member should get a minimum of 15 to 20 swings a day. In order to accomplish this, coaches need to keep everything moving at a brisk pace. Each hitter should attack the ball aggressively, and the player who is throwing batting practice should concentrate on throwing strikes.

As the hitter steps to the plate, he should execute a sacrifice bunt on the first pitch, a hit-and-run on the second pitch, and then take 8 regular swings. After the last swing, the hitter should "think second" and proceed to run each base as if he were in an actual game. This will serve as a review on proper baserunning techniques. Hitters should wear helmets at bat and once they get on base.

The next hitter follows the same format as the first hitter—executes a sacrifice bunt, followed by a hit-and-run and 8 swings. The previous hitter, who is now on base, should execute all the baserunning techniques at each base appropriate to the way the hitter performs at the plate (review baserunning techniques in Chapter 3).

While players hit and run bases, the coaches, assisted by an alternate first baseman, hit fungos to the infielders and outfielders. The infielders and catchers should hit while the outfielders and pitchers shag balls, field fungos, and cycle through the other drills. Then the outfielders and pitchers could take their turn at bat.

Catchers should catch for only five hitters in a row in order to stay alert and fresh. Pitchers shouldn't throw more than 40 pitches at batting practice. If they want to work on their pitches further, they should throw to a catcher in the bullpen. While the pitcher is working on batting practice his catcher should inform him how many pitches pass through the strike zone between the hitter's crotch and knee areas. Pitchers should work at developing this important habit and should strive for a 70% success ratio. If infielders, outfielders, and catchers pitch batting practice, they should follow the same guidelines. This allows everyone's arm to remain fresh and ready for action in additional drills.

If the infielders and catchers hit first, all the other players except the hitter and the base runner should be off to the side of the field working on sacrifice and drag bunting, fake bunt-and-swings, simulating swings, or bat drills until their turn comes. After the infielders and catchers complete their first round of hitting, they should switch places with the outfielders and the pitchers and follow the same hitting, bunting, and baserunning procedures. The player acting as "feeder" for the pitcher stands at the edge of the outfield grass, approximately 6 feet behind second base. This player supplies the pitcher with balls as quickly as possible following each hitter. Since this job soon gets boring, no player should act as "feeder" for more than three hitters in a row.

At the end of the first round of batting practice, the groups should change places again and begin the second round promptly. Each player gets 5 or 6 swings during the second round. The basic procedures used in the first round can also be used in the second round. The two rounds should take no longer than 90 minutes for a group of 15 players (see Fig. 12-4).

Several times a week batting practice can be supplemented with the Must Swing Pitches Drill.

---

## MUST SWING PITCHES

*Age Group:* 8 and up.

*Purpose:* To encourage aggressiveness at the plate while developing sensitive visual concentration, better bat control, and a keener sense of appropriate contact points.

*Equipment:* Bat, balls, gloves, helmets.

*Procedure:* The hitter is allowed only 5 pitches thrown at half speed. The hitter must swing at each pitch regardless of where it is thrown. The batter tries to hit each pitch to the *opposite* field without popping up, except a belt-high inside pitch, which the hitter must "pull."

---

This drill will stop players from trying to pull all pitches and will encourage hitting outside pitches to the opposite field more. Hitters will hit fewer pop-ups since they must get on top of each pitch in order to perform this drill correctly. The major skills involved in batting practice are listed below for easy reference.

| *Skill* | *Page* |
|---|---|
| Hitting mechanics | 3 |
| Hit-and-run | 18 |
| Fake bunt-and-swing | 138 |
| Sacrifice and drag bunts | 25 |
| Baserunning techniques | 29 |

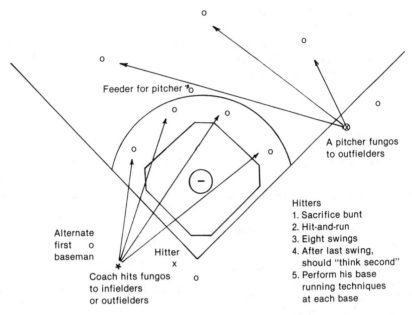

Feeder for pitcher

A pitcher fungos
to outfielders

Hitters
1. Sacrifice bunt
2. Hit-and-run
3. Eight swings
4. After last swing,
   should "think second"
5. Perform his base
   running techniques
   at each base

Alternate
first
baseman

Hitter

Coach hits fungos
to infielders
or outfielders

**Figure 12-4**  Batting practice diagram.

The next four drills combine hitting and fielding, hitting and running, or fielding and running.

## PEPPER GAME DRILL

*Age Group:* 8 and up.

*Purpose:* To develop bat control and fundamentals of fielding and throwing.

*Equipment:* Bats, balls, gloves, three-colored home plates (see Appendix B for instructions).

*Procedure:* Players work in groups of three. One player is the hitter and the other two players are fielders. The two defensive players stand approximately 30-60 feet from the hitter and 10-12 feet apart. The defensive player with the ball executes a skip and throw to the hitter, being careful to throw a strike across the plate. The hitter should use a three-colored home plate to be aware of contact point areas. (A glove could also serve as home plate.) The hitter should strive to make contact with the ball appropriately in the various contact areas (see p. 11). The hitter should try to hit the ball on the ground to give the fielders fielding opportunities. After 20 swings the players should rotate.

Hitters should assume a stance that is slightly open toward the fielders and should choke up on the bat several inches for better bat control. Additional bat control can be taught by having hitters use only the lead or follow hands. This will emphasize the importance of having strong fingers, hands, and forearms for effective bat control. If the hitter is weak from the elbows to the finger tips, this drill will be difficult, and one should remind him of the necessity for developing strength in the hands and arms (see Appendix A, especially the use of Rolley, for further information).

Hitters can keep score by counting the number of consecutive swings without a missed or foul ball. Players can play a game by counting 1 point against the hitter for a caught line drive, 2 points for a caught ground ball, and 3 points for a ball hit too high or too wide for the fielders to catch. When fielders get 21 points, the next player becomes the hitter.

Older players can use a system where a hitter loses his remaining swings if he swings and misses or if he hits a fly ball over the fielder's head or too far to the side. Fielders may also make the drill more fun by tossing the ball to each other before throwing the pitch to the hitter.

## SACRIFICE BUNT
## AND RUNNING PRACTICE

*Age Group:* 10 and up.

*Purpose:* To work on sacrifice bunts and running for a sacrifice or a steal.

*Equipment:* Two bases, bat, balls, gloves, helmets.

*Procedure:* Two or three players act as runners, starting at first base and taking the appropriate type of lead, ready to go to second base as soon as the league rules permit. Bunters and runners should wear helmets. Runners should be wearing long pants and should practice various slides into second base. This drill should be administered on soft grass to avoid abrasions during sliding. A defensive team (catcher, first baseman, second baseman, third baseman, pitcher) pitches and fields the bunts and throws to the appropriate base. Each bunter gets 5 bunts, then players rotate.

## TAGGING-UP

*Purpose:* To have players practice tagging up after a fly ball.

*Equipment:* Third base, home plate (see Appendix B), gloves, ball, helmets.

*Procedure:* Set up third base and home plate at regulation distance. Three players start at third base, two players are in the thrower position, (about where the shortstop would be), and two players are at the left fielder's position. The first runner stands at third base. The thrower throws to the left fielder. When the fielder catches the ball, the coach tells the runner to "go." Some advanced base runners may prefer to watch the ball enter the fielder's glove and simultaneously run. The runner may either sprint past home plate or simply take three hard steps in order to draw the throw. The runner should not try to score unless he knows he will be safe. The runner should carefully consider the direction and depth of the fly ball in his decision to score or to fake and draw the throw. The left fielder throws back to the next thrower. Runners should wear helmets.

The drill can include a catcher at home plate to provide practice for outfielders throwing to home plate, relay throws, and the catcher's making tag plays at home plate. When using a catcher, the left fielder throws to home plate with the thrower acting as cutoff. To avoid injury runners should not slide during the drill but should peel off to the side as they reach home plate. Players rotate as indicated on the figures. After a few turns, the next runner may serve as the base coach.

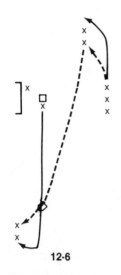

**12-6**

## TEAM DEFENSIVE DRILLS (SITUATIONS)

*Purpose:* Provides players with opportunities to execute individual skills under game conditions.

*Equipment:* Gloves, bat, ball, complete field, helmets.

*Procedure:* Players fill all defensive positions. Remaining players serve as base runners and get in a line at home plate. Runners should wear helmets. The coach calls the number of outs and then hits a ground or fly ball. The runner does not leave home plate until the coach hits the ball to give the same effect as a base runner in a game. Alternatively, the base runners can call the number of outs, hit the ball to the fielders, and proceed to run the bases.

The coach should position runners and hit balls to provide opportunities for cutoffs and relays, bunt coverage, run-downs, double plays and defensing singles, extra base hits, and all types of ground and fly balls. If the drill is administered with game situations in mind, there will be many opportunities for instruction on game strategy, fundamentals, and rules. Coaches may be placed at first and third base coaching boxes so that runners may respond to helpful instructions from the base coaches. Base runners and fielders should rotate so that all players participate equally.

### Intra-Squad Games

Intra-squad games give teams the opportunity to practice many offensive and defensive game situations under competitive conditions. Players generally enjoy competitive events during practice and work hard at them. Intra-squad games can be scheduled often after players learn basic skills.

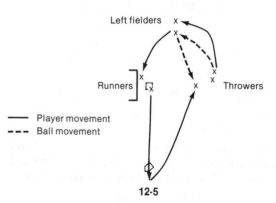

Left fielders

Runners          Throwers

—— Player movement
- - - Ball movement

**12-5**

## MINI INTRA-SQUAD

*Age Groups:* 5-7 (use hitting tees), 8-9 (coach pitches), 10 and up (regular).

*Purpose:* To provide a practice game with all defensive positions covered when there are not enough players for two full teams.

*Equipment:* Bats, gloves, ball, catching equipment, infield setup, helmets.

*Procedure:* The entire team is divided into three equal mini-squads, each with its own pitcher and catcher. One mini-squad hits while the other two combine to fill the defensive positions.

The game may be scored on a point system, with a point awarded for each hitter reaching base by any means and a point for each run scored. This method of scoring challenges the defensive team to execute effectively and consistently.

After every 3 outs, the bases should be cleared of any runners. Each hitter on each mini-squad is allowed to appear at the plate three times before a different mini-squad becomes the offensive team. The squad with the most points wins the game.

The coach can pitch against each mini-squad, or regular pitchers can be used. Competitiveness is often heightened if the coach allows each mini-squad to choose the pitcher they wish to hit against.

## ONE PITCH INTRA-SQUAD

*Purpose:* To provide a variety of baserunning and defensive situations.

*Equipment:* Bats, gloves, ball, catching equipment, infield setup, helmets.

*Procedure:* The team divides into two equal squads, or three mini-squads if there are not enough players to fill two 9-person teams. The game can be scored like the mini-squad game described above.

The offensive team provides its own pitcher, who should deliver an easy pitch to hit. Each hitter is allowed only one pitch. A swing and miss, "taking" a pitch, and foul balls are considered outs. The pitcher must be able to throw strikes.

After the third out, the next team hustles in to take its turn as the offensive team. As soon as the new team's first hitter and the pitcher are ready, the pitcher may pitch. This rule requires everyone to hustle on and off of the field, adding a fitness factor to the game. Since the pitches are easy to hit, the catcher needs only a mask for protection and therefore will not need to spend much time changing gear.

## EXTENDED BAG GAME

*Purpose:* Provides several learning opportunities for game skills in an enjoyable game.

*Equipment:* Bats, gloves, ball, catching equipment, infield setup, helmets.

*Procedure:* Divide the team into two equal squads. There can be as few as five or six players on each squad. First base is extended another one-third regulation distance farther down the line (see Fig. 12-7).

The rules are:

- There are 6 outs per half inning.
- After the sixth out, the half inning is over and the two squads switch.
- Each team supplies its own pitcher, who tries to deliver easy pitches to hit.
- Each hitter is allowed only one pitch.
- Swings and misses, taking pitches, and foul balls are outs. The hitter must try to hit the ball fair.
- If the hitter hits a fair fly that is caught, he is out.
- If the hitter hits a fair ground ball, he must sprint to the extended first base and touch that base before a fielder fields the ball and throws to *second base*. If the throw reaches *second base* and is caught before the hitter reaches first base, the hitter is out. If the hitter reaches first base before the throw reaches second base, the hitter is safe.
- The runner on first must stay on first until the next ball is hit. If the ball is hit on the ground, the runner must run back to home.
- When a ground ball is hit with a runner on first, the defensive team can throw to second to get the hitter out, or throw home to get the runner out.
- The runner going home is safe if he beats the throw to home.
- All plays at home and second are force outs, so there should be no sliding.
- A runner on first can tag on a fly and attempt to score.
- If a runner is off first base when a fly or line drive is caught, the fielder can throw to second base to try to "double up" the runner.

Score the extended bag game by points rather than runs. Each time a player reaches the extended first base safely or crosses home plate safely, the offensive team gets a point. The squad scoring the most points wins. The game should last about 5 innings.

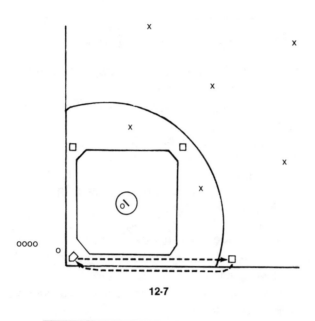

**12-7**

## Offensive Game Strategy

Coaches should consider the following suggestions carefully when developing their offensive game strategy.

### Hit-and-Run

The hit-and-run may be used when there is a runner on first base or possibly runners on first and third. The runner on third should use the regular third base techniques. Here are the best times to hit-and-run:

• A runner with excellent speed is on first base and a hitter with excellent bat control is at the plate. There can be any number of outs.

• If the count is 2-0, 3-1, or 3-2, the next pitch will probably be a fast ball near the strike zone which the hitter will be able to hit.

• If there is a slow runner at first base, a slow runner at bat, and less than 2 outs, a hit-and-run can help prevent the double play. The hitter must make contact by hitting down through the ball.

• If the score is close, the hit-and-run can help increase a team's offensive momentum.

• If the team at bat is several runs ahead, the hit-and-run can help keep the pressure on the defense.

### Bunt-and-Run

When the score is close and the team at bat is facing an effective pitcher, a properly executed bunt-and-run can be the turning point in a tight game. The play

usually is performed with a runner on first base trying to advance to third on a drag bunt, or a runner on second base trying to advance to home on a bunt. The runner breaking from first base must check the quality of the bunt while stealing second base. If the ball is popped up, the runner must quickly return to first.

Essentially, the base running technique for the bunt-and-run is the same as the hit-and-run. The hitter tries to bunt the ball so that the third baseman must make the play and leave third base open. The bunt-and-run is also effective with runners on first and third, since the runner on third might score on the bunt.

### Fake Bunt-and-Swing

When the score is close and the team at bat is facing an effective pitcher, a properly executed fake bunt-and-swing might produce a cheap single or a misplayed fielder's choice, and can be the turning point in a close game. Usually it is executed with a runner on first base only, but it can also be effective with runners at first and third.

The base runner breaking from first uses the same techniques as used for the hit-and-run and bunt-and-run. The hitter pivots into a sacrifice bunt position when the pitcher pauses in the stretch. The hitter wants the infielders to think that he is about to hit a sacrifice bunt. Then as the pitcher delivers the pitch, the runner attempts to steal second base, and the hitter slides his hands together on the bat and punches the ball to an open area in the infield. The hitter's main objective is to hit the ball on the ground in order to protect the runner stealing second and set the infielders up for commiting an error.

### Steals

1. Generally, steals are used when the score is close or the team at bat is several runs ahead.

2. The steal is effective against a pitcher who can be timed in the stretch and pause prior to each delivery.

3. The steal is effective against a right-handed pitcher who picks his left foot up high and puts it down slowly.

4. The steal is effective against a weak-throwing catcher, a catcher who is slow getting the throw on its way, or a catcher whose throws are erratic.

5. If there are runners on first, first and second, or all 3 bases, with 2 outs, runners should be moving on a 3-2 pitch.

6. The fake steal helps set up the regular steal and delay steal.

7. A fake bunt with no strikes help protect the runner stealing if the hitter uses the bat to hide the ball from the catcher.

8. A fast runner can steal home plate if the runner gets a long lead and an immediate break off the pitcher's motion. It helps if the hitter at the plate is right-handed. Stealing home is most effective against pitchers with slow, easy motions, especially left-handers. Usually, stealing home should be attempted with 2 outs.

9. Regular, early, and delayed first and third steals can be executed with any number of outs. They are most effective against inexperienced pitchers and catchers.

10. The delayed steal is an effective baserunning maneuver with runners at first, or first and third, provided that it is preceded by a fake steal and extended lead.

11. An attempted steal of third is most effective against a pitcher who checks the runner only once at the stretch position, or against a shortstop or second baseman who allows the runner to get a long lead. It will help protect the runner if the batter at the plate is right-handed, since such a hitter tends to block the catcher's view of third base thus making it a more difficult throw.

*Note:* The regular steal, early steal, delayed steal, fake steal, steal of third, and steal of home should all be a regular part of a player's drill system.

## Sacrifice Bunt

1. Sacrifice bunts are effective when the team at bat is one run behind, even, or ahead.

2. Usually the sacrifice bunt should be saved for the later innings, but if the team at bat is facing an effective pitcher the sacrifice bunt should be attempted at any time.

3. Sacrifice bunts can be used with runners at first, or first and second, especially if a consistent hitter is coming to the plate following the sacrifice.

4. A sacrifice bunt can be attempted anytime there is a weak hitter at the plate with a runner at first base and less than 2 outs, or a runner at second and no outs.

## Squeeze Bunt

The squeeze bunt can be executed as a "safe squeeze," requiring the runner to break for home only if the batter lays down a well placed bunt, or an "all out squeeze," requiring the runner to break for home as soon as the pitch is on its way to the plate.

1. A squeeze bunt is effective against a pitcher using a full motion when there are less than 2 outs, a runner on third, and the score is close.

2. Consider a squeeze late in the game when the team at bat is facing an effective pitcher and the score is close.

3. The squeeze is more effective with a right-handed hitter at the plate, since the hitter will block some of the catcher's view of the runner.

4. Use an all out squeeze only with an excellent bunter at the plate. The hitter must bunt the ball in order to protect the runner.

## Special First and Third Maneuvers

*Bunt-and-Run.* When there are runners at first and third, and less than 2 outs, the runner at first could try to steal second, while the hitter drag bunts trying to get a base hit. The runner at third may attempt to score if the bunt is well placed.

*Steals.* The regular, early, and delayed steal can be executed with any number of outs. Emphasize the early or delayed steal with 2 outs and 2 strikes on the hitter. These steals are especially effective with a weak hitter at the plate.

*Fake Bunt-and-Swing.* When there are runners at first and third and less than 2 outs, the hitter should execute the fake bunt-and-swing. The runner on third decides whether or not to score on the ground ball. The runner at first attempts to steal second base.

# Defensive Game Strategy

Effective defensive game strategy starts with precision and correct mechanics of fundamental fielding skills. If a team is well-drilled in fielding, throwing, and catching, they will commit few errors and will perform well during games. Coaches should consider the following suggestions when the conditions arise.

1. If there are runners on second and third with less than 2 outs, and the game is close, intentionally walk the next hitter in order to set up the double play at any base. This is especially true if the player at bat is a strong hitter.

2. If there are runners on first and third and the runners try an early, regular, or delayed steal, the defensive players' primary concern is the runner on third base.

3. The defensive players' primary concern in all bunt situations is to get an out. The lead runner is the best runner to get out, but if there is any doubt, the throw should always be made to first base for the sure out.

4. Pick-offs are most effective in critical situations. The defense must be careful not to throw the ball away.

5. The overall defensive philosophy should be to play effective fundamental defense by trying to eliminate bases-on-balls, errors, mental mistakes, and continually trying to get the leadoff batter out each inning.

6. If the leadoff hitter in the last half of the last inning hits a triple, and the score is tied, the defense should intentionally walk the next two hitters to set up a force-out at the plate. The infield should move in near the infield grass. The outfield should pull in close since a long fly will score the winning run.

7. Anytime the defense is behind, tied, or one run ahead, and there is a runner on third, or second and third, the first and third basemen should play even with the bag, and the second baseman and shortstop should play two strides behind the base path so they can try to throw the runner out at the plate on a ground ball.

8. If the score is tied or there is a 1-run difference, and runners are on first and third with less than 2 outs, the first and third baseman should play just behind the base path and the shortstop and second baseman should play at double play depth (four to five strides behind the base path).

Infielders should practice turning double plays with runners at various bases. If there are runners at first and third, first and second, or all three bases, the infielders must decide whether to complete the full double play or get a force out at second followed by an instant throw to home or third. The decision should be based on (a) how hard the ball is hit, (b) the direction it is hit, (c) whether the hitter is left-handed or right-handed, and (d) the speed of the hitter. The primary objective is to turn the double play, or get one sure out without allowing a run to score.

## Scouting

Information usually is gathered in bits and pieces when compiling a complete scouting report. Almost any information can be helpful. The more often scouts or coaches watch a ball club or single player, the more information they are able to accumulate.

Scouting reports can be useful to players who know how to use them. A scouting report is mainly a storehouse of information, which should be used at advantageous times. It is important to note that ball players must do what they do best and not make major adjustments just to fit the scouting report. Ball players will want to use their strong points against their opponents' weak points. Scouting reports should be studied carefully, however, so that any useful information can be utilized as appropriate during a game.

The following outline can serve as a guide for assembling a general resumé of a team's strengths and weaknesses. If it is used properly, the information will help coaches prepare their teams for games. Coaches can also use this outline to "scout" their own teams to help them better assess their own strengths and weaknesses.

## Scouting Outline

### I. Pitching Charts (see p. 17)

- How many pitches are thrown per inning?
- What type of pitches are delivered each inning?
- What is the pitcher's most effective pitch?
- Which pitch is thrown when the count is 2-0, 3-1, or 3-2?
- What is the sequence of pitches?

### II. Habits of the Pitcher

- How does the pitcher react with runners on base?
- Can runners steal easily off the pitcher?
- What type of pick-off moves does the pitcher have?
- How does the pitcher field his position?
- Does the pitcher expose the type of pitch before the delivery?
- What type of competitor is the pitcher?

### III. Hitting Resumé

- Which hitters are power hitters and which are contact hitters?
- What pitch do various hitters hit best?
- Are there mechanical flaws in stance or swing?
- Are there major strengths and weaknesses in their strike zone?
- What types of competitors are they?

### IV. Catcher's Throwing Ability

- Does the catcher like to throw to all bases?
- How quick are his throwing actions?
- How accurate are his throws?

## V. Outfielders' and Infielders' Mechanics

• Do players know their positions and play them well?

• How do they react to difficult plays, such as first and third situations?

• What type of pick-off plays do they use?

• How well does each of them field and throw?

## VI. General Aptitude of the Team

• How well-drilled are they in fundamentals of various phases of baseball?

• How do they respond to changing situations?

• Do they keep their composure throughout pressure situations and critical circumstances?

## VII. Coaches' Signs

• What types of signs do they use?

• How many different signs do they have?

## VIII. Team Attitude

• How do they play when they are behind?

• Do they let down when they are ahead?

• Do they play well together?

## Drill Summary

Workouts should be structured in a manner to encourage each player to cycle through a system of drills. Such a procedure will reduce the amount of standing and watching to a minimum and will promote a more effective learning environment. Since the amount of time available for most practice sessions is limited, the coach should stress organization and effective management at each workout.

Once the coach introduces the drill system to the players, he should allow them the freedom to select the order in which they pursue each drill within the system. The major requirement should be that the players hustle from one drill to another, spending no more than five minutes on each drill. Such a system should continue through batting practice and should only be interupted for team drills which demand the simultaneous participation of each team member. Therefore, it is extremely important for the coach to become familiar with the drills listed below and outlined in earlier chapters. Please refer to the designated pages for review.

| Hitting Drills (Chapter 1) | Page |
|---|---|
| Hip Turner | 8 |
| Wrist Roller | 9 |
| Throwing Bats | 9 |
| Lead and Follow Hand Swings | 10 |
| Bat Press | 10 |
| Three-Colored Home Plate and Contact Points | 11 |
| Hitting Off a Tee | 12 |
| Whiffle or Sock Ball | 14 |
| Whiffle or Sock Ball on a String | 14 |
| Contact Point | 14 |
| Simulating Swings | 15 |
| Colored Ball | 16 |
| Number of Fingers | 16 |

| Bunting Drills (Chapter 2) | Page |
|---|---|
| Catch the Ball Bunt | 26 |
| Accurate Sacrifice Bunting | 27 |
| Rapid-Fire Bunting | 28 |

| Baserunning Drills (Chapter 3) | Page |
|---|---|
| Running Past First Base | 29 |
| Rounding First Base—Thinking Second | 31 |
| Running From Home Plate to First Base | 31 |
| Stop and Go | 31 |
| Lead and Pick-Off | 36 |
| Running the Bases | 38 |
| Assuming Leads and Baserunning Techniques | 38 |
| Complete Baserunning | 39 |

| Sliding Drills (Chapter 4) | Page |
|---|---|
| Sliding on Damp Grass | 43 |
| Around the Bases | 43 |
| Baserunning and Coaching | 44 |

| Individual Infield Drills (Chapter 5) | Page |
|---|---|
| Set-Sprint | 51 |
| Crossover Step | 52 |
| Crossover-Reaction | 53 |
| Flick the Ball | 54 |
| Arm Action | 55 |
| Skip and Throw for Points | 55 |
| Rhythm | 56 |
| Short Hop | 56 |
| Short Hop Goal | 56 |
| Backhand | 57 |
| Fly Balls Overhead | 57 |
| Reaction-Position | 58 |
| Freeze | 59 |
| Simulation | 59 |
| Shadow | 60 |

*Positional Infield Drills (Chapter 6 and Chapter 11)*   *Page*

Receiving Tosses   70
Ground Balls Into Double Plays   70
Double Play Practice   70
Double Play Practice With Runners   71
Pop-Ups for Catchers   74
Catchers Throwing From the Stance   74
Catcher Making Tag Plays at Home   75
Shift Drill for Catchers   124

*Infield Defensive Situation Drills (Chapter 7)*   *Page*

Run-Down   77
First and Third Steal Situation   80
Scramble   81
Stuffed or Wooden Glove   81

*Outfield Drills (Chapter 8)*   *Page*

Toe-Running   86
Outfield Ground Ball—Fly Ball   89
Balls Lying At the Fence   89
Balls Hit Off the Fence   90
Outfield Teamwork   93

*Team Defensive Situation Drills (Chapter 9)*   *Page*

Five Player Cutoff and Relay   98
Cutoff and Relay System   98
Team Throwing for Points   100
Three Player   100
Short Base Situations   101
Individual Position   101
Game Situation (Simulation)   101
Formal Infield and Outfield   102

*Pitching Drills (Chapter 10)*   *Page*

Pitcher's Bunny Hop   112
50 Pitch Change-Up   116
Tarp Target   116
Hit the Spot Pitching   116
Pitcher's Control   116
Pick-Off   120

*Drill Systems and Multipurpose Drills (Chapter 12)*   *Page*

Station Drill System   131
Fungo Stations   132
Pick-Offs—Bunt Coverage—Covering First Base   132
Batting Practice   134
Must Swing Pitches   134
Pepper Game   135
Sacrifice Bunt and Running Practice   135
"Tagging-Up"   136
Team Defensive (Situations)   136
Mini Intra-Squad   137
One Pitch Intra-Squad   137
Extended Bag Game   137

## Seasonal Plan

Every coach should construct his own plan for the season in order to more adequately prepare his team as the season progresses. Duplicate copies of the plan should be made and given to all players so that every team member better understands the skills he is expected to perform during the season. It is very important that the coach develop his seasonal plan with the intent of improving game skills. He should strive to design each practice in a manner that will bring the team to a state of readiness for the first game and will keep them prepared throughout the season. This requires the coach to sensitively appraise and carefully evaluate his players as the season continues. Without such coaching techniques and planning procedures, a productive season is very unlikely.

The Table of Contents shows the components of a well planned developmental program. Notice that it includes all the teaching points considered to be important in a comprehensive developmental program. Each coach should examine the Contents carefully, *then proceed to construct his own season plan*. For further information on constructing a seasonal plan, see Chapter 8 of *Coaching Young Athletes*.

# APPENDICES

Appendix A: Baseball Conditioning

Appendix B: Constructing Instructional Aids

# APPENDIX A

# Baseball Conditioning

Extensive stretching and conditioning is generally not necessary for young ball players, but as they get older, especially after puberty, a strenuous physical fitness program will enable them to perform up to their maximum ability. In this appendix, conditioning drills are described which are especially useful for baseball players.

## Strength and Flexibility

The combination of strength and flexibility may be difficult to achieve, but almost every phase of baseball requires a high degree of both. The drills and exercises described in this chapter will increase flexibility and enhance development of general strength and muscle tone where most needed.

*Warning:* When administering strength exercises with preadolescents, *use only light weights that will not overtax the children's physical structure*. When doing flexibility exercises with *anyone*, stretch slowly until there is slight discomfort or a slight, tingling pain. Then, hold for 5 seconds and relax. *Do not bounce!* Bouncing can reduce flexibility and injure muscles and joints.

## Endurance

Running and jumping rope are excellent ways to increase endurance, but they tend to bore many athletes if pursued constantly. Several drills are presented here which coaches may use to condition athletes while they perform fielding skills.

## How to Use Drills

Some of the drills in this section are specifically referred to in other parts of the book. In addition to using the drills as specified there, coaches may use these drills as a prepractice warm-up or as a strength program if performed in numerous repetitions, or they could incorporate many of them into the practice. Stretching exercises and some strength exercises, done lightly, can be an effective pregame warm-up as well. Coaches may want to require that players pursue certain of these drills on their own outside of practice.

## Strength and Flexibility Drills

### Jumping Jacks

Players should keep their elbows straight in order to encourage proper mobility of the shoulder. Players should touch the sides of their legs and clap their hands high over their heads (see Figs. A-1 to A-6).

### Three Point Stretch

Players should spread their feet wide apart and (a) touch the ground behind their bodies, (b) touch their elbows on the ground, and (c) touch their toes (see Figs. A-7 to A-9).

### Rise on Toes

Players raise up on their toes and simultaneously spread their fingers wide apart with their palms facing

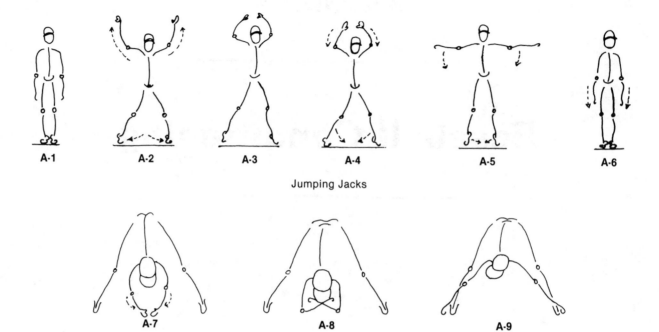

A-1    A-2    A-3    A-4    A-5    A-6

Jumping Jacks

A-7           A-8           A-9

Three Point Stretch

an imaginary, incoming ball as though they are going to catch it. When players' heels come back to the ground they squeeze their fists as tightly as possible to loosen and tone the muscles in their fingers, hands, and forearms (see Figs. A-10, A-11).

## Bunny Hops

Players jump as high and far as possible to either side, landing only on the balls of the feet each time.

This exercise develops balance and power (see Figs. A-12 to A-16).

## Scissor Claps

Players thrust their legs apart as if taking a giant step, trying to step as far as possible and clap their hands between their legs during each step. Players should keep their heads up and backs straight (see Figs. A-17 to A-19). Repeat briskly.

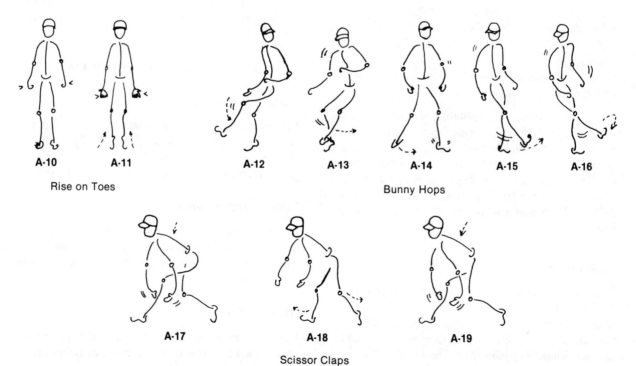

A-10    A-11              A-12    A-13    A-14    A-15    A-16

Rise on Toes                              Bunny Hops

A-17              A-18              A-19

Scissor Claps

## Sit Ups

Players should keep their feet flat on the floor and knees bent to prevent back strain. Each repetition is done by quickly thrusting the arms forward to develop quick upper body movements, which will help players with the fundamentals of throwing (see Figs. A-20 to A-22).

## Leg Rolls

Players place their hands behind their necks and perform a circular movement with their legs by bending the knees, raising the legs up, and then gradually straightening them out as the feet get near the ground. Players should not let their heels touch the ground (see Figs. A-23 to A-27).

## Jack Knife

Players perform a half leg roll and a half sit up by thrusting the chest up to meet their knees. Then they straighten their bodies without allowing their heads or heels to touch the ground (see Figs. A-28 to A-30).

## Arm Rolls

Players hold their arms away from the sides of their bodies and roll them forward in a circular pattern. They gradually increase the size of the path until a full range of motion occurs in the arms and shoulders. Once this is completed, they should repeat the cycle backwards (see Figs. A-31 to A-34).

A-20    A-21    A-22

Sit Ups

A-23    A-24    A-25    A-26    A-27

Leg Rolls

A-28    A-29    A-30

Jack Knife

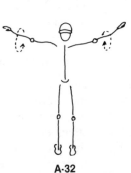

A-31    A-32    A-33    A-34

Arm Rolls

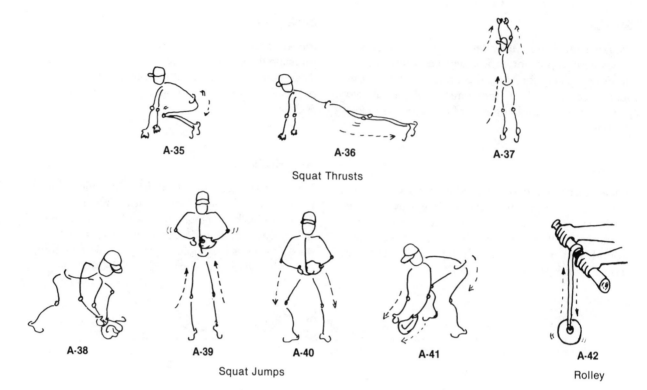

A-35                    A-36                    A-37

Squat Thrusts

A-38          A-39          A-40               A-41                A-42

Squat Jumps                                                        Rolley

## Squat Thrusts

Players squat, place their fingertips on the ground, then thrust their legs backward. They then thrust their legs forward and jump as high as they can, stretching their arms up as though attempting to catch a line drive hit over their head (see Figs. A-35 to A-37).

## Squat Jump

Players assume a fielding position with fingertips touching the ground in front of the body. They then jump as high as they can and land softly on the balls of their feet in another fielding position (see Figs. A-38 to A-41). This drill may be performed by having the players alternate between a fielding and a backhand position.

## Using the Rolley

Instructions for making the rolley are in Appendix B. Players should hold the wooden handle in both hands with the arms extended away from the chest. They should roll the weight up and down by moving the hands and wrists. They should be challenged to roll the weight up and down a specific number of times per week, and the player or coach can chart each player's progress. This exercise strengthens players' wrists, forearms and hands (see Fig. A-42). Fifty repetitions is a recommended daily goal for all players.

## Using Hand Grippers

Hand grippers are an inexpensive item that can be purchased in most sporting goods stores. Players can perform several exercises with them. They can squeeze the grippers as many times as possible with each hand, or they can try to hold a dime between the handles for as long as possible.

These exercises develop strength in the hands, wrists, and forearms, which are critical areas for the success of a hitter. The added strength will also promote better glove action and hand control during fielding, since strength, speed, and quickness are closely related.

## Isometric Swing Strengthener

Players press the bat as hard as possible against a fixed object such as a pole or wall during various phases of the swing. This develops muscle tone and stamina.

## Bat Extension Drill

Another series of bat exercises that increases strength in the arms, wrists, and hands is performed by holding the bat in one hand and extending the arm in a straight outward position—either directly in front, to the side, or over the head. Then the bat is moved in a straight or circular direction. Strength should increase in proportion to the number of daily repetitions.

## Endurance Drills

The following drills are examples of the many drills coaches may use to increase their players' endurance if they use some imagination.

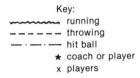

Key:
〰〰〰 running
— — — — throwing
— · — · — hit ball
★ coach or player
x players

1. Players sprint across the outfield while tossing a ball back and forth with a partner, remaining about 5 feet apart. Gloves are optional (see Fig. A-43).

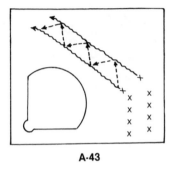

**A-43**

2. Players form a single line and run after short fly balls thrown by a coach or another player. After catching the ball, the player runs the ball back to the thrower (see Fig. A-44).

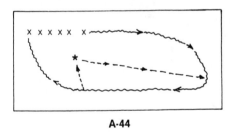

**A-44**

3. Players get into pairs and make each other run for short fly balls (see Fig. A-45).

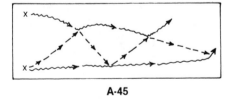

**A-45**

4. Players get in pairs, one circling around the other and staying about 30 feet away. While running, the player catches 25 balls tossed by the partner and continues to run while tossing the ball back to the partner in the center. After 25 tosses, players trade places (see Fig. A-46).

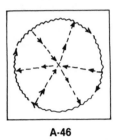

**A-46**

5. Players get in pairs and stand about 10 feet apart. They have 2 balls and no gloves. One player tosses the balls to the partner, throwing short ground balls to alternate sides while the partner fields the balls. After 25 tosses, players change positions (see Fig. A-47).

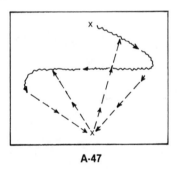

**A-47**

6. Players form a single line in the outfield while the coach or another player hits high, long fly balls to each player. After fielding the ball, each player throws it back and gets at the end of a waiting line which is formed in a different part of the outfield (see Fig. A-48).

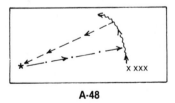

**A-48**

# APPENDIX B

# Constructing Instructional Aids

## Half-and-Half Colored Baseballs

Find the midpoint between the narrow seams of a baseball and mark it. Continue marking the midpoints between the seams as the seams get wider apart. Using something that will bend around the ball, keeping a straight line, for example, a string, connect all the marks so that the ball is now divided exactly in half. Color half of the ball using a permanent marker. The ball should now look just like the ball in Figure B-1. Divide another ball in half as in Figure B-2. Several different colors can be used so these balls can also be used in the Colored Ball Drill.

B-1                    B-2

## Personal Strike Zone

The player should hang a tape measure on a wall with the 0 inch position on the floor. The player then assumes a normal batting stance. A parent, coach, or another player makes a mark at the middle of the player's chest and the top of the knees. Subtract the number of inches at the top of the knees from the number of inches at the player's chest to get the length of the player's strike zone. The width of the strike zone is 17 inches. Cut a rectangle out of poster board that is 17 inches by the length of the strike zone, and divide it into three parts like the strike zone in Figure B-3. When using the strike zone, players should hang it so that the bottom is at the top of their knees when they're in a normal batting stance. Hitters can draw baseballs on the strike zone to represent various pitches as in Figure B-3. Pitchers can draw a 2-inch border on each side and a 4-inch border on the base (see Fig. B-4) to outline the best location for their pitches.

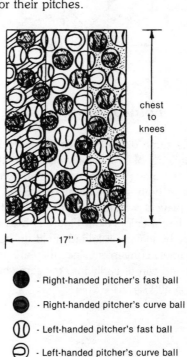

chest to knees

17"

- Right-handed pitcher's fast ball

- Right-handed pitcher's curve ball

- Left-handed pitcher's fast ball

- Left-handed pitcher's curve ball

B-3

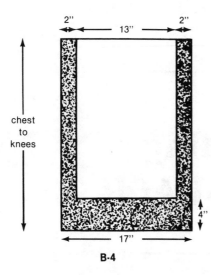

B-4

## Three-Colored Home Plate

Cut a home plate out of ¼-inch plywood (first choice) or poster board (second choice) using the dimensions on Figure B-5. Color each section a different color.

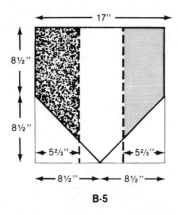

B-5

## Fold-Up Home Plate

Using the same dimensions as in Figure B-5, cut a home plate out of ¾-inch plywood. Cut the plate exactly in half along the dotted lines shown in Figure B-6. Hinge both sections together. Sand the wood well so players won't get splinters. Paint the plate three different colors as in Figure B-5 or use it as a half plate by leaving it folded. Fold-up home plates are extremely convenient since they are inexpensive to build and can fit easily into the same bag used to carry bats and balls.

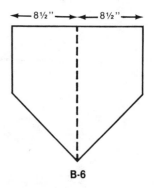

B-6

## Boxes and Triangles

### Box

Player should assume the position shown in Figure B-7 and have a friend, parent, or coach take the measurements from shoulder to shoulder, and from shoulder to elbow. Cut a box out of poster board using those dimensions.

### Triangle

Player should assume the position shown in Figure B-8 and have a friend, parent, or coach take measurements from shoulder or armpit to the knee on the same side of the body, and to the opposite hip. Cut a triangle out of poster board using those dimensions.

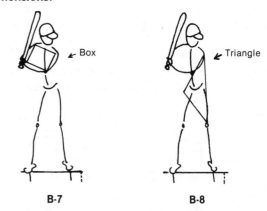

B-7                    B-8

## Rolley

A rolley can be made with the end of a bat or any other piece of wood about 12 inches long and 1½ inches in diameter. Drill a hole through the wood at the center, put a 2½-foot cord through it and tie a knot at one end. At the other end tie a 3-pound weight (see Fig. B-9). As players get older and taller, they can use heavier weights and longer cords. Make sure that the wood is sanded well and won't cause splinters.

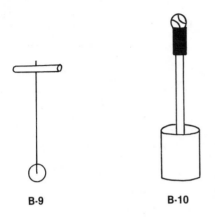

B-9                    B-10

## Hitting Tees

Use an empty gallon paint can. Place a broomstick in the can and fill with ready mixed cement. Allow the cement to harden for a day. Cut several lengths of radiator hose with an inside diameter of 1½ inches, from 2 inches to 10 inches long. Place one end of the hose on the broomstick, the length depending on the player's height and the type of ball he wants to practice. The ball is placed on top of the hose. Each team should have at least three tees. The shortest one should have a broomstick that is a few inches shorter than the bottom of the shortest player's strike zone, and the tallest should be about belt high for the tallest player.

Instead of using paint cans and cement, hitting tees can be made out of 5-gallon oil cans filled three-quarters full of sand. With this method, the broomsticks can be taken out of the can when transporting the tees, and extra baseballs can be kept in the can (see Fig. B-10).

## Jump Rope

Use a plastic sectioned rope of ½-inch nylon cord. To measure for length, put both ends of the rope under one armpit. The rope should drag on the ground 3 inches.

## Stuffed or Wooden Glove

Take an old catcher's mitt and stuff it with a very firm piece of foam rubber so that it has no pocket. Or trace the outline of a catcher's mitt on a piece of ¾-inch plywood and cut it out. Sand the wood well. On the back of the wood, attach a strong, 1½-inch × 6-inch piece of leather. There should be enough room for players to get their hands between the leather and the wood, but not enough so that the glove will slip off.

## Tarp Target

Tie a large piece of old carpet on an 8 foot by 8 foot section of chain link fence. Place a tarp on the target and outline, in paint or tape, an appropriate strike zone with a dotted line across the crotch area, (see Fig. B-11). Additional sections can be added to the strike zone if desired.

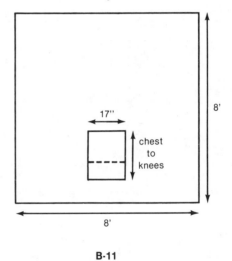

B-11

## Colored Balls

Use baseballs or tennis balls. Either color the whole ball using a permanent marker, or put a thick stripe around the ball. Make sure the colors can be easily distinguished from one another.